## *Praise and Outrage for* The Poor Gringo Guide

"Hilarious ... A Mexican *Joy of Cooking* run amuck ..."
— *¡Buen Provecho!*

"... Disgraceful ... a desecration of Mexico and its cuisine ... this gringo should be shot and deported ..."
— **Former Mexican ambassador to Tuvalu**

"A crazy gringo with a recipe for skullduggery ..."
— ***The Chili Insider***

"PETA will sink their teeth into these recipes ..."
— ***Scullery Digest***

"Sebastian Dangerfield meets Diana Kennedy ... A bean burrito will never taste the same ..."
— ***Gourmand Magazine***

"Omnivores rejoice! Vegans take cover! Miles Pickerel is loose!"
— ***The Uncommon Culinarian***

"You won't find these menu items at Chipotle."
— **Juan Chavez, former dishwasher and deported Mexican**

"... The gorditas are absolutely lardicious! ... Sow offally bad, they're good ..."
— ***Corpulent Cooking***
(posted at heavy-weights.com)

"One gringo's gastronomic march to madness."
—**M. S. Holm,** *Tacos and Tequila Are My Friends*

... Miles Standish Pickerel is no gourmet, not even by the loosest translation of a drunken Francophile. He is a slam-it-down, toss-it-on-the-fire, meat-an'-tater, elbows-on-the-table, fork-clicking, chew-with-his-mouth-open kind of fellow. His former mother-in-law rarely had him over for dinner. He is a graduate of the Walt Whitman School of Cooking, where liberal substitutions are encouraged and "Song of Myself" is finding a pubic hair in your taco ...
—**From the Foreword**

# The Poor Gringo Guide to Mexican Cooking

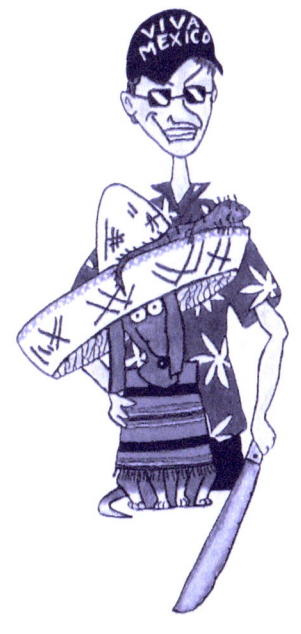

M. S. Pickerel

Copyright © 2009 by M. S. Pickerel

Sentry Books
An Imprint of Great West Publishing

www.sentrybooks.com

All rights reserved. No part of this publication may be reproduced, stored in a retrieval system or transmitted, in any form, or by any means, electronic, mechanical, recorded, photocopied, or otherwise, without the prior permission of the copyright owner, except by a reviewer who may quote brief passages in a review.

Library of Congress Control Number: 2008940076

Book design and layout by Jonathan Gullery

Printed in the United States of America

**Publisher's Cataloging-in-Publication**
*(Provided by Quality Books, Inc.)*

Pickerel, M. S. (Miles Standish), author.
  The poor gringo guide to Mexican cooking / M.S. Pickerel ; illustrator, Susan Say-less.
    pages cm
  Includes index.
  LCCN 2008940076
  ISBN 978-0-9796199-2-2 (hardcover)
  ISBN 978-0-9796199-4-6 (paperback)
  ISBN 978-0-9974553-4-2 (electronic book)

  1. Cooking, Mexican. 2. Cookbooks. I. Sayles, Susana, illustrator. II. Title.

TX716.M4P53 2009          641.5972
                          QBI16-1052

Hardcover ISBN: 978-0-9974553-6-6
Hardcover ISBN: 978-0-9796199-2-2
Paperback ISBN: 978-0-9796199-4-6

To Ladrón:
Canine Companion
Dinner for Six

# Contents

Acknowledgments (*Agradecimientos*) .................... 8
Foreword (*Introducción*) .................... 9
Your Chef Today (*Su Chef al Día*) .................... 11
How Pickerel Turned Culinary (*Como Fué Que
    Pickerel se Tornó Culinario*) .................... 16
Pickerel's Kitchen (*La Cocina de Pickerel*) .................... 16
Essentials and Utensils (*Los Utensilios y lo Esencial*) .................... 17
Ingredients (*Ingredientes*) .................... 21
Preferred Brands (*Marcas Preferidas*) .................... 28
Pickerel's Pointers (*Consejos de Pickerel*) .................... 30
Beans (*Frijoles*) .................... 33
Tortillas (*Tortillas*) .................... 45
Leftover Tortillas, Tattered Tortillas, and Stale Tortillas
    (*Sobras de Tortilla, Tortillas Maltratadas y Tortillas Duras*) ....... 53
Sauces (*Salsas*) .................... 71
Chili Peppers (*Chiles*) .................... 85
Eggs (*Huevos*) .................... 97
Potatoes (*Papas*) .................... 109
Rice (*Arroz*) .................... 117
From the Garden (*Del Jardín*) .................... 125
Poultry (*Aves*) .................... 139
Fish and More (*Pescado y Más*) .................... 151
Farm, Field, and Front Porch (*Granja, Campo y Porche*) .................... 171
Soups and Broths (*Sopas y Caldos*) .................... 193
Deep-Fried (*Fritangas*) .................... 207
Lime Recipes (*Recetas con Limón*) .................... 217
Desserts (*Postres*) .................... 223
Beverages (*Bebidas Refrescantes*) .................... 235
Appendix (*Apéndice*) .................... 247
Glossary (*Glosario*) .................... 251
Index (*Indice*) .................... 257

# *Acknowledgments*

Pickerel wishes to thank his ex-wife, Miriam, for making a precipitous exit from their unholy matrimony. If not for her timely departure, Pickerel would have chosen conjugal homicide over culinary mayhem. To local farmers, Pickerel expresses his sincerest gratitude. Their unguarded fields provided fresh fruits and vegetables that otherwise would have been purchased. Pickerel remains indebted to his neighbors—especially those who unsuspectingly allowed their poultry and pets to wander out of sight and into Pickerel's front yard. He cannot imagine what these recipes would taste like without their generous contribution. Special thanks also go to Mexican health inspectors, underpaid wildlife officials, and corrupt law enforcement personnel (all of whom shall remain nameless) for allowing the author to despoil public domains, trespass on private property, and swindle innocent natives in the pursuit of no cost ingredients. For creating appropriately outrageous illustrations to go with this text, the author embraces (from a distance) the taciturn and talented Susan Say-less. To Shea Spindler: your gimlet eye leaves Pickerel in editorial awe. Sarah Garibaldi, LDG, thank you for the graphic tweaking. Not to be taken for granted are the tildes and accents added to these pages by H. Vargas: the only person on the planet who understands Spanish as written by Pickerel. And to everyone at Endle Literary Agency, Sentry Books, and Great West Publishing, thank you for daring to allow this deviant sally into Mexican cuisine to go to print. You will not be forgiven.

# *Foreword*

Pickerel has prepared, eaten, and—most importantly—digested every dish in these pages. Many fires have charred his grill. His pots are black, his bean masher worn. *The Poor Gringo Guide to Mexican Cooking* is, between recipes, the story of Pickerel himself—a poor gringo masquerading as a sane one.

Pickerel lives in Mexico for many reasons. The sea is near. The nights are warm. The women are friendly. So are the husbands. He is poor here for others, which have nothing to do with his cooking.

Pickerel is no gourmet, not even by the loosest translation of a drunken Francophile. He is a slam-it-down, toss-it-on-the-fire, meat-an'-tater, elbows-on-the-table, fork-clicking, chew-with-his-mouth-open kind of fellow. His former mother-in-law rarely had him over for dinner. He is a graduate of the Walt Whitman School of Cooking, where liberal substitutions are encouraged and "Song of Myself" is finding a pubic hair in your taco.

Pickerel does not promise that you will get fat on his poor gringo fare. In fact, you may get thin. The only promise Pickerel does make—if his cooking guide is followed—is regular and satisfactory bowel movements. This he guarantees, upon proof, or your money back.

Oh, yes.

Pickerel pretends to know nothing of culinary terms. He also mixes metric and English measures (both liquid and dry) at his convenience. His Spanish translation of food items and cooking directions is colloquial, if not ungrammatical. And he borrows, bargains, or steals most of his ingredients.

Purists read no further.

# *Your Chef Today*

Your chef for this impertinent culinary onslaught is Miles S. Pickerel, at your service. Middle name is service. However, S is for Standish—a momentary resurfacing of the puritanical consciousness on his mother's side.

Autobiographically speaking, Miles Standish Pickerel (It is he speaking here, preserving the neutral voice of the disembodied; Pickerel is allergic to first-person singular and plural. It makes him itch.) appeared on the planet one rainy morning in June 1950 at 221 Longwood Avenue, Boston, Massachusetts. His arrival was inconspicuous enough—one more boomer in Beantown. That afternoon, across Muddy River, the Red Sox played a twilight double-header against the Yankees, losing both games. Pickerel's mother fondly recalls that her son cried all night. To this day, he continues to wail in one implacable voice or another, even in the telling of his favorite recipes.

Pickerel's first distinct recollection is that of trying to throw pabulum at a Goodyear blimp as it passed low over his daybed, obstructing his view of the universe. He was two at the time. Next came the unpleasant memory of his maternal grandmother—a stern, fearsome woman with cold Britannic blood—forcing him to eat a boiled egg from an eggcup. Forty years later, Pickerel still runs from hardboiled eggs.

His first social encounter with fellow small-fry Freudians like himself was on the sidewalk of Ditson Street, downtown Dorchester, where he pushed Grady Goss, age three, off the curb for not giving Pickerel half the sidewalk. Grady ran home to his mother, scraped up and bawling, while Pickerel marched victoriously foreward. He remains a sidewalk pusher to this day.

Then his formal education began. For young Pickerel, this was an overwhelming event overshadowed by abundant paper, Crayolas, wet paint, Play-Doh, and glue. There was a big person mixed up in it somewhere, calling herself a teacher, but Pickerel acknowledged her existence only when she began to shriek. The whole experience was so thoroughly enjoyable that life since has never stopped being kindergarten. Pickerel misses the chaos to this day.

Regarding Pickerel's adolescent years, he will say only this: he was a typical teenage boy—he liked to eat, drive fast, watch porn, and play with his peter. As for the debauched collegiate days that followed and his subsequent (albeit perverse) embarkation into the adult world, Pickerel will say nothing. Nothing best describes that chapter of his life.

# *How Pickerel Turned Culinary*

When Pickerel's wife, Miriam, departed their two-room, dirt-floor hacienda one August morning in 1997, taking the children but leaving the dog, Pickerel faced the cruel culinary realities of the world for the first time in his life. He had spent the last thirty years intentionally bent on not stirring a pot or washing a dirty tablespoon. In a pinch, he would butter toast, boil a tea bag, or turn a saltshaker, but nothing more.

He had lived with his mother until the very last episode of *Gunsmoke* aired in September 1985. Constitutionally speaking, he was old enough to become president of the United States, and, though Pickerel was never elected or nominated, his mother catered to his smallest palatal whim as if he had been. Seafood Newberg served over oven-warmed toast for breakfast. Swedish meatballs skewered on toothpicks during televised Celtics games. Pickerel's mother baked beans and brown bread every Saturday at six sharp (when Pickerel was tuning into *Hee Haw*). On Sundays, she prepared a thick-crusted shepherd's pie (supplicated by her one and only begotten son, sometimes preacher, sometimes parishioner of her heart). She made Pickerel corn bread on rainy November mornings, and she boiled corned beef and cabbage every Tuesday in March. When Pickerel turned pale, she fried him a pan of liver and onions, and on his birthday, she prepared his favorite dish: salmon soufflé. She cooked an old-world beef Stroganoff that warmed Pickerel's bilges even when he gobbled it cold, which he did sometimes, straight from the Westinghouse at two in the morning after surviving on gin and pistachios for twelve hours without intermission. What Stroganoff! What a *madre!*

Then Pickerel met Miriam, and the planet heaved slightly from the collision. Young Miriam. Innocent Miriam. Sweet but sugar-free Miriam. She was studying interior design at a local junior college. Pickerel was an ergophobic associate professor of biological sciences at the same institution. They came from opposite ends of the great *Via Lactea*—he, a devious black hole, she, an ingenuous twinkle, twinkle. But Pickerel didn't care if the universe was expanding. He was not looking for fast-snapping neurons, an engaging personality, or even new upholstery. He was looking for high growth in mutual funds. He was looking for stock options, T-bills, and a junior partnership in the family lumber business in Brazil. Pickerel could bring himself to rape the tropical landscape. Yes, he could! Apart from abundant wealth, Pickerel was also looking for one thing more in his future: an abundant woman—not one with hidden beauty or factory options, but one with well-converted carbohydrates in all the right quarters.

How Miriam managed to usurp Pickerel's good sense, deluding him into seeing abundance where abundance was not, is a long and mournful tale that Pickerel still drowns himself bibaciously to forget. It has no place here, where thorough digestion is sought and a loose bowel is a culinary crime.

Instead, let Pickerel say this: Miriam turned out a very decent meatloaf. Yes. Also a mean dish of scalloped potatoes. And her macaroni and cheese (old Norwegian recipe from her mother) never once made it as far as the dog's dish in the backyard.

Stateside, Miriam cut a persuasive figure pushing her shopping cart down the supermarket aisles, sagaciously eyeing bar codes. Years of convenience shopping had tuned her prehensile grip for the instant, the frozen, the freeze-dried, and the prettily packaged. In the kitchen, she was a dervish between the microwave and the toaster oven. She knew all the settings—the wattage for thawing frozen broccoli, the seconds needed to silence Orville Redenbacher. Her electric can opener was never lonesome, her Crock-Pot never cool. She was well on the way to turning instant herself—Miriam in a minute. Just add water and nuke.

Then she followed the Great Solitaire (aka Miles Pickerel) to Mexico—25° 45° N, 108° 57° W, to be exact—and Quaker Oatmeal never tasted the same. A two-burner gas stove with a deceased pilot light turned out to be a shocking welcome. So was the sink. More precisely, the lack of sink. "Where does the water go?" was the question Miriam posed upon peering into the depths of a plastic dishpan perched on a rickety wooden stand. Obviously, Miriam had never had the pleasure of tossing dirty dishwater out the back door. "And the hot water?" she asked meekly, observing the solitary cold-water tap with its musical drip. Pickerel pointed at the high noon sun and smiled. After all, such was the price of living in the romantic dream fields of a dangerous Latino land.

At the beginning, Miriam bravely trooped it out. She beat their beans without a blender. She hand strangled Pickerel's morning juice. Daily, she made the dusty pilgrimage to the local market where she haggled in bad Spanish over fresh carp and the price of ripe mangos. Briskly, she returned over the cobbles, her woven bag full of corn to husk, peas to shell, and fish to gut.

Pickerel did his part too. He found a cottonwood stump upon which Miriam could strike cutlery. He purchased a clattering electric fan to blow hot wind upon the flies. And he grew demanding with the landlord. Said

Pickerel in his most exigent voice, "*Señor*, the holes in the kitchen roof must be plugged. *Pero ya!*" When Miriam was not laboring under summer showers, she was speckled with tropical sunlight. Poor Miriam. She tried. She really did.

Then came the Pickerel progeny, unexpected and plural—Rose and Roselyn—the twins, a double whammy of vanilla frizzes and Colgate smiles—and heirs to the Pickerel misfortune. Their arrival sent Miriam's adventurous spirit into a nosedive while launching her nest-building instincts into the stratosphere. Pretending to be poor had been fun. As for the real thing, Miriam saw no future in it. "To hell with doing without," were her exact words. Suddenly, indoor plumbing became essential, hot water a necessity, and the lack of window screens a serious health hazard. Soon Pickerel found himself on Miriam's list of things to fix. No longer was she willing to accept his God-given right to prevaricate. Nor was she disposed to tolerate his walking phallus or his intemperate squandering of the family peso. Pickerel's tiny business of biological supply was still in the early stages of liftoff. His monthly check from the VA did not always make a timely landing in the hands of Miriam. Usually it landed not at all, due to urgent debt in other sectors. Remnant cash was often rerouted to El Toro Manchado (The Spotted Bull), Pickerel's favorite retail outlet for distilled beverages.

Miriam's brisk step to the market turned to a trudge. Dusty streets took their toll. The untimely concurrence of a trash collectors' strike and an outbreak of dengue fever fouled her mood. Frequent visits by the landlord trying to ambush Pickerel for back rent became a constant Miriam mortification. And simply living with Pickerel was enough to make her believe she had died and gone to hell in a *chiquihuite*.\*

In due course, Miriam's shadow grew willowy while the substance of the woman grew frazzled and wild—a dandelion gone to seed.

One morning, with eggs frying on the stove for breakfast, the bottled butane ran out. No gas, no eggs. When Miriam called for help, Pickerel jumped to his feet, quickly suggesting that she fire up the charcoal grill. Miriam refused. Instead, she laughed a strange laugh, one from the abyss. Then she shrieked, "Miles, get me some gas this instant!" Pickerel farted, rather loudly, and then he smiled. He may have grinned.

That was it. Miriam retreated, hands over ears, paint peelings on the ceiling stirring in her wake. Within the hour she was gone, twins in tow, and Pickerel suddenly found himself alone with one dog, no breakfast, and

---

\* Tortilla basket made from woven grass.

cold eggs congealing on a gasless stove.

What to do? he asked himself as he stared at the lace of eggs clinging to the edge of the frying pan. He looked to Ladrón for an answer—the dog that two months later would mysteriously disappear on the same day Chacha Machado (Pickerel's first housekeeper) served a very decent pozole* for a dinner party of six—and then the answer came to him.

Pickerel would cook. Yes. He would fire that charcoal grill, refry those eggs, and he would eat them inside a warm tortilla—Miriam be damned. Then Pickerel did it, a new king in his kitchen, and even Ladrón got a lick.

The next day he dared to boil his first pot of beans. A week later, he was eating refried topped with grated ranch cheese. Within the month, squash blossom quesadillas filled Pickerel's plate, *frijoles* on the side.

Every dish in this poor gringo's guide came after that—recipes borrowed from neighbors, offered by friends, stolen from taco stands, or taught to Pickerel by female culinary consorts passing through his kitchen in the tsunamic wake of Miriam.

To this day, Pickerel continues his gastronomic march to madness. And he still gets gas.

---

\* A stew made with meat and hominy in a red chili sauce.

# Pickerel's Kitchen

Welcome to Tabachines 212 Ote., Pickerel's address in an unnamed city. Observe the front yard—an oblong plat of weeds enclosed by a rusted wrought-iron fence topped with rust-cankered pikes (tetanus is Pickerel's first defense against creditor climbers). And behold Pickerel's blue-painted front door, dented with kick marks—these left from the days when Miriam believed door locks could keep Pickerel from entering his castle in a drunken rage at early antemeridian hours.

*Pásale, pásale.* Yes, come in. *Mi casa es tu casa.*

No tour today, however. Instead, let us head straight to Pickerel's kitchen (*cocina*) at the rear of his humble abode. Pickerel calls it his scullery turned culinary, his galley-in-the-alley—a three-sided lean-to that opens onto a low-walled patio where rare red bougainvillea once grew until Pickerel repeatedly peed upon them for obstructing his view of the neighborhood. Now when Pickerel cooks, he is able to gaze unhindered upon nearby wash lines and genuflecting washerwomen.

But enough of Pickerel's voyeuristic pastimes. To the kitchen and what you will need there to prepare your poor gringo cuisine.

# Essentials and Utensils

Pickerel's poor gringo kitchen would not be complete without the following instruments of culinary mayhem.

**Bean masher**—*Moledor de frijol.* A plastic or wooden instrument of bean demise.

**Bean spoon**—*Cuchara para guisar.* For cooking beans. Must be long-handled; wooden or plastic. Never use a metal spoon. Beans will behave badly.

**Blender**—*Licuadora.* The presence of an electric appliance in Pickerel's kitchen is a tacit acknowledgment that science is grand and the manual eggbeater is dead. He considers his four-speed, turbo Facimix of Brazilian fabrication to be the most important advancement in thorough digestion since Tums. Even plain water tastes better with froth. And in the preparation of his unheralded, maguey milkshake, Pickerel would be helpless without it.

**Cheese grater**—*Raspador de queso.* If cheese is milk's leap toward immortality, then a cheese grater is what? A triturating time machine? For poor gringos, a hand grater will do. Ask Santa for an upgrade to a box grater.

**Colander**—*Escurridor.* Pickerel made his own by going crazy with an ice pick on a #10 coffee can.

**Cookware**—*Batería de cocina.* The centerpiece of Pickerel's cookware is his bean pot: a 10-liter, enameled ironware receptacle blackened with many bean incarnations. His biggest pot is an aluminum stockpot (*olla*), 16-liter capacity that Pickerel sometimes turns upside down for a stool. His kitchen also boasts two porcelain saucepots (*cazuelas*) and a menagerie of banged-up, formerly nonstick saucepans (*cazos*) that Pickerel borrowed from (and did not return to) neighbors, housekeepers, and grieving widows. As for his skillets (*sartenes*), they are cast-iron, and Pickerel has three of them—eight, ten, and twelve-inchers (the last, a reflection of his rich fantasy life). Finally, there is Pickerel's *comal*—his griddle—an indispensable piece of flatware for cooking tortillas. Pickerel

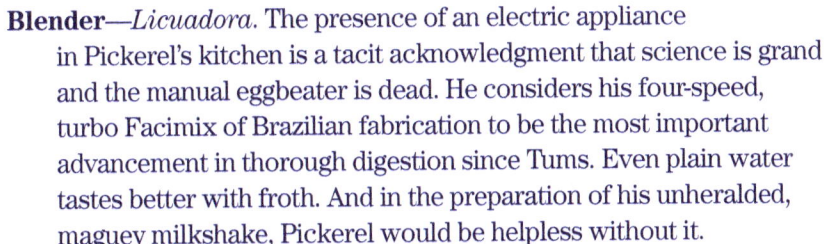

owns two—a thin, tin one (square 12" x 12" piece of sheet metal cut from nearby AC ductwork) for tortilla warming, and a heavy-duty, heat-holding, cast-iron job that Pickerel needs both hands to lift. On cold nights, he has slipped it between his bedcovers as a warmer.

**Corn grinder**—*Molino de maíz (granos)*. Pickerel uses his grinder to make green corn tamales. If you count among your culinary appliances a meat grinder or a food processor (Pickerel has neither), you may use one of these to grind corn for tamales. Purists use a *metate*. Alternatively, you may borrow a neighbor's *molino* if you promise to pay the owner back with warm, freshly made tamales. If your grinder is new, first grind 1/2 cup of uncooked rice and then grind 3 corn tortillas. This will eliminate any metal flavor. Also, be sure your grinder is fixed to a heavy/immovable object (bar counter, billiard table, or nearby fencepost). Hand grinding is a shaky, screw-loosening enterprise.

**Cutting board**—*Tabla para cortar*. Pickerel uses Miriam's cottonwood stump for fish gutting, poultry beheadings, and other animal dismemberments. For smaller jobs, he uses a pine board. Once a year he replaces his bloodstained and knife-marked plank for a new one, selected from a carpentry shop conveniently located across the street.

**Dishpan**—*Bandeja*. Pickerel uses a plastic dishpan for sorting beans, mixing tortilla dough, making green corn tamales, soaking dishes, and washing the racing stripes from his yellowed undershorts.

**Fire**—*Fuego*. Pickerel's kitchen has multiple options. *Número uno* is his gas stove (*estufa*), a Mabe three-burner (burner number four inoperable since Doña Cuca, Pickerel's purveyor of cold-blooded vertebrates, plugged it with blackened reptile glue while cauterizing broken iguana tails). (See *Stewed Iguana*, page 191.)

Never one to depend on a timely supply of gas, Pickerel has backup—his charcoal grill (*parrilla*). He buys his charcoal (*carbón*) from friend and local burner Pablo Quemado, a sooty-faced man who charges Pickerel the ridiculously low price of thirty pesos (about three dollars) for one bulging onion sack of charred *déndron* (enough to last Pickerel two weeks). In return, Pickerel prescribes his soon-to-be-patented tequila vaporizer as treatment for Pablo's stage-one black lung disease. (Pickerel—known as *El Doctor* in the neighborhood—dispenses his ample medical knowledge to the natives at no charge, though donations are gratefully accepted.) So Pablo and Pickerel are back-scratching buddies until organ failure (Pablo's *pulmones* and Pickerel's liver) do they part.

Finally, option three in Pickerel's incendiary arsenal is the pit—his backyard barbeque pit (*hoyo*). Pickerel dug it one midnight while Miriam slept. It began as a shallow grave—last resting place for a quarrelsome spouse—then grew less rectangular and more cylindrical as Pickerel's hands blistered, his back wearied, and sobriety set in. Later, Pickerel tossed in a layer of large, round stones (highly recommended for thermal retention), and then he acquired an appropriately sized cover (the hood off a 1979 Oldsmobile Delta 88, mint condition) from an unconvicted felon working at a local garage. (To hear more of this hero, read Pickerel's forthcoming *The Poor Gringo Guide to Mexican Mechanics*.) Pickerel inaugurated his pit the afternoon he not so accidentally ran over a goat grazing too close to the shoulder of a country road. Pickerel outran the goat keeper (an old man with a herding cane) to the carcass, and in moments, he was motoring back to town with the dead goat in the trunk of his car. Pit side, Pickerel invited neighbors to gather wood and supply him with aluminum foil and free labor. Within the hour, one chopped up, chili-basted, and foil-wrapped goat was slow cooking under a dirt-covered Oldsmobile hood. (See *Fired Tequila Goat*, page 189.)

**Lime squeezer**—*Exprimidor de limón*. The cast-iron variety lasts longer than the aluminum kind. Pickerel's squeezer has turned green with a thousand lime confessions.

**Meat pounder**—*Machacador* or *marrito para carne*. Hammer-like device with a dentated head used to pound tough meat. Pickerel lost his the day Manuela Picas (green card aspirant with a temper) threw it at him. She missed but hit a window instead, sending his meat pounder into the street. As Pickerel ran to fetch it (he was going to *machacar* Manuela for breaking his window), a passing urchin found it and was already setting a new world record for the 100-meter dash in bare feet. Pickerel now uses a smooth, flat-bottomed stone (fist-size) for his meat pounder.

**Metate**—*Metate*. Also known as the Aztec blender. A flat, rectangular stone mortar used for grinding corn, chilies, and cacao. Pickerel owned one until it was carried off by his landlord in lieu of back rent. Now he grinds his corn in a *molino*. (See *Corn Grinder*, page 18)

**Mortar and pestle**—*Molcajete y tejolote*. If purchased new, both of these must be cured prior to use (to avoid mineral shedding). Pickerel has no idea how to do this. He acquired his mortar and pestle used from Reyna de Los Reyes, a post-Miriam tenant who dreamed of permanent residency. When she precipitously exited  Pickerel's life never to return (after discovering Pickerel's stash of embalmed cats—her calico kitty among them—curing behind the latrine ... Did Pickerel mention that he dabbles in the biological supply business?), she took her Virgin of Guadalupe votive candles but left the *molcajete*—mostly because it was too heavy to run with. (Reyna's black basalt mortar is a relic the size of a pre-Columbian chamber pot.) Now that Pickerel calls it his own, he pulverizes spices, garlic, and coriander with the thoroughness of a possessed alchemist transmuting lust to love.

**Rolling bottle**—*Rodillo*. Instead of a rolling pin, Pickerel uses a rolling bottle to flatten his flour tortilla dough. He recommends a long-necked beer bottle, preferably 1/2-liter size, preferably Pacifico brand, preferably full (and cold). When not making flour tortillas, Pickerel remains entirely unbiased in his preference for bottled beer.

**Steamer**—*Olla vaporera*. Pickerel's steamer consists of a dozen stones (golf ball-size) laid in the bottom of a tall pot. He adds just enough water to cover the stones, and he positions two circles of mosquito screen (cut to fit the diameter of his pot) over the stones. On the screen, he places the ingredient(s) to be steamed, covers the pot, and places it over high heat.

**Strainer**—*Colador*. Pickerel uses a short length of mosquito screen removed from the window after the landlord made repairs.

**Tongs**—*Pinzas*. Essential for toasting chilies and roasting onions over charcoal. Pickerel uses a short culm of *carrizo* (poor cousin of sugarcane) cut lengthwise with the end attached as a hinge. This device Pickerel borrowed from local urchins who bring live scorpions and tarantulas to Pickerel's small business of biological supply. A burning chili is not unlike an enraged arachnid.

**Tortilla basket**—*Chiquihuite*. A woven basket to keep tortillas warm.

**Tortilla press**—*Prensa de tortilla*. A simple engine of tortilla torture used to squeeze the skinny out of tortilla dough. Two flat and perfectly round cast-iron plates hinged together with a lever. Absolutely medieval.

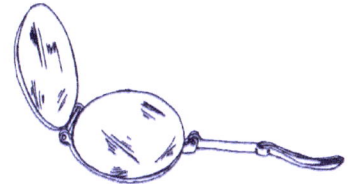

## Ingredients

***Carne machaca***. Salted, pounded, dried, and shredded meat made from beef or other mammalian quadrupeds.

Pickerel used to make his own *machaca* (recipe to follow) until rumors of missing pets and an uncommon scarcity of domestic rodents alarmed his neighborhood. Pickerel added his angst-ridden voice to the *barrio* hubbub—visibly concerned for the safety of his longtime canine companion, Ladrón (though not for the welfare of annoying rodents, of which, coincidentally, he had none)—but the purported pet and pest bogeyman was never sighted, much less apprehended.

Pickerel now buys his *machaca* from the lowest-priced *machaca* vendor within bicycling distance of his humble abode. He does not inquire about the meat's origin or its species. He understands that low price means low quality, low pedigree, and low to the ground. Pickerel figures that all meat—after salting, pounding, drying, and shredding—acquires its own distinctly flavorful anonymity in *machaca*.

# *Recipe for making machaca from any fresh, healthy, mystery meat*

Credit for this recipe goes to Ramon Recodo, a Sonorense cab driver currently operating with a suspended taxi license after a customer reported him for stopping on a busy street to retrieve roadkill while the taximeter was running.

*Ingredientes* (to make 400 grams or about 1 lb of machaca)
   1 kg of thinly sliced strips of boneless meat; the less fat, the better (1 *kg de tiras finamente rebanadas de carne deshuesada; entre menos grasosa, mejor*)
   1/2 cup or 1/4 kg salt (1/2 *tasa o 1/4 kilo de sal*)

*Equipo*
   Your meat pounder (*su machacador de carne*)
   12 clothespins (12 *ganchos para ropa*)
   A wash line (*un tendedero*)
   2 square yards of mosquito netting (2 *yardas cuadradas de tela mosquitero*)
   Blender (*licuadora*)

*Preparación*
   Using a meat pounder (*machacador*), pound meat on hard surface to tenderize. Flatten each piece to the thickness of a hardbound book cover. Salt the first strip on both sides and lay on a plate. Salt the next strip (both sides) and place on top of the first. Salt all strips this way, laying each on top of the one before it. Cover and refrigerate strips over night.
   The next morning, remove meat from the refrigerator and hang strips on a wash line with clothespins. Shake excess salt off each strip. Cover with mosquito netting. Sun dry strips for 7 days.

> **Cautionary note:** Bring in meat at night (in Pickerel's neighborhood, *machaca* thieves—four- and two-legged—strike when the sun goes down) and on rainy days, refrigerating in the interim.

   After a week, strips should be dry but pliable. Place each in a blender, and blend until meat shreds into thin, hairlike fibers. One kilo of dried meat will fill a 2-quart blender with triturated fibers.
   Place shredded meat inside a plastic bag, knot tightly, and store in the

refrigerator. Use to scramble with eggs, to mix with fried vegetables, and to add to poor gringo soup. *Recipes to follow.*

## **Cheeses** (*Quesos*)

Since Pickerel eats on the south side of cheap street, he uses only three cheeses in his recipes: cheap, cheaper, and cheapest.

**Cheap**: *Queso Menonita* (Mennonite cheese), *queso de Chihuahua* (Chihuahua cheese), or *queso de Oaxaca* (Oaxacan cheese). Pale yellow or butter white, these cheeses are sold in wedges, wheels, or string balls. They can also be bought in hunks. Pickerel prefers the El Laurel brand made from Holstein milk by highland Mennonites who, when not recording positive population growth, dedicate themselves to making fine cheese. If your *lácteo* must melt—for quesadillas, stuffed chilies, or *frijoles puercos*—use this cheese.

**Cheaper**: *Queso de rancho* (ranch cheese) or *queso fresco* (fresh cheese). A mild, white cheese made from raw milk, soft ripened and lightly salty. Used for *botanas* (appetizers/snacks), to accompany bean broths and lentils, and to fill *tacos de abañil* (mason's tacos).

*Queso fresco oreado* (air-seasoned, fresh cheese). Firmer and drier than the soft-ripened variety with a deeper cream color. Used in potato soup, to stuff peppers, and to crumble on *antojitos* (whim snacks to satisfy a food craving—gastronomical equivalent of lust for a quickie).

*Queso para rallar* (grating cheese) or *queso blanco duro* (hard white cheese). Two names for a dry grating cheese used in *chilaquiles* and to top refried beans, enchiladas, tostadas, *sopes*, gorditas, and other *antojitos*.

**Cheapest**: *Panela* (basket cheese). A fresh, unripened white cheese made from unpasteurized milk. Curds are clabbered, salted, and molded into a woven-grass basket that leaves a textured impression on the cheese. May be air-seasoned to achieve additional firmness. Used in *botanas*.

*Queso asadera*—Unmolded, fresh cheese (not to be confused with *queso asadero*—aged, melting cheese) made from packed, whole curds that are air-seasoned. Pickerel uses this poor gringo cheese as a beer snack.

*Requesón*—Fresh, mild, soft cheese made from the curds of cooked whey, spreadable and similar to ricotta. Easily flavored with salt for filling enchiladas and flautas, or with sugar and honey for desserts.

## *Herbs and Spices* (*Hierbas y especias*)

Pickerel uses the following in his kitchen:

Bay leaf (*laurel*)—Long-leaf variety.

Coriander (*cilantro*)—Pickerel picks his with roots and places it in water to keep it fresh.

Pepper (*pimienta entera*)—Peppercorns. Pickerel grinds them with his mortar and pestle (*molcajete y tejolote*) to make ground pepper (*pimienta molida*).

Oregano (*orégano*)—Use only the whole-leaf variety, then pulverize between fingertips.

Salt (*sal*)—Sea salt is Pickerel's preference.

Cinnamon (*canela*)—Use the loose bark variety: long, fragrant quills stealing the show at market spice stalls.

## *Hominy* (*Nixtamal*)

Ask for *nixtamal* or *maíz para pozole* at your local market or corner grocery. These white corn kernels are already soaked, boiled in lime, and ready for cooking.

Pickerel once tried to make his own hominy using a sack of agricultural lime stolen from a farmer's field. However, the experiment failed when the corn kernels began to smoke, blister, and turn black. Pickerel now buys his hominy from Don Tuerto, the blind hominy man (occupational accident). Pickerel still uses the lime in his latrine.

## *Lime* (*Limón*)

Pickerel uses the Mexican sour lime to marinate veggies, tenderize meat, cook fish, flavor broths, chase tequila, mix Margaritas, sanitize the drinking end of a beer bottle, and to keep flies from entering the same. Pickerel plucks his fruit from the thorny branches of his own lime tree—a privileged angiosperm that has miraculously survived the high acidic (uric) content of Pickerel's backyard soil.

## *Shrimp powder* (*Polvo de camarón*)

Although Pickerel lives near shrimp-infested waters and he is often spotted during riptide advisories scouting local beaches for ownerless boats and bikini-clad damsels, there are no shrimp in his recipes—not whole ones, anyway. Pickerel cannot afford shrimp. He can, however, afford shrimp heads, as these are free for the taking from nearby shrimp-peeling plants.

Once a year, during shrimp season, Pickerel makes his pilgrimage to the Mar del Cortez, a local peeler, where he gets permission to gather freshly snapped shrimp heads (*cabezas de camarón*) as they move down the plant conveyer toward a fishmeal rendering truck. Pickerel is not alone. The conveyor is crowded with shrimp head enthusiasts, some scrounging kitty food, others wanting to make their own fertilizer, but most doing what Pickerel is doing—collecting shrimp heads to make shrimp powder.

Here is Pickerel's recipe.

After washing thoroughly, boil 2 kilos of freshly removed shrimp heads in a large pot. Drain, cool, and lay out in the sun to dry. Pickerel uses his flat rooftop for this (although neighbors complain about the stink), covering the heads with mosquito screen to keep off flies. To avoid shrimp mold, be sure heads cool before drying. If the days are cloudy, refrigerate until the sun comes out. Dry until crisp. Grind finely with mortar and pestle (*molcajete y tejolote*) or in blender (*licuadora*). Store in a sealed container.

Pickerel uses shrimp powder in the following crustaceanless dishes:
**Shrimp Head Omelet** (page 108)
**Potato Shrimp Cakes** (page 114)
**Shrimp Ball Soup** (page 160)

## *String beans* (*Ejotes*)
The green beans used in these recipes (and harvested by Pickerel himself from local bean fields) have a tough, fibrous string running the length of their pod seams. Ideal for poor gringo flossing (yes, Pickerel flosses, but only when green beans are in season), this green thread is the reason why Pickerel unfashionably refers to these unripe legumes as "string beans." Any stringless green bean may be substituted.

## *Tomatoes* (*Tomates* or *Jitomates*)
Because Pickerel resides in tomato country, *jitomates*—as the natives call them—are heavy hitters in his vegetable lineup. This also explains why Pickerel never buys tomatoes (or any other ingredients he can be borrow, beg, bargain, or bag). Instead, he heads into nearby fields where the generosity of unsuspecting farmers provides Pickerel's poor gringo pantry with Roma, red plum, and cherry tomatoes.

A thin weed among the vines, Pickerel begins his foray into the fields at dawn, farting wantonly and peeing carefully as he listens to the whispers of early morning pickers fornicating between the rows. By the time the sun comes up, Pickerel is one among the harvest throng of girls, casting his willowy shadow across their bent figures. They giggle behind bandana-covered faces as he bids them a friendly *"buenas días."* Close he has been to their sweet soil sweat and warm tomato smell, and he has dreamed of lying beneath the shady vines with one or all of them. Dreamed, yes. Beyond that, the only thing Pickerel has fondled in tomato fields are plump and succulent size Ds to garnish his noonday salad.

Did Pickerel mention he is also a friend to the tomato farmer? At no charge, Pickerel removes hornworms and chinches from the farmer's plants (botanical pests are a big seller in biological supply). Pickerel catches snakes and pesky, tomato-eating rodents. He shares the farmer's joy when frost hits Florida, and he shares in outrageously high tomato profits when José Cuervo flows freely at the Spotted Bull. Pickerel also translates for tomato buyers new to town. (Their cold storage tans and short-sleeved shirts fresh out of hibernation make them easy for Pickerel to pick out on the crowded railroad platform.) They arrive looking wary, green themselves, yet ready for picking. Pickerel is hospitable, serviceable, just another friendly 'mericun on his way to hell. From directions to erections, Pickerel is full of suggestions, with a safe hotel in between.

> **Health note**: Except in recipes where tomatoes are boiled or broiled, wash well before using. Pickerel goes the extra step and peels the skin. He has walked in enough tomato fields to see what pickers do with tomatoes. No specifics needed. Let your imagination plummet.

Pickerel's connection to tomato country does not end here. One night our hero was driving his 1978 Chevy Nova at a death-demeaning speed on the narrow and windy San Blas road. His blood-tequila level hovered just under the legal limit of designated fool. In the backseat of the Chevy Nova was half the starting lineup of the Tomateros—tomato country's winter-league, Triple A baseball club. Riding shotgun was Eulalio Rodriquez, the Tomatero third-base coach. After a victory party (eleventh inning win over the Cañeros) at the Spotted Bull, Pickerel had magnanimously offered to drive team members to the Sufragio train station to catch the Bala, a midnight bullet train to Nogales.

Speeding through the tropical night, Pickerel did not see the black horse standing in the middle of the San Blas road. (He had turned to grab the shirtfront of the highly intoxicated Tomatero shortstop for daring to suggest that Babe Ruth was gay.) But Pickerel did hear the third-base coach scream, *"Caballo! Caballo!"* just as the hood of his Chevy Nova suddenly lifted in front of them. A loud crunching noise filled the car, followed by an explosive clash of glass. Cries and curses punctuated the abrupt end of forward motion. Then a feeble whinny touched the night.

Such was the demise of Pickerel's Chevy Nova. End of the horse, too (see *Pan-broiled Horse in Tomato Sauce*, *Aztec Soup*, and *Cortez-On-Foot Burritos*). As for Pickerel's passengers—all of whom walked the final quarter mile to Sufragio (except Eulalio, who sprinted to the train station restroom to wash off horse blood)—not one Tomatero was bruised. No small feat for tomatoes hitting a horse at high speed.

Pickerel also lived to lie another day.

## *Tomato puree* (*Pure de tomate*)

A few miles down the poorly paved road from Pickerel's humble abode is the old Heinz tomato plant, now run by the natives after a successful expropriation. The white steam of departing tomato souls rises from its tin roof, while inside, the Piranesian engines of puree manufacture—cauldrons of scalding water, sharp-bladed choppers, and the endless auger—suggest why Hoffa was never found.

Pickerel has taken the tour many times (once he even gave it), and he returns religiously each month to pick up the free samples offered to every visitor. Pickerel thinks of these small gifts as ongoing compensation in the name of the expropriated. Also, they are why Pickerel never finds himself without tomato puree.

## *Vanilla* (*Vainilla*)

Pickerel is not about to chronicle Mexico's fall from vanilla glory. The Totonacas grew it. Montecuzoma drank it. Cortez shipped it. Today, Mexican vanilla bottlers fake it. Suffice it to say, Pickerel's cupboard stocks no vanilla essence, no vanilla extracts, no flavorings, pastes, or powders. Neither does Pickerel believe any vanilla bottle label that reads "coumarin free."* He knows too many Mexican health inspectors to trust this advertising claim.

Instead, Pickerel uses only vanilla beans to flavor his recipes. These he smuggles in his suitcase (through agricultural inspection stations) every time he returns from Veracruz—Mexico's vanilla state.

Already boiled, sweated, and bundled, two dozen bean pods fit easily inside a Samsonite when packed between Bermuda shorts and boxer briefs. (Weeks after his trip, Pickerel's private acreage retains a faint vanilla flavor—as reported by women exploring that region.) Once

---

\* Coumarin, an extract of the tonka bean, smells like vanilla, tastes like vanilla, and makes your liver bleed. Pickerel, who already has enough liver damage for one lifetime, needs no help from coumarin-adulterated vanilla.

unpacked, bean pods store best in a tight-lidded jar kept in a cool, dark place such as a fruit cellar or an underground thermonuclear bomb shelter. Avoid refrigeration. Pickerel uses his dirt-floored closet.

## *Preferred Brands*

Pickerel shamelessly promotes the following brands (*marcas*) in the hope that one or all of their manufacturers will realize increased sales from his endorsement and gratefully offer him stock options. Until that day, price-possessed Pickerel will continue to pull the cheapest sardines off the shelf.

**THE BASICS** (*Los Basicos*):
- **Wheat flour** (*harina de trigo*): Alteña, Corerepe, or Del Valle
- **Corn flour** (*harina de maíz*): Maseca
- **Roasted corn flour** (*pinole de flor*): Siglo XX—Used for breading and beverages.
- **Vegetable shortening** (*manteca vegetal*): Inca
- **Margarine** (*margarina*): Primavera
- **Semisweet chocolate** (*chocolate*): Abuelita
- **White rice, long-grain, unconverted** (*arroz blanco*): San Martin or Del Marqués
- **Pastas** (*pastas*): Vesta or Romana
- **Vinegar** (*vinagre*): La Costeña
- **Tomato puree** (*puré de tomate*): Del Fuerte or La Costeña—Sold in 200 gram boxes that approximate 1 cup (250 ml).
- **Powdered or cubed bouillon** (*consomé en polvo*): Knorr Suiza or Maggi—Pickerel has squeezed a week's worth of broth from a single bouillon cube. Much cheaper than boiling bones, but not as savory.
- **Mole sauce concentrate** (*mole en pasta*): Mole Doña María
- **Canned tuna** (*atún enlatado*): Dolores
- **Green olives** (*aceitunas*): Búfalo

**COOKING OILS** (*Aceites para Cocinar*):
- **Canola oil** (*aceite de canola*): Capullo
- **Corn oil** (*aceite de maíz*): La Gloria
- **Safflower oil** (*aceite de cártamo*): Aurora—Pickerel's preference for deep-frying.

**CANNED CHILI PEPPERS** (*Chiles Enlatadas*):
- **Pickled chilies** (*chiles curtidas*): La Morena
- **Pickled jalapeños** (*jalapeños en escabeche*): La Costeña—Pickerel recommends the sectioned chilies mixed with sliced carrots and onions.
- **Chipotle peppers** (*chile chipotle adobado*): Herdez or San Marcos—Chipotle peppers in adobado sauce are ripened red jalapeño peppers, dried, smoked, and seasoned with a sour vinegar paste of herbs and spices.

**BOTTLED SAUCES** (*Salsas Embotelladas*):
- **Salsa Ranchera**—Thick, dark brown sauce made by Clemente Jacques from jalapeño, serrano, poblano, and chipotle peppers steeped in cider vinegar. Warm capsaicin sea with a fruity undercurrent.
- **Salsa Huichol**—Made with *chile cascabel*, the rattle chili, from the Nayar Huichol Mountains of Nayarit. Mild, earthy flavor with nuts somewhere in the background. Low on the Scoville scale. Best sauce for any lime-covered concoction.
- **Salsa La Guacamaya**—Look for the Scarlet macao with a chili in its claw on the label. Made in Sinaloa from Cora peppers.
- **Salsa Rio Mayo**—Made by the Gutiérrez family in Navajoa, Sonora. Mild flavor of cumin underneath.
- **Salsa Cholula**—Distinctive wooden cap. Tangy hot from Jalisco. Made from piquín peppers and red *chile de árbol*, the tree chili.
- **Salsa en Polvo Tajín**—Chili powder. In the Totonac language, *Tajín* means place of thunder—gastrically apropos for this mixture of ground piquín peppers, salt, and dehydrated lime juice dispensed from a plastic shaker.

# Pickerel's Pointers

### *Charring and peeling fresh chilies* (tatemando y pelando chiles frescos)

The first time Pickerel prepared a stuffed chili, he neglected to char and peel its waxy skin. Days later, chili wax still decorated his unflossed teeth, giving his already lecherous smile unearthly highlights.

Char a chili by placing it over a medium flame and rotating it slowly until the skin blisters and blackens. Small chilies (serrano, habanero) may be skewered on a fork (*tenedor*), while larger chilies (Anaheim, poblano, moron, *pimiento verde*) may be rotated with tongs (*pinzas*). Char evenly, including folds and creases, allowing the skin to burn and crinkle into blackened curls. When chili has charred, place in a plastic bag (a bread bag will work, but make sure chili is not on fire), and allow it to sweat (*sudar*). This makes the blistered chili skin easier to peel and lets the chili season. Remove from bag after 10 minutes and place under running water (or in standing water if, as in Pickerel's house, none is running that day). Gently stroke chili to remove skin (a mini-masturbation). The charred layer will shed in large pieces or peel away in flakes. Skinless chilies are tender and slippery—just limp, green vegetable flesh.

> **Safety note**: Capsaicin (the alkaloid that gives a chili its heat) clings tenaciously to human skin. Wash hands thoroughly after handling chilies and before rubbing eyes, blowing nose, or touching anus.

### *Deveining chili peppers* (desvenando chiles)

Devein charred chilies *after* sweating and peeling (see above). Fresh chilies should be deveined and left seedless before cooking—except in the preparation of certain salsas.

**For recipes with chili stem attached** (soused chilies, stuffed chilies): Insert the tip of a kitchen knife below the stem and make a small vertical slit. Through this slit, insert knife and cut the seed trunk loose from the base of the chili stem. Enlarge the vertical slit enough to maneuver the knife inside chili without tearing it. Remove veins by scraping gently with the tip of the knife and extracting veins with fingers. Wash well to flush loose seeds.

**For recipes with chili stem detached** (chilies with cheese, in broths, and in vegetable dishes): Sever stem and cut the chili lengthwise, almost to the tip. Remove the seed trunk and separate veins from chili by filleting with knife. Wash well to flush loose seeds.

### *Shredding meat* (*deshebrando carne*)
Authentic poor gringo cuisine requires low-priced meat (when neither rustled nor run-over quadrupeds are available). Pickerel chooses only those retail cuts found on the underside of grazing bovines and equines—brisket, eye of round, bottom round, flank, or skirt steak. Pickerel poaches this meat (*frito en agua*), and then he uses his fingertips and a fork to shred it into stringy fibers (*deshebrar*) for preparing tacos, tostadas, flautas, gorditas, and burritos. Pickerel trims his nicotine-stained nails before pinching any protein between his willowy widgets.

### *Pounding meat* (*machacando carne*)
Pickerel recommends using a meat pounder (*machacador de carne*) to tenderize tough meat (beef, horse, or frog) in recipes that do not call for meat to be poached and shredded (see above).

### *Frying onions* (*acitronando cebolla*)
For best flavor, fry onions gently and without browning until soft. Fry garlic the same.

### *Emergency rations: beans, tortillas, and sauces*
(*raciones de emergencia: frijol, tortillas y salsas*)
Pickerel keeps a pan of *frijoles* (boiled, stir-mashed, fried, or refried) in a state of continual standby at the back of his aged and thermally challenged Mabe refrigerator. When he makes tortillas, he cooks enough to endure both a personal and a worldwide economic crisis—albeit one that lasts no more than a week. And at least one salsa—boiled, roasted, or fresh—resides at the bottom of a crusty-edged bowl, ready for action at the dip of a spoon.

In a pickle, a poor gringo needs no more.

# Beans

## Frijoles

*"No man goes hungry where there are beans..."*
Pancho Villa Slim
Bean farmer, Guasave, Sinaloa

Beans Cooked in a Pot

Horsemen Beans

Stir-Mashed Beans

Fried and Refried Beans

Pork-Style Beans

Speckled Hen

Stir-Mashed Speckled Hen

Come with Pickerel on the great tour of beans. First boiled. Then mashed. Later fried. Next refried. Then refried ad infinitum. Amazingly, after this, they are still beans. No other legume on the planet can brag so many reincarnations.

**Buying beans**: When Pickerel was new to the world of beans, he purchased the prepackaged, store-bought variety, ignoring repeated warnings from native bean experts and a local legume inspector. That changed after Pickerel culled a cupful of smooth, round river stones (pretending to be beans) from a kilo of packaged *frijoles*. Pickerel now buys his beans from Pepe Cervantes, owner of Pepe's bean stall in the plazuela *mercado* or market. Pepe sells his *frijoles* in large woven baskets where a customer can run his arms elbow deep into a heap of beans and pull out fistfuls to sift between his fingers. Pickerel does this every time he buys beans—not because he is fishing for sticks and stones (Pepe is the most honest bean vendor on the planet), but because Pickerel likes the feel of swimming in beans. Pepe scoops his *frijoles* onto an antique balance-beam scale, weighs them with a gimlet eye, then pours them into whatever container you remembered to bring (Pickerel often brings only his pockets). As for variety, Pepe offers a bean for every season—the sulfur-colored *azufrado*, the deep yellow *canario*, the white *alubia*, the black bean from Veracruz, the small purple *Flor de Mayo* (not to be confused with the Jack Palance flick filmed in Topolobambo), and Pickerel's favorite, the soft brown *mayacoba*.

**Social note**: Every market has a Pepe. To find one, wander into your local *mercado* looking like a stupid gringo in search of a lost spouse (or a lost gringo in search of a stupid spouse). Wear Bermuda shorts—pale legs in a Mexican market always grab the attention of idle onlookers. Pick out your nearest gawker and say very slowly, "*Amigo. Dónde están los frijoles?*" If subject fails to answer or stares at you with mouth open, find a new stranger. Repeat, "*Amigo. Dónde están los frijoles?*" And so on. Eventually someone will escort you to the local equivalent of Pepe the bean seller. And though it means nothing, tell him Pickerel sent you.

**Cleaning beans**: Remove arthropods, broken beans, smashed beans, spotted beans, half beans, blackies, dwarfs, giants, or any bean that looks like it might grow up into a socially deviant legume if given moist earth. Pickerel works for a homogeneous and classless society of bean. One kilo of beans may take as long as an hour to clean. Pickerel invariably enlists children, idle guests, and passing neighbors to help him clean his beans.

***Washing beans***: Wash well. Pickerel uses a mosquito screen borrowed from his neighbor's window to sluice his beans. He has washed as much as forty fingernails full of soil from a single kilo of beans.

***Bean pot*** (*Olla para frijol*): Pickerel uses a 10-liter pot to boil his beans.

# Beans Cooked in a Pot
## *Frijoles de Olla*

*Ingredientes* (to feed one gringo for one week if he eats only beans)
- 1 kg beans (1 *kilo de frijol*), any variety
- 8 liters cold water (8 *litros de agua fria*)
- 2 tbsp salt (2 *cucharadas de sal*)
- 2 sprigs *epazote* if boiling black beans (See *Epazote* below.)

*Equipo*
- Bean pot (*olla*)

*Preparación*

Clean and wash beans. Pour into bean pot. Cover with water *twice* the bean depth. Bring water to a fast boil. Do not stir—they will surface ensemble. When beans rise, add remainder of cold water. Bring to boil again. Cover and cook over low flame. In 1 hour, add salt. Pickerel tosses in multifingered "pinches" as if he was casting a spell on the whole affair. Add *epazote* (if needed). Again, do not stir. By this hour, Pickerel's beans are the color of his unswept dirt floor. His kitchen is warm with the vapor of bean, ripe with the smell of prehistoric cotyledons rooted on the whirling Pangaea ...

*(Please note: When Pickerel rhapsodizes, it is his sigmoid flexure speaking.)*

When beans have boiled for 2 hours, remove cover and spoon a few *frijoles* into your palm, allowing them to cool. (Wash hands first if, like Pickerel, bean-boiling interlude was spent self-administering a coconut oil enema.) Test for tenderness by placing bean in mouth and pressing it between tongue and gums *only*. Bean should be soft in the center, easily mashed. If you must enlist teeth, then the bean is not cooked. Boil for another 30 minutes and try again. The older the bean, the longer the boil.

Serve in a deep bowl (*tazón hondo*) with flour tortillas on the side. (See *Flour Tortillas*, page 49.) A spoon is handy but not required. Rolled-up tortillas work well. Dip each tortilla into the bean broth, then mop and suck.

---

**Epazote**: A strong-scented herb (dried or fresh) found in any market spice stall; it looks like mint and smells like turpentine before it is cooked. Pickerel, who has experimented extensively with the flatulent effects of boiled beans, has observed that epazote makes him fart less—but only after eating black beans. In all other bean varieties, Pickerel detected no difference.

# Horsemen Beans
## *Frijoles Charros*

For those who wish to go beyond the boiled bean and take their *frijoles* to the savory outdoors where Mexican cowboys ride bare-bottomed and Mexican horse thieves call their mothers on cell phones, go *charro*.

*Ingredientes* (six servings)
   1/4 kg slab bacon *(1/4 kilo de tocino en barra*—Pickerel buys his with rind.)
   2 large tomatoes (2 *tomates grandes*)
   1/2 medium onion (1/2 *cebolla mediana*)
   1 serrano chili pepper (1 *chile serrano*)
   4 sprigs of coriander (4 *ramitas de cilantro*)
   4 liters of boiled beans in their broth (See *Beans Cooked in a Pot*, page 36.)

*Equipo*
   Deep skillet with cover (*sartén honda con tapadera*)

*Preparación*
   Heat skillet. Dice bacon, tomato, onion, and chili. Mince coriander leaves and thinnest stems. Place bacon in skillet and cook until it sweats (not crisp). Do not drain grease. Add tomato, onion, chili, and coriander. Mix well. Cover and simmer over low heat.
   Bring beans to a boil. When bacon sputters and onion softens, add contents of skillet to boiling beans. Stir, cover, and bring beans to a boil again.
   Serve in bowl (*tazón*) with warm tortillas on the side.

> Horsemen beans go well with grilled steer, if you have one. Otherwise, you may eat them outside under the stars—as Pickerel does—and dream of stampedes.

# Stir-Mashed Beans
## *Frijoles Guisados*

> **A word on old beans:** Several varieties of bean may be stored for as long as two years before they become the happy home to tiny bean bores (gorgojos del frijol). Although the additional protein has never humbled Pickerel's hardy constitution (nor his high opinion of stir-mashed bean bore), he knows that not at all poor gringos share his digestive insouciance. So beware of bean bores! Local merchants often hoard beans in back storerooms in anticipation of a bean shortage. The closest Pickerel has ever come to killing an unconfessed Catholic was over the high price of hoarded beans. But that's another story.

*Ingredientes* (four servings)
1/4 cup cooking oil (1/4 *taza de aceite para cocinar*)
4 cups boiled beans (4 *tazas de frijoles cocidos*) (See Beans Cooked in a Pot, page 36.)

*Equipo*
Deep skillet (*sartén honda*) Choose one with nothing on its schedule. Beans are likely to reside there all week.
Bean masher (*moledor de frijol*)

*Preparación*

Heat oil in skillet over *low flame*. Spoon in beans (beans only; no broth yet). Hot oil will jump out of the skillet when beans are added, so be prepared to take evasive action. Pickerel strips down to his dirty white undershirt when he stir-mashes beans.

With masher in hand, squash beans into hot oil with a firm but gentle rocking motion. Walk the masher forward into unsquashed territory. Do not pound! Repeat: Do not pound! Wet beans on hot oil will travel. Ask Pickerel. His kitchen walls scream errant bean.

As beans turn mushy, spoon in broth. Continue to mash. Work for the consistency of runny mashed potatoes. Beans should remain recognizable (not blended), but at some point, the word *mashed* becomes sacred, and you will know your *frijoles* have been squashed enough.

Serve with corn or flour tortillas.

# Fried and Refried Beans
## *Frijoles Fritos y Refritos*

The saga of the bean never ends. First boiled, then stir-mashed, then fried and refried, and then refried again. Pickerel looks upon it not so much as a story of lingering demise, rather as a tale of infinite resurrection.

When Pickerel was at his lowest affordable self-purchasing price, he ate beans every day. His life, in the short-term, had become a week of beans. Each day hinged upon his appetite for beans as if some dietary epiphany had come to him in a dream. Sunday began with Pickerel boiling 2 kilos of beans. Steam poured skyward through the holes in his kitchen roof. On Monday, he tapped half his reserve and took it *charro*. The other half moved to Tuesday, when it became stir-mashed by noon, with the making of tortillas somewhere in the background. On Wednesday, fried beans picked up something on the side—cheese, rice, eggs—while Thursday refried searched desperately for anything on the side. Friday, Pickerel entertained only the broth, which he celebrated as bean soup.

By Saturday, Pickerel had turned a medium shade of bean—his tissues filled with nitrogenous proteins and his lower intestine loaded with organic chemistry in the gaseous state. On Sunday, Pickerel ate out. Actually, he walked the streets inhaling deeply the aroma of broiled beef wafting from crowded sidewalk taco stands. Even this was more satisfying than eating beans.

*Ingredientes* (three servings)
- 2 tbsp cooking oil (2 *cucharadas de aceite para cocinar*—or enough to cover the bottom of a small skillet)
- 3 cups leftover stir-mashed beans (3 *tazas de frijol guisado*) (See *Stir-Mashed Beans*, page 38.)

*Equipo*
Small skillet (*sartén chica*)

*Preparación*
Heat oil in skillet, spoon in stir-mashed beans, and stir over medium heat. Do not cover. Allow the hot oil to break those hydro-beanie bonds. When beans bubble, your mission is concluding. Stir once more, remove from fire, and let cool.

You now have fried beans—thicker, drier, slower to get off the burro.

When you deliver them onto a plate, they should cling grudgingly to your serving spoon (*cuchara de guisa*).

To refry, you must only fry again. Hot oil, fried beans, more elbow in the stirring.

With each refry, beans thicken and solidify. To depart from a serving spoon, they must be thrown at your plate, tomahawk style. If plate shatters (or if aftershocks are felt), the life of refried has ended. Wash the crusty edges from your blackened bean pan and start again.

# Pork-Style Beans
## *Frijoles Puercos*

These are the Benito Juarez of beans—heroic and deserving of their own holiday. Since they are flavored with something Pickerel's poor gringo budget rarely affords—pork sausage—he prepares them only when he has:
- (A) Cashed his VA check.
- (B) Found sausage in the neighbor's fridge while babysitting neighbor's kid.
- (C) Killed a pig.

*Ingredientes* (eight servings)
- 1/2 kg cooked beans in a pot (1/2 *kilo de frijoles de olla*) (See *Beans Cooked in a Pot*, page 36.)
- 1/8 cup pickled chilies (1/8 *taza de jalapeños en escabeche*) (See *Canned Chili Peppers*, page 29.) Any pickled chili (*chile curtida*) will do, but Pickerel prefers jalapeños.
- 1/2 cup margarine (1/2 *taza de margarina*)
- 1/4 kg pork sausage (1/4 *kilo de chorizo de puerco*) (See *Chorizo* sidebar.)
- 1/4 cup Salsa Ranchera (1/4 *taza de Salsa Ranchera*) (See *Bottled Sauces*, page 29.)
- 1/4 kg Chihuahua cheese (1/4 *kilo de queso de Chihuahua*) (See *Cheeses*, page 23.)

*Equipo*
- Blender (*licuadora*)
- Large saucepot (*cazuela grande*)
- Large skillet (*sartén grande*)

**Chorizo**: Every pueblo has its choriceros or sausage makers, some reputable, others, shall we say, Pickerelian. Pickerel formally purchased his chorizo from Chino Ley, a local butcher and midnight rustler of livestock. Then one morning, as Miriam was about to scramble eggs with chorizo, she discovered one whole pig eye staring up at her from inside a pork sausage package. The twins were fascinated, but Miriam refused to let chorizo enter their unhappy home again. Pickerel has since switched vendors, and he can truthfully report that not once has he found identifiable ophthalmic organs in his pork sausage (the errant eyelash, maybe, but Pickerel is not one to split hairs). For those who prefer the hygienic high ground of commercially made chorizo, Pickerel recommends the Chata brand, preferably ranch-style. Tangy vinegar background spiced with the flavor of smoked poblano chilies, toasted coriander seeds, and no peeping pig eyes.

*Preparación*

Pour cooked beans (with broth) from bean pot into blender. If you boiled 1 kilo of dry beans (See *Beans Cooked in a Pot*, page 36.), use half (volume) of your cooked beans for this recipe—an amount that will fill two to three blenders. Blend beans at lowest setting and pour into saucepot.

Mince chilies. Melt margarine in skillet. Add chorizo and fry over low flame. When chorizo browns, add to blended beans in the saucepot. Mix well and simmer over low heat until beans bubble. Add Salsa Ranchera, minced chilies, and cheese. Stir until this *lácteo* loses its soul.

   Serve with corn chips or broken tostadas. No spoon needed. Just dip. You may even lick your fingers.

# Speckled Hen
## Gallina Pinta

Except for the time Pickerel ran over a neighborhood chicken crossing a muddy street, the only speckled hen he puts in a pot is the kind made with whole, white hominy boiled with brown beans. This inexpensive soup-stew for peasants and poor gringos is "speckled" without the hen.

*Ingredientes* (four servings)
- 1 cup beans (1 *taza de frijol*) (See Beans, page 34.)
- 1 cup white hominy (1 *taza de nixtamal*) (See Hominy, page 24.)
- 1/4 thinly sliced medium onion (1/4 *cebolla mediana en rebandas delgadas*)
- 1 tbsp salt (1 *cucharada de sal*)

*Equipo*
- Large bowl (*tazón grande*)
- Saucepot (*cazuela*)

*Preparación*

Clean beans. (See *Cleaning Beans*, page 34.) Place hominy in large bowl with cold water and rub grains vigorously between hands to shuck off the thin sheaths from kernels. Rinse well to remove sheaths and the dark "eye" at the base of each kernel.

Add washed hominy to saucepot with 2 liters of cold water. Bring to a boil. Kernels will split at the base and open—flower—in about 30 minutes.

When hominy has flowered, add beans and continue to boil until beans have cooked. (See *Beans Cooked in a Pot*, page 36.) Add sliced onion and salt. Cover and simmer on low heat for 5 minutes.

Serve in bowl (*tazón*) with a sprinkle of grated ranch cheese on top and corn tortillas on the side.

# Stir-Mashed Speckled Hen
## Gallina Pinta Guisada

*Ingredientes* (four servings)
    1/4 cup cooking oil (1/4 *taza de aceite para cocinar*)
    4 cups speckled hen (4 *tazas de gallina pinta*) See *Speckled Hen* previous page.

*Equipo*
    Deep skillet (*sartén honda*)
    Bean masher (*moledor de frijol*)

*Preparación*

Over a low flame, heat oil in skillet. Spoon in speckled hen—more hominy and beans than broth. Mash the beans and hominy together with a firm but gentle rocking motion of masher. Do not pound. Spoon in broth—enough to give the mixture a runny consistency—and continue to mash until beans and hominy lose their identity—the equivalent of speckled hen run over.

Serve with warm corn tortillas.

# Tortillas

## Tortillas

*"Those damn gringos had me making tortillas up there..."*
*Rodolfo Neri Vela*
*First Mexican astronaut*

Corn Tortillas

Flour Tortillas

Sweet Whole Wheat Tortillas

Once upon a time, Pickerel bought his tortillas at a little tortilla foundry (*tortillería*) down the street. He stood at the tortilla counter like a pilgrim before La Virgen Morena, watching the thin moons of cooked corn roll off a hot conveyor and into the sudoriferous hands of the widowed proprietress. Pickerel was a regular. The widow was friendly. Conversation warmed over steaming piles of tortillas. One morning Pickerel suggested that they stroll among the sacks of milled corn in the back storeroom—make love upon the sacred starch.

Pickerel now holds the world record for a spurned seducer sprinting two city blocks with a kilo of unpaid tortillas under each arm.

Today he makes his own, eating as many as a dozen tortillas at a meal—enough to stretch his pyloric sphincter with a contented but distended stomach. And when Pickerel's pockets cling frugally to a few pesos, homemade tortillas are his low-cost carbo fuel (aside from beer). This staple of the pre-Columbian corn worshipers not only offers Pickerel sustenance, but also serves variously as his plate, fork, spoon, bowl-mopper, napkin, and sunshade. *Vivan las tortillas!*

# Corn Tortillas
## Tortillas de Maíz

*Ingredientes* (makes about forty tortillas)
    4 cups corn flour (4 *tazas de harina de maíz nixtamalizado*)
    1/2 tsp salt (1/2 *cucharadita de sal*)
    2-1/2 cups hot (not boiling) water (2-1/2 *tazas de agua caliente; no herviendo*)

*Equipo*
    Large mixing bowl (*tazón grande para mezclar*) or small dishpan (*bandeja chica*)
    Tortilla press (*prensa de tortilla*)
    2 small sheets of plastic (2 *hojas chicas de plástico*); cut a bread bag in half
    Griddle (*comal*)
    Tortilla basket (*chiquihuite*) or dish with cover (*recipiente con tapadera*)
    Dishcloth (*servilleta de tela*)

*Preparación*
    In bowl or dishpan, combine corn flour, salt, and half the requisite water into soft dough. Knead well. Pickerel adds the remaining water in spurts until the dough reaches a pliant consistency (that of Silly Putty—Pickerel's favorite toy, even today).
    Heat griddle. It should be very hot. Stoke that fire.
    Take a thick pinch of dough and make a sphere the size of a ping-pong ball. Gently press between palms, leaving flat spots on opposite sides. Your tortilla is ready for pressing.

### *Option 1—tortilla press:*

    Open tortilla press. Lay one plastic sheet on the bottom plate and place dough ball on it in the center of press. Lay second sheet on top of ball, close press, grab handle, and push down hard. Pickerel applies the entire six feet of his lanky timber to the handle, grinning diabolically as he imagines Miriam's head inside instead of tortilla dough. (Tortilla pressing is excellent therapy for anger management.) Don't worry about squeezing the dough too thin. The handle of the tortilla press halts at the full horizontal position. Lift handle, open press, and peel away the top sheet of plastic. Gently lift the second sheet with the tortilla. This thin expanse of corn dough has to separate from the plastic sheet without fractures or folds. Do this by placing your free hand on the tortilla and then flipping it over so the plastic is on top. Next, peel the plastic from the tortilla. As Pickerel holds the corn fritter, he does a quick trill with his fingers (as if he was playing the piano upside down) to keep it from sticking to the sweaty pastures of his palm. The tortilla is now ready for the griddle.

### Option 2—pan press:

Place the dough ball between two sheets of plastic and press on any flat surface with the bottom of a heavy frying pan. Do not twist or rotate pan. Just push and grunt. Push evenly. Grunt loudly. Once dough is flat, remove plastic sheets as detailed above.

> **Note**: Only purists and tortilla vendors worry about the shape of their tortillas. Whichever method Pickerel chooses, he finds that his tortillas end up not round but in the shape of cumulus clouds gathering for the summer monsoons.

Place pressed dough on the hot griddle. Cook 1 minute and flip. You will see brown "cooked" spots on the face of tortilla. Leave on the griddle another minute. Flip again. Tortilla will start to puff as the heated air trapped between the cooked layers rises. Tap this bulge with fingertips to spread puffiness evenly (cowards use a dishcloth), and then give the tortilla a half turn (clockwise or counter). Cook for 30 seconds, remove from griddle, and place in your tortilla basket or covered dish. Pickerel stacks as many as twenty in his *chiquihuite,* keeping them warm inside a folded dishcloth (*servilleta de tela*) and ready to eat.

> **Side note**: Pickerel stores leftover tortillas in his Westinghouse, reheating them on his griddle whenever his heart palpitates for corn. If you do not wish to cook 40 tortillas at once, you may save the dough in a plastic bag, refrigerate, and cook according to your own palpitations.

# *Flour Tortillas*
## Tortillas de Harina

*Ingredientes* (for thirty tortillas)
- 1 tbsp salt (1 *cucharada de sal*)
- 3 cups warm water (3 *tazas de agua tibia*)
- 1 kg wheat flour (1 *kilo de harina de trigo*)
- 3/4 cup vegetable shortening or lard (3/4 *taza de manteca vegetal* or *manteca de puerco*)

*Equipo*
- Small mixing bowl (*tazón grande para mezclar*)
- Large mixing bowl (*tazón grande para mezclar*) or small dishpan (*bandeja chica*)
- Smooth board or other flat surface
- Rolling bottle (*rodillo*)
- Griddle (*comal*)
- Dishcloth (*servilleta de tela*)

*Preparación*

In small mixing bowl, add salt to warm water and stir until dissolved. Combine flour and shortening in large mixing bowl. Mix well. Pickerel squeezes fistfuls of flour and shortening, allowing them to ooze between his fingers. From the small bowl, add half the warm salty water to the flour mixture (Pickerel sprinkles his like rain). Knead dough until soft and pliant. You are *amasando*—massaging the *masa*, or dough. Add water as needed until the consistency is such that you can elevate the entire dough mass on two fingers and it will not droop to either side. There are those who let their dough repose two hours after kneading. Not Pickerel. When this poor gringo makes flour tortillas, it is because (a) he is hungry, or (b) he has pilfered something that he urgently needs to hide inside a tortilla (such as the *machaca* from his neighbor's rooftop). Pickerel cannot wait two hours.

Make golf ball-size dough balls between hands. Flatten each with a slap.

Sprinkle flour on a smooth board. Take the rolling bottle and flatten the first dough ball to the size of a large pancake. Lift, rotate 90 degrees, and roll again. Then again—lift, rotate, and roll. And again. You are rolling toward roundness, but also with full knowledge that a pancake-shaped piece of dough flattened by a beer bottle on a board may take many shapes. To prevent dough from sticking to your hands, bottle, or board, sprinkle flour liberally on all surfaces. If the dough wrinkles or tears as you roll it, squeeze it back into a ball and roll it again. Work for an even thickness—ten pages of your favorite paperback book is ideal.

Heat griddle over a medium flame.

Lift tortilla from board. If the dough is well kneaded and rolled to the right thickness, the tortilla can be held in one hand, its edges draped over your fingertips like a damp washcloth. Next, toss it to your other hand (make sure free hand is not clutching the beer bottle). Toss between both hands, slowly at first, back and forth, catching, tossing. You are *torteando*—stretching the tortilla. Practice will make you Pickerelian, if not perfect. A tortilla is larger than your hands and unevenly under the influence of gravity. It resists a game of pitch and catch. Once you get the hang of it, do it faster. As you clap the tortilla back and forth, make it slam against your palms. The tortilla will get bigger, thinner. This makes for a lighter, softer tortilla.

> **Side Note:** For those who have long fingernails, arthritic hands, or who do not want to be seen tossing tortilla dough like a lunatic playing patty-cake with himself, you may skip this part and place your 10-page-thick tortilla directly on the griddle.

The griddle must be hot. The tortilla should hiss, its edges turning yellow, as soon as it touches the griddle. If not, add more heat. The center of the tortilla will turn yellow next. Watch the surface for bubbling. At the first sign of bubbles, flip tortilla over. Almost immediately, the tortilla will begin to inflate. Press lightly with fingertips (cowards use a dishcloth) to push out the air. Rotate the tortilla 90 degrees and leave for 5 seconds. Remove, place inside a folded dishcloth, and go on to the next.

If a tortilla has shiny spots when it comes off the griddle, it is too thick. If it comes off with holes, it is too thin. When the tortilla is just right, you will be able to peel away the front from the back and fill it as if it were a paper-thin sandwich.

# Sweet Whole Wheat Tortillas
## *Tortillas de Trigo*

Pickerel's dessert tortillas—made when he has company (not including live-in maids and green card aspirants).

*Ingredientes* (for thirty tortillas)
- 1 cone (1/4 kg) dark brown, unrefined sugar (1 *cono* [1/4 *kilo*] *de piloncillo*) See *Piloncillo* sidebar.
- 3 cups water (3 *tazas de agua*)
- 1 kg whole wheat flour (1 *kilo de harina de trigo integral*)
- 1/2 tsp salt (1/2 *cucharadita de sal*)
- 1/2 tsp baking powder (1/2 *cucharadita de polvo para hornear*)
- 3/4 cup vegetable shortening or lard (3/4 *taza de manteca vegetal* or *manteca de puerco*)

*Equipo*
- Large mixing bowl (*tazón grande para mezclar*) or small dishpan (*bandeja chica*)
- Saucepan (*cazo*)
- Smooth board or other flat surface
- Rolling bottle (*rodillo*)
- Griddle (*comal*)

> **Piloncillo**: Sometimes called panocha, but not by feminists or women etymologically sensitive to a word that dares to share its meaning with the female reproductive organ (whose suggestive similitude with a rich, dark-colored sweet is left for the reader to determine), this is Mexico's (and Pickerel's) cheapest substitute for refined sugar (*azúcar refinada*) and brown sugar (*azúcar mascabado*). Made from sugar cane juice mechanically crushed from cane stalks, then boiled to syrup and molded into truncated cones (*conos*) or small hard bricks (*barras*), this sweetener has high molasses content.

*Preparación*

Place *piloncillo* in saucepan with water. Bring to low boil and cover. Stir occasionally until sugar dissolves. Let cool.

Combine flour, salt, and baking powder in mixing bowl. Add shortening and sugared water. Work mixture with hands. Pickerel breaks a first-class sweat when he makes this dough. He pounds. He presses. He kneads. He folds. Pickerel knows the end is near when he can lift the dough one-handed, elevate it, pump fake to the left, pump fake to the right, then dish to Jordan at the top of the key. If the dough holds together, it is ready for the griddle. (For those unfamiliar with basketball terminology, knead dough until soft and pliant but not droopy.)

Heat griddle and make golf ball-size dough balls. Roll to roundness following the directions for plain flour tortillas. (See *Flour Tortillas*, page 49.)

Do not hand toss sweet tortillas. Instead, place each on the griddle and cook 60 seconds on both sides (twice as long as plain flour) or until the tortilla is firm.

Allow to cool before serving. Tortillas should be hard and crisp like a tostada, with the flavor of molasses in the background.

# Leftover Tortillas, Tattered Tortillas, and Stale Tortillas

## Sobras de Tortilla, Tortillas Maltratadas y Tortillas Duras

*"La mujer y las tortillas, calientes han de ser."*
"A woman and tortillas, warm they should be."
Popular Mexican refrain never uttered by Elvia Carrillo Puerto
Mexico's first feminist

Mason's Tacos
Bean Tacos
Dangerously Crisp Tortillas with Toppings
Tattered Tortillas with Veggies
Tattered Tortilla Casserole
Tomatoed Tortillas
Tortillas Rolled with Cheese
Tortillas Rolled with Beans
Cheap Cheese Red Enchiladas
Cheap Cheese Green Enchiladas
Squash Blossom Quesadillas

As Pickerel has yet to perfect his recipe for tortilla mash whisky, he puts his corn tortillas—be they leftover, tattered, or stale—to other culinary ends. Take for example, his poor gringo cornrug. Start with a leftover corn tortilla reheated on a griddle (*comal*). Add a dollop of butter, spread thinly, sprinkle on a pinch of salt, roll up the tortilla like a rug, and eat.

> **Warning**: *Melted butter may drip from the end of cornrug onto shirtfront or pants. For this reason, Pickerel eats cornrugs only when lounging in his underwear (or without it).*

## *Mason's Tacos*
### Tacos de Albañil

Mexican masons (the bricklayers, not the brotherhood) are itinerant tradesmen who prefer to eat lunch fast and cheap. A quick and economical noon meal leaves more time and money at the end of the day to get drunk (usually with Pickerel at the Spotted Bull). The *taco de albañil* is the quickest way to miser three food groups under a masonic belt without dropping the trowel or too many pesos. A mason's taco is also an ideal fast food for impoverished gringo travelers and famished fugitives on the run.

*Ingredientes*
- 1/4 kg fresh cheese purchased from nearest corner grocery (1/4 *kilo de queso fresco de la tienda de la esquina más cercana*) (See Cheeses, page 23.)
- 1/4 kg warm corn tortillas purchased from nearest *tortillaría* or 8 homemade corn tortillas (1/4 *kilo de tortillas de maíz calientitas de la tortillería más cercana u ocho tortillas de maíz recién hechas en casa*) (See Tortillas, page 46.)
- Favorite bottled sauce brought from pantry (*su salsa favorita embotellada de la alacena*) (See Bottled Sauces, page 29.)

*Preparación*
Slice cheese. Fill tortilla. Sprinkle sauce. Fold tortilla. Eat fast.

# Bean Tacos
## *Tacos de Frijol*

The two staples of Mexican cooking—beans and tortillas—come together in this essential poor gringo plug of hunger. Pickerel cooks his bean tacos right on the grill, no griddle between tortilla and fire. The simple fusion of corn and bean has gotten him through many meatless days and Miriam-free nights. **Social note**: Drunken Mexicans road testing their English on Pickerel often call this combination a "taco bean," as in, "Eh, Picaro, ju wanna taco bean?"

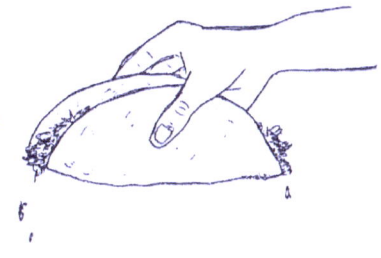

*Ingredientes* (for six bean tacos)
- 1 cup stir-mashed, fried, or refried beans (1 *taza de frijol guisado, frito o refrito*) (See *Beans*, pages 38/39.)
- 6 corn tortillas (6 *tortillas de maíz*) (See *Corn Tortillas*, page 47.)
- Hot sauce (*salsa picante*) (See *Sauces*, page 71, and *Bottled Sauces*, page 71.)

> Every tortilla has two sides: a thin side for spreading butter, beans, or any other filling and a thick side for holding the tortilla. The thin side is the one with a rice paper face that peels if scratched and crinkles if charred.

*Equipo*
- Saucepan (*cazo*)
- Griddle (*comal*) or grill (*parrilla*)

*Preparación*

Heat beans in saucepan. Warm tortillas on griddle or grill (cold tortillas will crack if folded). Spoon warm beans onto the thin side of a warm tortilla. Spread beans evenly with the back of spoon. Fold tortilla in half. Place on griddle or grill.

Turn tacos every few minutes over low heat. The best bean taco is slow cooked—tortilla browning on both sides, edges turning crisp. Bean steam will pour out the ends. When the tortilla turns hard, remove from fire and let cool. This may take 5 minutes or more. If in a hurry, open tortilla with a fork (*tenedor*) and allow steam to escape from bean inferno.

Flavor with your favorite bottled sauce or with a salsa you made yourself. (See *Fired Chili Sauce*, page 82.) Either way, a bean taco is the straightest road to poor gringo heaven.

# Dangerously Crisp Tortillas with Toppings
## Tostadas

For this recipe, Pickerel hangs a dozen leftover tortillas on his wash line (*tendedero*) to dry in the sun. Pickerel does not worry about flies or dirty clothespins, but he does avoid windy days. Once, his entire wash line of leftover T's blew into the neighbor's backyard. Pickerel had to scale his neighbor's wall—one topped with broken glass (in Pickerel's *barrio* good fences make lacerated neighbors)—to retrieve his wayward tortillas before Manola, the neighbor's female Chihuahua with a Doberman mean streak, awoke from her canine siesta. (Of Manola you will hear more, when Pickerel makes his *machaca* with eggs—fondly referred to as Manola *machaca*.)

> After making Dangerously Crisp Tortillas with Toppings, use leftover beans, broth, meat, sauce, and veggies to make gorditas. (See Little Fat Ones, page 212.)

## Tostadas for Seven
(Seven days or until you get sick of them)

When Pickerel makes tostadas, he does not cook again for a week. His multistage production—the equivalent of a five-act culinary musical opening on Broadway—leaves him limp, lustless, and longing for the Bahamas. However, the payoff is big: a week's worth of dangerously crisp tortillas topped with meat, beans, veggies, and sauce—plus broth to wash them down.

### Preproduction—Beans and Tortillas

*Ingredientes*
- 2 cups of stir-mashed beans (2 *tazas de frijol guisado*) (See *Stir-Mashed Beans*, page 38.)
- 2 dozen leftover tortillas (2 *docenas de tortillas para recalentar*)
- 1/2 liter cooking oil (1/2 *litro de aceite para cocinar*)

*Equipo*
- Saucepan (*cazo*)
- Deep skillet (*sartén honda*)

*Preparación*

### For beans

Warm in saucepan over low heat.

### For tortillas/tostadas

Pickerel air-dries his tortillas—to economize cooking oil, to preserve our dwindling reserves of fossil fuels, and to avoid producing dangerous greenhouse gases over Mexico (Pickerel cannot resist sounding environmentally safe). Those without wash lines may deep-fry their leftover T's to achieve the same dangerously wind-blown crispness desired of all tostadas.

Heat oil in skillet. When hot, slip in tortillas, three at a time. Turn once. Fry until golden. Remove and stand upright to drain excess oil on kitchen towels (*toallas de cocina*) or, Pickerel style, on old newspapers untouched by dog (*papel periodico*).

### Act I: The meat (*La carne*)

The first of many crossroads in a poor gringo's search for low-cost (or no-cost) animal protein. Farm-raised or wild? Pet or stray? Mammal or not? The options for tostada meat, though many, are subject to local laws, seasonal availability, and how fast you can run, drive, or throw a tomahawk. Culinarily speaking, Pickerel prefers meat that, once poached (*frito en agua*), shreds easily with the fingertips. (See *Shredding Meat*, page 31.) Examples: chicken breast (*pechuga de pollo*), flank or skirt steak (*falda de res*), heel or eye of round (*cuete*), brisket or bottom round (*guasano*), thigh from a free-range turkey (*pierna de pavo*)—preferably within the range of Pickerel. Although Pickerel has prepared tostadas with meat from other species (which he will not identify for fear of reprisals from the local wildlife inspector and neighborhood canophiles), not once has he ventured outside the chordate phylum. So whatever your protein of choice, be assured that neither dinner guests nor in-laws (yes, Pickerel has dared to experiment) will identify it taxonomically. In the end, when mouths open wide for that first bite of tostada, the mystery of the meat remains buried under a haystack of lettuce and onions. Its flavor and chewiness—no matter how distinctive—will be lost in a medley of beans, bouillon broth, sauce, and cheese. Pickerel guarantees it.

*Ingredientes*
- 1 kg meat (1 *kilo de carne*)
- 1/2 onion (1/2 *cebolla*)
- 4 garlic cloves, unpeeled (4 *dientes de ajo, sin pelar*)
- Bouillon powder (*consomé en polvo*): 1 tsp chicken bouillon for poultry (*1 cucharadita de consomé de pollo para aves*) or 2 tsp beef bouillon for everything else (2 *cucharaditas de consomé de res para todo lo demas*)
- 2 tbsp salt (2 *cucharadas de sal*)
- 1 tsp peppercorns (1 *cucharadita de pimienta entera*)

*Equipo*
- Stockpot (*olla*)

*Preparación*

Place meat (whole or chopped in large pieces) in 4 liters of water with onion (unsliced), garlic, bouillon powder, salt, and peppercorns. Cover and boil over low heat for 2 hours (3 if meat is untamed). Test with fork (*tenedor*). When tender, remove from broth and let cool. Using a fork and/or your fingers, shred meat into fibers no thicker than a toothpick. (See *Shredding Meat*, page 31.)

Set shredded meat aside. Save stock to make broth (see below).

### Act II: Broth (Caldo)

*Ingredientes*
- 2 large tomatoes (2 *tomates grandes*)
- 3 liters of leftover meat stock (3 *litros de caldo de carne*)
- 1 tbsp cooking oil (1 *cucharada de aceite para cocinar*)

*Equipo*
- Blender (*licuadora*)
- Large saucepot, at least 4 qts (*cazuela grande, por los menos 4 litros*)
- Strainer (*colador*) Pickerel uses mosquito screen.

*Preparación*

Add uncut tomatoes to meat stock. Cover and cook 10 minutes over low flame. Have blender washed and ready. Pluck tomatoes from stock, remove skins, and drop into blender with 2 tablespoons of stock. Blend until smooth.

In saucepot, heat oil. Add blended tomato and fry over low flame until it bubbles and thickens. Pour meat stock into the saucepot with fried tomato, using strainer to remove garlic and onion. Careful—hot stock hitting hot tomato! Stir, cover, and simmer over low heat for 30 minutes. Leave covered.

## Act III: Sauce *(Salsa)*

*Ingredientes*
- 2 cups of prepared broth—see above (2 *tazas de caldo ya preparada—ver nota arriba*)
- 4 medium tomatoes (4 *tomates medianos*)
- 5 serrano chilies (5 *chiles serranos*)
- 1/2 medium onion (1/2 *cebolla mediana*)
- 1 garlic clove, peeled (1 *diente de ajo, pelado*)
- 1/2 tsp salt (1/2 *cucharadita de sal*)
- 1/4 tsp ground pepper (1/4 *cucharadita de pimienta molida*)
- A pinch of ground, whole-leaf oregano (*una pizca de hoja de orégano molido*)

*Equipo*
- Saucepan (*cazo*)
- Blender (*licuadora*)

*Preparación*

In saucepan with broth, add tomato, chili, onion, garlic, salt, pepper, oregano, and 2 cups of water. Cover and bring to a boil. Lower heat, remove cover, and cook until the chilies soften (test with fork) and half the broth is left. Cool. Remove chili stems and tomato skins with fork. Add contents of saucepan to blender and blend until smooth.

## Act IV: The veggie and cheese topping *(Verdura y queso)*

*Ingredientes*
- 3 medium cucumbers (3 *pepinos medianos*)
- 3 medium tomatoes (3 *tomates medianos*)
- 5 radishes (5 *rábanos*)
- 1/2 crisphead lettuce (1/2 *lechuga iceberg*)
- 1/4 kg hard white cheese for grating (1/4 *kilo de queso blanco duro para rallar*) (See *Cheeses*, page 23.)
- 2 medium onions (2 *cebollas medianas*) Pickerel prefers red onion (*cebolla morada*) for his tostada topping.
- 5 limes (5 *limones*)
- 1 tsp salt (1 *cucharadita de sal*)
- 3 tbsp vinegar (3 *cucharadas de vinagre*) Pickerel uses white cane vinegar.

*Equipo*
- Cheese grater (*raspador de queso*)
- Serving bowls (*tazones hondos*)
- Lime squeezer (*exprimidor de limón*)

*Preparación*

Peal and slice cucumbers thinly. Peel and slice tomatoes. Slice radishes. Chop lettuce finely. Grate cheese. Place all of the above in separate bowls (*tazones*).

Halve onions, slice into rainbows, and place in bowl (*tazón*). Slice 4 limes. Squeeze onto onions. Add salt, vinegar, and 1/2 cup of warm water (*agua tibia*). Mix, cover, and marinate 15 minutes.

### Act V: The finale (*El final*)

Pour a cupful of broth (Pickerel fills a mug). Squeeze in half a lime. Stir.

Spread a thin layer of warm beans across each crisp tortilla. Follow with a heaping spoonful of shredded meat. Add veggies next—lettuce first, tomato, cucumber, then radish. Layer carefully. Add a forkful of onions, spreading them evenly across the tostada. Sprinkle grated cheese on top and spoon on sauce—as much as you dare.

Your tostada should look like a haystack—one teetering with a symphony of colors and flavors. Take care that the crispy tortilla doesn't break as you lift it.

Option #1: Spoon on broth and take a bite, grabbing a little of everything: crunchy tortilla with the taste of bean, chewy meat, soft veggies, cheese, and salsa.

Option #2: Do not spoon on broth. Instead, take a bite, grab a little of everything, and then wash it down with a sip of broth.

# Tattered Tortillas with Veggies
## Sopitas con Verdura

*Ingredientes* (one serving)
- 3 corn tortillas (3 *tortillas de maíz*)
- 1 medium tomato (1 *tomate mediano*)
- 1/4 small onion (1/4 *cebolla chica*)
- 1/2 Anaheim chili, deveined and seedless (1/2 *chile largo-verde sin venas, ni semillas*) (See *Deveining Chili Peppers*, page 30.)
- 2 tbsp cooking oil (2 *cucharadas de aceite para cocinar*)
- 1/4 tsp salt (1/4 *cucharadita de sal*)

*Equipo*
- Large skillet (*sartén grande*)

*Preparación*

Stack tortillas, cut into strips, and then crosscut into postage stamp-size squares. Peel tomato and chop finely. Dice onion and chili.

Heat oil in skillet. Add tortilla squares. Sprinkle with salt and stir.

Cook until crisp and golden. Push to one side of the pan to make room for veggies. Fry tomato, onion, and chili in same pan until they are steamy. Push tortilla squares back into the middle of pan and mix with veggies.

Serve with a dash of your favorite bottled sauce across the top and fried beans on the side.

# Tattered Tortilla Casserole
## Chilaquiles Rojos

*Ingredientes* (three servings)
- 2 cups red chili sauce (2 *tazas de chile colorado*) (See *Red Chili Sauce*, page 81.)
- 10 corn tortillas (10 *tortillas de maíz*)
- 1 cup grated ranch cheese (1 *taza de queso de rancho rallado*)
- 3 tbsp cooking oil (3 *cucharadas de aceite para cocinar*)
- 1/2 small onion, thinly sliced (1/2 *cebolla chica, cortada en rebandas delgadas*)

*Equipo*
- Large skillet (*sartén grande*)

*Preparación*

Warm chili sauce. Stack tortillas and cut in quarters. Open each tortilla triangle (separate the two layers, thin from thicker) and fill with a three-finger pinch of cheese.

> Substitute green tomato sauce for the red to prepare chilaquiles verdes. (See Green Tomato Sauce, page 76.)

Heat oil in skillet. Place filled tortilla triangles in oil *thin side up*. The thick side must fry first; otherwise, the filling will spill. Position as many tortilla triangles as you can fit into the skillet. Flip each at the first sign of browning. The thin side will take less time. Fry tortilla triangles until golden and crisp.

Keep flame low. Spoon in red chili sauce. Cover triangles, making sure sauce seeps into all the tortilla spaces. Sprinkle on the remainder of cheese. Place raw onion rings on top. Cover and remove from heat. Let sit 3 minutes. Serve with stir-mashed or refried beans on the side.

# *Tomatoed Tortillas*
## Entomatadas

From local etymologists, Pickerel has sought out derivation of the word *entomatada*, this Jericho of puree impoverishment. The closest root word he has found is *intomatoeds* (pronounced in-toe-may-toads): past tense of the verb *intomato*, first person singular of the infinitive "to intomato," whose derivation might very well be: V. [Sp., Fr. *inletomataput*: into-the-tomato-put (1604) {of Nahuatl origin; more at *putatomatoin*}].

That said, Pickerel recommends his tomatoed tortillas for breakfast. And let the record state that Pickerel never breakfasts before wetting his appetite on the morning paper. This he borrows from neighbors (late-risers all) who enjoy home delivery (yes, Pickerel plays fair—he rotates his subscribers from day-to-day). Pickerel uses the sports page to kindle his grill. The financial news he puts down for the dog. All remaining sections he saves for absorbent purposes: to keep the floor of his latrine dry and to catch the excess cooking oil that drips from his deep-fried tostadas, flautas, and gorditas.

*Ingredientes* (two servings)
    2 tbsp cooking oil (2 *cucharadas de aceite para cocinar*)
    1 cup tomato puree (1 *taza de puré de tomate*)
    6 corn tortillas (6 *tortillas de maíz*)
    1 cup grated ranch cheese (1 *taza de queso de rancho rallado*)

*Equipo*
    Small skillet (*sartén chica*), no smaller than a tortilla
    Shallow bowl *(plato hondo)*

*Preparación*
    Heat oil in skillet. Warm puree and pour into shallow bowl. Place the first tortilla in puree. Dunk it. Both sides should get red. Lift and drain excess puree into the bowl. Slip tortilla into the hot oil. Use a spatula (*espátula*) for this. Tomato puree and hot oil have a long-standing feud. Bystanders take cover. Even the willowy Pickerel keeps his distance, approaching only to flip the tomatoed tortilla onto its back. Thirty seconds per side is enough.

    Lift tomatoed tortilla from oil. It should be limp, about to fall apart, its bright tomato-red color darkened by the heat of battle. Place on a plate, thin side up. Sprinkle with cheese. Roll up tortilla with cheese inside. Pickerel tries to be neat, even orientally artistic, when he rolls a tomatoed tortilla newly delivered from angry oil, but hot tortillas make fingertips hurry.

Do the next tortilla. When all tomatoed tortillas are rolled, sprinkle with remaining cheese and serve with refried beans on the side. Then you may *putatomatoin*.

## *Tortillas Rolled with Cheese*
### *Revolcadas*

*Ingredientes* (two servings)
- 2 tbsp cooking oil (2 *cucharadas de aceite para cocinar*)
- 1/4 small onion (1/4 *cebolla chica*)
- 1 cup grated ranch cheese (1 *taza de queso de rancho rallado*)
- 6 corn tortillas (6 *tortillas de maíz*)

*Equipo*
Small skillet (*sartén chica*), no smaller than a tortilla

*Preparación*

Heat oil in skillet. Dice onion finely and mix well with grated cheese.

Slip first tortilla into hot oil. As soon as tortilla inflates, flip over. You do not want a crisp tortilla but one that is soft enough to roll. Remove tortilla and place on a plate. Slip in the next. Pickerel stacks his lightly fried tortillas thin side up, one upon another until the last one is cooked.

Spoon 2 tablespoons of cheese and onion mix onto the thin side of each tortilla. Roll into burritos and press the ends so cheese won't fall out. Lay them side by side on your plate. Leave enough cheese for a generous sprinkle across the top.

Serve with stir-mashed beans on the side and a dash of Salsa Ranchera. (See *Bottled Sauces*, page 29.) Crunchy onion + Soft cheese + Warm tortilla = Poor gringo bliss.

# Tortillas Rolled with Beans
## *Enfrijoladas*

*Ingredientes* (two servings)
- 1/2 small onion (1/2 *cebolla chica*)
- 1 lime (1 *limón*)
- 1/2 tsp salt (1/2 *cucharadita de sal*)
- 1 tbsp vinegar (1 *cucharada de vinagre*) Pickerel uses white cane vinegar.
- 1/4 crisphead lettuce (1/4 *lechuga iceberg*)
- 1/2 carrot (1/2 *zanahoria*)
- 1 cup stir-mashed beans (1 *taza de frijoles guisados*)
    (See *Stir-Mashed Beans*, page 38.)
- 3 tbsp cooking oil (3 *cucharadas de aceite para cocinar*)
- 8 corn tortillas (8 *tortillas de maíz*)
- 1/4 cup grated ranch cheese (1/4 *taza de queso de rancho rallado*)

*Equipo*
- Lime squeezer (*exprimidor de limón*)
- Small bowl (*tazón chico*)
- Small skillet (*sartén chica*), no smaller than a tortilla

*Preparación*

Slice onion into rainbows and place in bowl (*tazón*). Slice lime. Squeeze onto onions. Add salt, vinegar, and 1/4 cup of warm water (*agua tibia*). Mix, cover, and marinate 15 minutes.

Shred lettuce. Peel carrot and grate finely. Warm beans. Heat oil in skillet.

Slip first tortilla into hot oil. As soon as tortilla inflates, flip over. You do not want a crisp tortilla but one that is soft enough to roll. Remove tortilla and place on a plate. Slip in the next. Pickerel stacks his lightly fried tortillas one upon another thin side up, until the last one is cooked.

Spoon 2 tablespoons of warmed beans onto the thin side of each tortilla. Roll each tortilla into a burrito and press ends so the beans won't fall out. Lay them side by side on your plate.

Next to *enfrijoladas*, place lettuce topped with grated carrot, marinated onion, and a generous sprinkle of grated cheese. Serve with a dash of Salsa Ranchera. (See *Bottled Sauces*, page 29.)

# Cheap Cheese Red Enchiladas
## Enchiladas Rojas de Queso

*Ingredientes* (two servings)
- 1 small white onion (1 *cebolla chica*)
- 2 limes (2 *limones*)
- 1 tsp salt (1 *cucharadita de sal*)
- 2 tbsp vinegar (2 *cucharadas de vinagre*) Pickerel uses white cane vinegar.
- 3 tbsp cooking oil (3 *cucharadas de aceite para cocinar*)
- 1/2 cup red chili sauce (1/2 *taza de salsa de chile colorado*)
    (See *Red Chili Sauce*, page 81.)
- 6 corn tortillas (6 *tortillas de maíz*)
- 1-1/4 cups grated ranch cheese (1-1/4 *tazas de queso de rancho rallado*)
- 1 cup chopped crisphead lettuce (1 *taza de lechuga iceberg picada*)

*Equipo*
- 2 small skillets (2 *sartenes chicas*), no smaller than a tortilla
- Lime squeezer (*exprimidor de limón*)
- Small bowl (*tazón chico*)

*Preparación*

Halve onion, slice into rainbows, and place in bowl (*tazón*). Slice limes. Squeeze onto onions. Add salt, vinegar, and 1/3 cup of warm water (*agua tibia*). Mix, cover, and marinate 15 minutes.

In the first skillet, heat 1 tablespoon of oil. When oil is hot, add red chili sauce. Cook on high heat for 5 minutes, stirring frequently. Sauce will thicken and darken. Keep warm over low flame.

In the second skillet, heat 2 tablespoons of oil. When hot, slip in the first tortilla. Fry quickly, flipping once. Tortilla should remain soft enough to roll.

With spatula (*espátula*), remove tortilla from oil, drain, and dip in sauce (Pickerel positions his sauce skillet nearby). Cover both sides with sauce, remove, and place thin side up on a plate. Spoon on ample cheese (6 enchiladas = 1/6 cup per tortilla). Roll tortilla and position at the edge of plate. Cover to keep warm while you prepare the other five enchiladas, placing each side by side. **Note:** Rolling soft tortillas dipped in warm chili sauce is a finger-messy business. Have a towel handy (or wear an old T-shirt for wiping, as Pickerel does).

When the last tortilla is in position, top with chopped lettuce and forkfuls of marinated onion. Sprinkle with leftover cheese. Your red enchiladas are ready for liftoff. Serve with fried beans on the side.

# Cheap Cheese Green Enchiladas
## Enchiladas Verdes de Queso

*Ingredientes* (two servings)
- 3 tbsp cooking oil (3 *cucharadas de aceite para cocinar*)
- 1 cup green tomato sauce (1 *taza de salsa verde*)
   (See Green Tomato Sauce, page 76.)
- 6 corn tortillas (6 *tortillas de maíz*)
- 1-1/4 cups grated ranch cheese (1-1/4 *tazas de queso de rancho rallado*)

*Equipo*
- 2 small skillets (2 *sartenes chicas*), no smaller than a tortilla

*Preparación*

In the first skillet, heat 1 tablespoon of oil. When oil is hot, add green tomato sauce. Cook until sauce thickens to a bisque-like consistency. Keep warm over low flame.

In the second skillet, heat 2 tablespoons of oil. When hot, slip in the first tortilla. Fry quickly, flipping once. Tortilla should remain soft enough to roll.

With spatula (*espátula*), remove tortilla from oil, drain, and dip in sauce (Pickerel positions his sauce skillet nearby). Cover both sides with sauce, remove, and place thin side up on a plate. Spoon on ample cheese (6 enchiladas = 1/6 cup per tortilla). Roll tortilla and position at the edge of plate. Cover to keep warm while you prepare the other five enchiladas, placing each side by side. When the last tortilla is in position, spoon extra sauce over enchiladas. Sprinkle with leftover cheese.

> In tribute to his adopted country and its tricolored flag, Pickerel paints his green- and white-capped enchiladas with a bright red swash of Salsa La Guacamaya. (See Bottled Sauces, page 29.) Patriotic Pickerel, last scoundrel in the bastion.

Serve immediately (otherwise tortillas turn soggy and fall apart) with refried beans on the side.

# Squash Blossom Quesadillas
## Quesadillas de Flor de Calabaza

The prestidigitatorial disappearance of squash blossoms from flowering zucchini fields and the simultaneous sighting of M. S. Pickerel in the vicinity are not a coincidence. To ensure self-pollination for the farmer (his crop, that is) and autumn squash for himself, Pickerel picks only one flower out of every thirty (boy and girl squash flowers room together, botanically speaking). Back in his kitchen, Pickerel removes stems and sepals (the only green part of a squash flower), but he leaves all reproductive organs intact (no comment). Occasionally, Pickerel finds squash bugs hiding among his petals (also squash bug turds), so he washes them well.

Poor gringos living distantly from squash fields may buy blossoms at their local market. Flowers from any squash will do—summer, winter, zucchini, pumpkin—when seasonally available. Sold by the kilo.

*Ingredientes* (two servings)
    24 squash blossoms (24 *flor de calabaza*), freshly picked
    1/4 kg Chihuahua cheese (1/4 *kilo de queso de Chihuahua*)
    Dough to make six corn tortillas (See *Corn Tortillas*, page 47.)

*Equipo*
    Cheese grater (*raspador de queso*)
    Tortilla press (*prensa de tortilla*)
    2 small sheets of plastic (2 *hojas chicas de plástico*); cut a bread bag in half
    Griddle (*comal*)
    Sharp kitchen knife (*cuchillo filoso*)

*Preparación*
   Chop blossoms. Grate cheese. Heat griddle. Make dough balls, press out the first tortilla (See *Corn Tortillas*, page 47.), and place on the heated griddle.

   After flipping tortilla, watch it inflate. Do *not* press out the air. Instead, let it rise and swell. Into this puffed-up toad of a tortilla, you will slip cheese and blossoms. Do this by slitting the tortilla along its outer edge with a sharp knife. Make the slit wide enough to drop in a three-finger pinch of both. Since the knife cut lets the hot tortilla air escape (deflating the toad), the slit must be propped open so both cheese and blossoms can enter. Do this with your fingers and the aid of the knife. Pickerel moves the tortilla from the griddle to an unheated surface long enough to prop it open and fill it. The object is to get the stuffed tortilla—now a quesadilla—back to the griddle so that the slit closes, the cheese melts, and the flowers cook. Flip again, and even again, pressing the quesadilla lightly to spread the melted cheese. You may leave your quesadilla on the griddle until the tortilla turns crispy, or you may remove it while the tortilla is soft and droopy.

Serve with nothing. The blend of melted cheese and crunchy flowers pressed between corn is, in Pickerel's humble opinion, virginally exquisite.

# Sauces

## Salsas

*Salsa ('sȯl-sə, 'säl- Sp) n 1. Sauce with rhythm*
*Samuel Juanson*
*Local Latino Lexicog*

Fresh Sauce with Lime

Cooked Sauce

Roasted Tomato Sauce

Boiled Tomato Sauce

Green Tomato Sauce

Guacamole

Red Chili Sauce

Fired Chili Sauce

In the days when penury left Pickerel counting the five food groups on two fingers, salsa was his savior. The formula: salsa + tortillas = meal.

Not one to embrace tedium, Pickerel allowed his salsa and tortillas to try different positions. One day, a rolled corn tortilla dipped deeply into warm tomato sauce. The next, a burnt chili salsa slipped snugly inside a folded tortilla. On other days, spoonfuls of fresh lime salsa rode wildly atop a toasted tortilla.

Although roadkill and rustled livestock have recently joined Pickerel's diet, salsas continue to preside at his table, sometimes flavoring, sometimes disguising the menu. The following are the sauces Pickerel still takes to the well.

## *Fresh Sauce with Lime*
### Salsa Fresca or Salsa Cruda or Salsa Bandera

*Ingredientes* (makes 1-1/2 cups)
- 2 medium tomatoes (2 *tomates medianos*)
- 1/2 small onion (1/2 *cebolla chica*)
- 3 small serrano chilies (3 *chiles serranos chicos*)
- 2 sprigs coriander (2 *ramitas de cilantro*)
- 1/2 lime (1/2 *limón*)
- 1/2 tsp salt (1/2 *cucharadita de sal*)

*Equipo*
- Large serving bowl (*tazón hondo*)
- Lime squeezer (*exprimidor de limón*)

*Preparación*

Peel tomatoes and chop finely with onion. Stem serranos and chop finely (seeds and veins). Mince coriander leaves and thinnest stems. Combine in a serving bowl (*tazón hondo*). Add salt. Squeeze lime over ingredients. Mix well. Serve fresh while the serrano is crunchy and the cilantro is crisp. Pickerel spoons fresh sauce on eggs and lentils and inside meat tacos. He also floats a hefty dollop in his bowl of boiled beans.

# Cooked Sauce
## *Salsa Cocida*

*Ingredientes* (makes 1-1/2 cups)
- 5 serrano chilies (5 *chiles serranos*)
- 3 large tomatoes (3 *tomates grandes*)
- 1 garlic clove, peeled (1 *diente de ajo, pelado*)
- 1/3 small onion (1/3 *cebolla chica*)
- 1/2 tsp ground pepper (1/2 *cucharadita de pimienta molida*)
- A pinch of ground, whole-leaf oregano (*una pizca de hoja de orégano molido*)
- 1/2 tsp chicken bouillon powder (1/2 *cucharadita de consomé de pollo en polvo*)
- 1/2 tsp salt (1/2 *cucharadita de sal*)

> Pickerel puts this sauce on fish and fritangas (anything fried). The ratio of chilies to tomatoes guarantees the first swallow will be a peristaltic descent into hell.

*Equipo*
- Saucepot (*cazuela*)
- Blender (*licuadora*)

*Preparación*

Remove chili stems and quarter tomatoes. Add to saucepot with garlic, onion, pepper, oregano, bouillon powder, and 1/2 liter of cold water. Cover and bring to a boil. Cook on low heat until the water is gone. With a fork (*tenedor*), remove the tomato skins (if stuck to pot bottom, leave there). Place remaining contents of saucepot into blender. Add salt. Blend on low setting for 30 seconds. Pour into a dish (you may help it along with a spoon), and serve warm.

# Roasted Tomato Sauce
## Salsa de Tomate Asado

*Ingredientes* (makes 1 cup)
- 3 medium tomatoes (3 *tomates medianos*)
- 1 shallot (1 *chalote*)
- 1 small garlic clove, unpeeled (1 *diente chico de ajo, sin pelar*)
- 12 peppercorns (12 *pimientas enteras*)
- 1/2 tsp salt (1/2 *cucharadita de sal*)

*Equipo*
- Griddle (*comal*)
- Tongs (*pinzas*)
- Mortar and pestle (*molcajete y tejolote*) or mixing bowl and bean masher (*tazón para mezclar y moledor de frijol*)

> A salsa without chili. Use on eggs, fish, broiled meats, lard-fried pork, and in combination with any other salsa inside tacos or on sopes.

*Preparación*

Heat griddle. Place tomatoes and shallot where griddle is the hottest. Place garlic on the edge for slow toasting. Tomatoes will turn and roll (due to the uneven heating of the water inside) as if trying to escape the griddle. This is the closest Pickerel comes to feeling sorry for a tomato.

Using tongs, turn tomatoes and shallot every few minutes, allowing them to blacken and blister on all sides. Toast garlic evenly. Tomatoes and shallot should cook in about 20 minutes. When squeezed with tongs, they should feel soft in the center.

Remove garlic when toasted on both sides. Peel the charred skin and place with peppercorns in the *molcajete* or mixing bowl. Grind until garlic pulp mixes with crushed pepper.

When tomatoes are cooked, grind one at a time into the garlic pulp. Remove charred tomato skins that resist grinding. After removing the stem and roots from shallot, grind into the tomato pulp. To pulverize onion layers, bear down with the *tejolote* or bean masher. Add salt, stir, and grind some more. Your textured sauce should have a smoky flavor and the burnt red color of brick. Serve warm.

# Boiled Tomato Sauce
## *Salsa de Tomate Cocido*

*Ingredientes* (makes 1-1/2 cups)
- 2 large tomatoes (2 *tomates grandes*)
- 1/2 onion *(1/2 cebolla)*
- 1 small garlic clove, peeled (1 *diente chico de ajo, pelado*)
- 1 tsp beef bouillon powder (1 *cucharadita de consomé de res en polvo*)
- 1 cup tomato puree (1 *taza de puré de tomate*)
- 1 tbsp cooking oil (1 *cucharada de aceite para cocinar*)
- 1 tsp salt (1 *cucharadita de sal*)
- 1/2 tsp ground pepper (1/2 *cucharadita de pimienta molida*)

> Pickerel spoons his tomato sauce on cabbage cakes, stuffed green chilies, fried cauliflower, potato shrimp cakes, and just plain scrambled eggs.

*Equipo*
- Saucepot (*cazuela*)
- Blender (*licuadora*)

*Preparación*

Quarter tomatoes, slice onion, and chop garlic, but not too finely. Place in saucepan with 1 liter of water and bring to a boil. Add bouillon powder, cover, and simmer for 5 minutes. Remove cover and mash tomatoes with a fork (*tenedor*). Allow to cool, remove tomato skins, and pour contents of saucepot into blender. Add tomato puree, salt, and pepper. Blend until smooth.

Heat oil in the empty saucepot. Add contents of blender. Fry tomato mixture over low flame until it bubbles and thickens. Your tomato sauce is ready.

# *Green Tomato Sauce*
## *Salsa Verde or Salsa de Tomatillo*

Not to be confused with green tomatoes (or unripe cape gooseberries), tomatillos are poor cousins of the ground cherry. Aztecs dined upon them long before the genes of Cortez swam down White River.

As for tomatillo stories, Pickerel has only one. Once upon a time, India Robles, a wide-bottomed field forager and Pickerel's would-be mistress-of-mayhem-with-a-machete, delivered tomatillos—freshly picked from dew-laden vines in the predawn darkness—to his doorstep for ten pesos a pail. A Pickerelian price. Then one morning, when the tropical sun was high, Pickerel made the mistake of trying to be his hospitable self. He said to India Robles, this tomatillo thief, "Come in out of the heat, India. Have a seat on the sofa, and let me get you something cool to drink." The invitation was innocent enough, but India mistook Pickerel's lecherous smile and the bulge in his pants (his pockets were full of limes) as preliminaries to a sofa seduction. What Pickerel saw next was the flash of sharpened steel, and then, as if the Force be with her, India Robles waved a bright-bladed machete at him—more precisely, at his crotch. Where this instrument of phallic downfall came from, Pickerel dared not ask, though there was only one place on wide-bottomed India where an 18-inch blade could hide without glinting in the sunlight.

Sadly, that was the last time Pickerel benefited from the low price of stolen tomatillos. He now buys them at his local market, and he suggests you do the same.

*Ingredientes* (makes 2 cups)
    12 green tomatoes (12 *tomatillos*)
    1 serrano chili (1 *chile serrano*)
    1 garlic clove, peeled (1 *diente de ajo, pelado*)
    1 tsp salt (1 *cucharadita de sal*)
    1/2 tsp chicken bouillon powder (1/2 *cucharadita de consomé de pollo en polvo*)

*Equipo*
- Saucepan (*cazo*) and colander (*escurridor*)
- Small plastic bag (a bread bag will work) for sweating charred chilies (*una bolsa de plástico chica para hacer sudar los chiles tatemados*)
- Blender (*licuadora*)

*Preparación*

After removing papery husks, wash tomatillos. Place in a saucepan with 3 cups of cold water. Boil tomatillos for 10 minutes or until they are soft. Drain in colander. Char serrano chili and peel skin. (See *Charring Chili Peppers*, page 30.) Sever stem and cut chili lengthwise to remove seeds and veins. (See *Deveining Chili Peppers*, page 30.) Place chili in blender with garlic, salt, bouillon powder, and boiled tomatillos. Do *not* add water. Blend until smooth. Your tomatillo sauce is ready for enchiladas, *chilaquiles*, and eggs. You may also refrigerate for later use.

SAUCES

# Guacamole
## *Guacamole*

Served as a sauce, relish, filling, topping, side dish, and dip, guacamole is the reason that Agustín de Iturbide—Mexico's liberator, emperor, and traitor (all in one short, disastrous lifetime)—decreed green as one of the three official colors of the Mexican flag (the others being red for chili and white for tortilla).

Although the bumpy, thick-skinned Haas variety remains the most popular avocado (*aguacate*) in Mexican market stalls, Pickerel prefers the creamier San Miguel variety (smooth-skinned, pear-shaped) or the regional criollo avocados (*paguas*) harvested from seed-grown (not grafted) trees. These oblong-shaped, papaya-size avocados are the true *agua-cates*—their yellowish green flesh being more watery than the fruit of commercial cultivars. They are cheaper, too, which gives them the edge when Pickerel revs his cost-cutting culinary engine into a guacamole-making frenzy.

> **Canine note**: Until the untimely disappearance of Ladrón, Pickerel's faithful canine companion, Pickerel benefited from a regular supply of dog-scavenged, dog-bitten avocados. Being the vagrant, busybody dog that he was—always out reading the pheromonal neighborhood newspapers—he discovered an avocado tree somewhere in his wanderings. Returning home triumphantly with a ripe avocado in his mouth, Ladrón resisted rendering unto Caesar what was Caesar's due. Usually Pickerel had to fight Ladrón for his share, and, no matter how complete the avocado extricated from Ladrón's bite, it always went into guacamole with teeth marks. (Ladrón—a dog with a botanical fetish—also fetched squashed mangos, blackened bananas, and the occasional coconut husk.)

Two guacamole recipes follow: one blended and creamy, best for spooning in tacos or topping tostadas; the other mashed with tomato, onion, chili, and cheese—rough and chunky—ready for a fork, a side of beans, or a warm corn tortilla.

### *For sauce*

*Ingredientes* (multiple servings—depends on who handles the spoon)
- 1 ripe avocado (1 *aguacate maduro*)
- 1/2 serrano chili (1/2 *chile serrano*)
- 1 slice of onion (1 *rebanada de cebolla*)
- 1/2 tsp salt (1/2 *cucharadita de sal*)

*Equipo*
>Small plastic bag (a bread bag will work) for sweating charred chilies (*una bolsa de plástico chica para hacer sudar los chiles tatemados*)
>Blender (*licuadora*)

*Preparación*

Wash avocado well. Cut lengthwise down to its seed, following circumference, and open avocado into halves. Peel skin and remove seed. Alternatively, remove seed and spoon avocado flesh from skin. Either way, ripe fruit is finger messy.

Char serrano chili and peel skin. (See *Charring Chili Peppers*, page 30.) Sever stem and cut chili lengthwise to remove seeds and veins. (See *Deveining Chili Peppers*, page 30.) Lop off a single slice of onion (1/4" thick).

Add avocado flesh to blender with salt, chili, onion, and 1-1/4 cups of water. Blend until smooth. You may need a spoon to remove guacamole from blender.

Serve immediately, before the delicate green color ages to the grim shade of overcooked peas. Cover and refrigerate to slow discoloration.

## For side dish

*Ingredientes* (two servings)
>1 ripe avocado (1 *aguacate maduro*)
>1 small tomato (1 *tomate chico*)
>1/2 serrano chili (1/2 *chile serrano*)
>1/2 small onion (1/2 *cebolla chica*)
>2 tbsp grated ranch cheese (2 *cucharadas de queso de rancho rallado*)
>1/2 tsp salt (1/2 *cucharadita de sal*)
>1/2 tsp ground pepper (1/2 *cucharadita de pimienta molida*)
>1 lime—optional (1 *limón—opcional*)

*Equipo*
>Small plastic bag (a bread bag will work) for sweating charred chilies (*una bolsa de plástico chica para hacer sudar los chiles tatemados*)
>Mixing bowl (*tazón para mezclar*)
>Fork (*tenedor*)
>Lime squeezer (*exprimidor de limón*)

*Preparación*

Wash avocado well. Cut lengthwise down to its seed, following circumference, and open avocado into halves. Peel skin and remove seed. Alternatively, remove seed and spoon avocado flesh from skin.

Peel tomato and dice finely. Mince onion. Char serrano chili and peel skin. (See *Charring Chili Peppers*, page 30.) Sever stem and cut chili lengthwise to remove seeds and veins. (See *Deveining Chili Peppers*, page 30.) Chop finely.

In the mixing bowl, add avocado, chili, tomato, onion, cheese, salt, and pepper. Mix ingredients with fork, leaving guacamole with a chunky consistency.

Traditionalists squeeze in lime, but Pickerel allows the avocado to lead the flavor parade in his guacamole—with or without a dog running alongside it.

# Red Chili Sauce
## Salsa de Chile Colorado

*Ingredientes* (makes 2-1/2 cups)
- 8 wide chilies (Ask for 8 *chiles anchos*—wrinkled, purplish black, and vaguely heart-shaped—sold by the kilo in any Mexican market and grocery.)
- 1 garlic clove, peeled (1 *diente de ajo, pelado*)
- 1/2 tbsp salt *(1/2 cucharada de sal)*

*Equipo*
- Saucepot (*cazuela*)
- Blender (*licuadora*)
- Strainer (*colador*) Pickerel uses mosquito screen.

*Preparación*

Stem chilies, open lengthwise, and remove seeds. Wash well and place in saucepot with 1 liter of cold water. Bring to a boil. Cover and cook for 10 minutes. The pungent essence of the chili soul will fill your scullery.

Chop garlic. No need for a drumroll—the blender massacres it.

Remove cooked chilies—they should be limp and detached from their waxy skins—and place in blender. Add garlic, salt, and a 1/2 liter of cold water. Blend (lowest setting recommended) until chilies turn into a dark maroon sea. Strain to remove the waxy bits of chili skin that survived the tempest. If sauce is too thick to pass through strainer, dilute with 1/4 cup of warm water. Tap strainer and employ the backside of a spoon to push sauce southward.

Use at once or cover and refrigerate. Before you do either, draw near and take a deep breath of your red chili sauce. Life is too short not to smell the chilies.

> Made with chiles anchos (ripened and dried poblano chilies), this sauce is the mantra of the chili faithful. Used in the preparation of Pickerel's enchiladas, chilaquiles, revolcadas, pozole, sopitas, red chili pork, red chili potatoes, and his soon-to-go-public dried carp egg cakes.

# Fired Chili Sauce
## *Salsa Tatemada*

> Pickerel uses this sauce on broiled meats and ranch-style eggs. (See Ranch-Style Eggs, page 99.) Also an excellent choice for spooning on tostadas and for dipping totopos (fried or baked tortilla chips).

*Tatemado*—from the Aztec word *tlatetlmati*: *tla*: **something**; *tetl*: **fire**; *mati*: **to place**—the scrabbled lexicon of a tribe who loved their T's. This is the only Aztec word Pickerel knows, so he speaks it whenever he can, but mostly at weenie roasts where ladies are present. ("Another *tatemado* dog, dear?")

*Ingredientes* (makes 1 cup)
- 3 medium tomatoes (3 *tomates medianos*)
- 2 serrano chilies (2 *chiles serranos*)
- 1/2 garlic clove, peeled (1/2 *diente de ajo, pelado*)
- 1 tsp ground, whole-leaf oregano (1 *cucharadita de hoja de orégano molido*)
- 12 peppercorns (12 *pimientas enteras*)
- 1/2 tsp salt *(1/2 cucharadita de sal)*

*Equipo*
- Charcoal fire (*fuego al carbón*) or stove flames (*llamas de la estufa*)
- Tongs (*pinzas*)
- Small plastic bag (a bread bag will work) for sweating charred chilies (*una bolsa de plástico chica para hacer sudar los chiles tatemados*)
- Mortar and pestle (*molcajete y tejolote*) or mixing bowl and bean masher (*tazón para mezclar y moledor de frijol*)

*Preparación*

Place tomatoes over open fire. For smoky flavor (and in deference to the Aztecs who had no bottled gas), Pickerel prefers a charcoal grill to a stove burner for broiling his tomatoes. Turn frequently with tongs. As the tomato skins blacken and blister, tomato juice will bubble out, signaling that the tomato core is cooking. When soft throughout, remove from fire and place in bowl (*tazón*).

Char chilies. (See *Charring Chili Peppers*, page 30.) Remove stems with knife (leave seeds and veins), and place chilies in bowl with tomatoes.

Place garlic in *molcajete* or mixing bowl with peppercorns and oregano (no stems). Grind all three to a peppery pulp. Add charred chilies and crush well. Do the same with the tomatoes, one at a time—watch for the squirting of hot tomato juice. Grind and stir. Add salt and grind again. Show no mercy. Remove blackened pieces of tomato skin that don't pulverize. Tomatoes and chilies will turn into a pulpy, reddish green sauce.

Pickerel serves his fired chili salsa right out of the *molcajete*.

# Chili Peppers

## chiles

*"Wish I had time for one more chili..."*
Dying words of Montecuzoma II
Ruler of the Aztec Empire

Stuffed Green Chilies

Soused Chilies

Fat Tortillas with Chili and Clotted Cream

Chili Water

Chilies in Cheese

Few gastronomical sensations compare to experiencing the burn of the same chili pepper twice. Pickerel has come to savor the entire passage through his long and lanky *barco*, though it was not always this way. Back in the days when IBS (irritable bowel syndrome) ruled his lower forty, Pickerel's mucous membranes blushed at the slightest inflammatory suggestion. A coconut milk enema was his only relief.

As the years passed, however, Pickerel's proteins grew less cantankerous (not Pickerel, only his proteins). Eventually capsaicin became as much a part of his tissues as ethanol, congeners, and persistent *crapula*. There came the day when he was eating *escabeche* with every taco, spooning salsas at breakfast, swallowing chilies raw, whole, cooked, you name it, all the while proselytizing Miriam on the value of chilies as a source of vitamin C. He even suggested C stood for chili (true or not, "Vitamin Chili" had a catchy ring).

Miriam would hear nothing of it. As with so many things in their unhappy union, while Pickerel grew to love chilies, Miriam grew to hate them. Eventually she barred the front door to anything remotely resembling a chili. She refused even to hold one by its tail. More tragically, she became insensible to the subtlety of its usage, incapable of appreciating its deeper meanings.

In the years when Pickerel reigned as the neighborhood's most gracious host, a frequent guest to his humble abode was a local musician—an accordionist of artistic proportions—who made Pickerel's acquaintance while serenading two lovelies on the sidewalk in front of the Spotted Bull. Pickerel knew him only as Chile, though that was not his Christian name. Pickerel never knew his Christian name, only his unholy one—Chile with a capital C.

The evening Pickerel introduced Chile to Miriam, she barely succeeded in containing her Margarita giggle.

"Chile? Oh, what a … what a curious name."

The only chili Miriam had met was in a Minneapolis supermarket—stumpy, sweet, and harmless: first name, Bell, last name, Pepper. Still, she was discreet enough to reserve further inquiry until Chile drifted off with a cold Tecate crooked in one arm and a *norteño* tune cascading from his squeezebox.

"Why do they call him that?" she whispered.

Pickerel took her gently by the arm. In those years, Pickerel saw himself as the patient mentor of Miriam, her knowledgeable guide in the Latino world of *doble sentido*.

"The name Chile," said Pickerel into Miriam's waxy deep, "is colloquial hereabouts for peter."

"Peter? I thought that was Pedro."

"Peter in the lowercase."

"Oh …"

"Peter the penis. He who has an exceptionally long one."

Accordion arpeggios swelled in the background. Miriam looked into the unblinking peepers of Pickerel. Even then, she suspected he was capable of the foulest prevarication. But for once, Pickerel was telling the truth.

"You mean …?"

Pickerel smiled.

New visions of hot sauce crossed Miriam's face. It was her first encounter with the deeper meanings of the vegetable world. Thereafter, she snuck eyefuls of Chile at every social occasion. Pickerel kept watchful vigil, lest her interest be misconstrued. Penetrating powers from the planet Krypton could not have been more obvious if Miriam had been leaping tall buildings in a single bound. Being of Puritan stock, however, she made no further comment.

So much for botanical metaphors. So much for Chile with a capital C. As for Miriam's cold Norwegian blood, of that you will hear more later.

Now a few words on Pickerel's favorite chilies.

For making sauces, he goes with the sharp bite of the unassuming serrano—fresh or charred. In pozole, he uses the guajillo and ancho chilies. The latter Pickerel cooks and liquefies in his Brazilian blender to make a red chili sauce for his cheap cheese enchiladas. For flavoring stir-fried veggies and stewed meat, the mild Anaheim—known in local markets as *chile largo-verde*—is Pickerel's top choice (seedless and deveined). The poblano chili he uses for stuffing. The wild chiltepin and its cultivated cousin, the piquín chili, he adds to hangover food (and to spice his fruit), while the burnt red chipotle (a ripened jalapeño, dried and smoked) goes into Pickerel's stewed marlin and Aztec soup. Bringing up the rear in his list of favorites is the meanest chili in the nightshade family—the jalapeño. Eaten raw, pickled, whole, in strips, in salsas—anyway it goes down—Pickerel enjoys the burn to the very last crook of his sigmoid. And, at a peso a pound, he hasn't found true intestinal discomfort at a better price. When his mother-in-law visited Mexico for the first time,

> **Social note**: Before substituting chilies indigenous to your area, Pickerel recommends consulting with a native— a native woman preferably. She who knows her chilies is an indispensable asset in any kitchen or bedroom.

Pickerel celebrated her untimely arrival by adding the thinnest sliver of jalapeño, finely minced, to her morning eggs—clandestinely, of course. "Well scrambled, please," ordered this woman, "with some catsup, dear." Pickerel, the model of cordiality, served them himself, hiding jalapeños under catsup. When the mother of Miriam precipitously exited their table, hand on throat, eyes rocketing from her head, Pickerel loudly railed against Mexican catsup bottlers, and then he accused local egg farmers of feeding their hens chili peppers.

Four recipes follow—four pure chili executions. Those looking for higher incendiary thrills on the Scoville scale may find their desired burn in one of Pickerel's sauces or from a bottled brand. (See *Bottled Sauces*, page 29.)

## Pickerel's Most Popular Chili Peppers

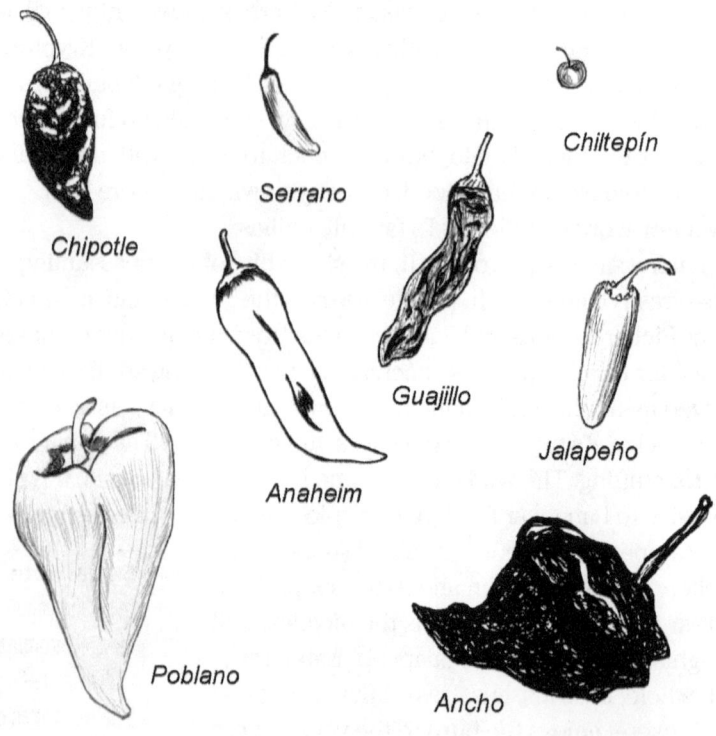

# Stuffed Green Chilies
## *Chiles Rellenos*

*Ingredientes* (three servings)

### For chilies
  6 poblano chilies (6 *chiles poblanos*)
  1/4 kg Chihuahua cheese (1/4 *kilo de queso de Chihuahua*)
  Toothpicks (*palillos*), preferably new
  1 egg (1 *huevo*)
  2 tbsp cooking oil (2 *cucharadas de aceite para cocinar*)

*Equipo*
  Tongs (*pinzas*)
  Small plastic bag (a bread bag will work) for sweating charred chilies (*una bolsa de plástico chica para hacer sudar los chiles tatemados*)
  Deep skillet (*sartén honda*)

### For sauce
  2 large tomatoes (2 *tomates grandes*)
  1/2 onion (1/2 *cebolla*)
  1/2 garlic clove, peeled (1/2 *diente de ajo, pelado*)
  1 tsp beef bouillon powder (1 *cucharadita de consomé de res en polvo*)
  1 cup tomato puree (1 *taza de puré de tomate*)
  1/2 tsp salt (1/2 *cucharadita de sal*)
  1 tbsp cooking oil (1 *cucharada de aceite para cocinar*)

*Equipo*
  Saucepot (*cazuela*)
  Blender (*licuadora*)

*Preparación*

Char chilies, sweat in plastic bag for 10 minutes, and place in water to remove skins. (See *Charring Chili Peppers*, page 30.) With a sharp knife, make a vertical slit below the chili stem. Through this slit, insert knife and cut the seed trunk loose from the base of the chili stem. Do not detach chili stem. Enlarge the vertical slit enough to maneuver the knife inside chili without tearing it. Remove veins by scraping gently with the tip of the knife and extracting veins with fingers. Wash out loose seeds.

Quarter tomatoes and slice onion. In a saucepot with 1 liter of water, bring tomatoes, onion, and garlic to a boil. Add bouillon powder, cover, and cook over low heat for 5 minutes. Remove cover and mash tomatoes with fork (*tenedor*). Allow broth to cool, remove tomato skins, and pour contents into blender. Add tomato puree and salt. Blend until smooth.

> **Personal note**: Pickerel saves his chili seeds to dry in the sun. Later, they travel in his shirt pocket, handy for masking the odor of malted barley on his breath. Pickerel has no money for Certs or Chiclets, so he pops a seed and bites hard, adding chili to his halitosis.

Heat 1 tablespoon of cooking oil in the same saucepot. Pour in contents of blender. Fry tomato mixture over low flame until it bubbles and thickens. Your sauce is ready. Keep warm.

Cut cheese in narrow rectangles—long French fries—and slip into each chili up to the tip. Do this through the slit made near the chili stem. As a rule, Pickerel stuffs as much cheese as he can fit or as much as he can afford—whichever fills his chilies first.

Close each cheese-filled chili by pinning the slit shut with a toothpick. Do this by gathering the chili flesh on either side of slit (between thumb and forefinger) and pushing toothpick in one side, out the other, then in again. Most chilies close with one toothpick. If the slit is large, use two.

After chilies are stuffed, crack egg and beat. (Pickerel beats the white separately to make it froth, then he adds the yolk.) Heat oil in skillet. Dip stuffed chilies into beaten egg and slide into hot oil. Cook over low flame, turning once, until cheese melts and egg batter turns honey-colored.

Serve in a deep dish, bathed in warm sauce, with corn tortillas on the side.

> **Warning**: Remove toothpicks before eating. Pickerel will spare you his horror story.

# Soused Chilies
## *Chiles en Escabeche*

One of Pickerel's muggy summer day dishes.

*Ingredientes* (three servings)
- 2 potatoes (2 *papas*)
- 2 carrots (2 *zanahorias*)
- 2 small zucchinis (2 *calabacitas*)
- 2 dozen string beans (2 *docenas de ejotes*)
- 1-1/2 tsp salt (1-1/2 *cucharadas de sal*)
- 2 small onions (2 *cebollas chicas*)
- 6 Anaheim chilies (6 *chiles largo-verde*)
- 1 tbsp cooking oil (1 *cucharada de aceite para cocinar*)
- 1 tsp peppercorns (1 *cuchardita de pimienta entera*)
- A pinch of ground, whole-leaf oregano (*una pizca de hoja de orégano molido*)
- 2 bay leaves (2 *hojas de laurel*)
- 1/2 cup vinegar (1/2 *taza de vinagre*) Pickerel uses white cane vinegar.

*Equipo*
- Small plastic bag (a bread bag will work) for sweating charred chilies (*una bolsa de plástico chica para hacer sudar los chiles tatemados*)
- 2 saucepots (2 *cazuelas*)
- Colander (*escurridor*)
- Small skillet (*sartén chica*)
- Covering dish (*recipiente con tapadera*)

*Preparación*

Peel potatoes and carrots. Cut in halves and slice into pencil-wide, pencil-thick strips. Cut squash to same size. Snap off bean ends, pull away fiber (See *String Beans*, page 25.), split lengthwise, and cut into bite-size pieces. Slice onions into rainbows.

Char chilies, sweat in plastic bag for 10 minutes, and place in water to remove skins. (See *Charring Chili Peppers*, page 30.) Open chilies lengthwise (about one-quarter length) and remove seed trunks and veins. (See *Deveining Chili Peppers*, page 30.) Leave stalks. Wash out loose seeds.

Heat water in saucepots. Parboil (*sancochar*) potatoes, carrots, beans, and squash (first potatoes, then carrots, and so on). Add 1/4 teaspoon of salt to each vegetable as it boils. Do not overcook squash. Veggies should end up on the soft side of crunch. Drain in colander and cool.

Insert ample strips of potato, carrot, bean, and squash into each opened chili. Place filled chilies in a covering dish (*recipiente con tapadera*).

Over low flame, heat oil in skillet and fry without browning (*acitronar*) onion slices. Stir in peppercorns, 1/2 tsp of salt, oregano, and bay leaves. Add vinegar. Stir well, cover, and cook over low heat. When mixture begins to bubble, pour onto chilies, spreading evenly. Cover, cool to room temperature, and refrigerate to chill.

Eat cold. To complete the sousing of his chilies (and himself), Pickerel washes down his *escabeche* with a six-pack of iced Tecate.

# *Fat Tortillas with Chili and Clotted Cream*
## Gordas con Natas y Chile Chiltepín

Pickerel longs for the days of milkmaids, when fair-skinned Tess was a maiden no more, and the milk of human kindness was precoital breakfast in bed. (Modern-day maidens beware—Pickerel is an early riser!)

For raw milk—needed for this recipe and for the regular relief of his ethylic-induced ulcer—Pickerel makes his ghostly appearance at local stables during the early morning milking hour. He loiters cowside, savoring the warm scents of freshly dropped dung as he watches the dairy farmer fondle the undercarriages of uncooperative bovines. Occasionally, Pickerel has lent a hand, helping the farmer hobble a heifer or hold a calf. Once, Pickerel even tried to milk a cow. He failed miserably, finding neither rhythm nor *lácteo*, while the cow—unaccustomed to Pickerel's willowy-fingered caresses—lowed in the sub-contra octave of bovid alarm. Neither man nor beast found the experience gratifying.

For this recipe, Pickerel departs from his local stable bearing a gallon of milk—still warm in a reusable wine carboy—at the ridiculously low price of almost free. (**Note**: Milk from Jersey cows gives the most cream, so pick your breed if you can.) If Pickerel was not such a cheapskate, he would remain in his castle until midmorning when the neighborhood milkman (a surly faced, hairy-handed fellow driving a prediluvian pickup) delivers raw milk to Pickerel's street. "*Leche bronca!*" he announces from a loudspeaker on his truck as women and children approach with empty pots and pitchers. The milkman fills these receptacles with dippers of a white liquid drawn from an unsanitary-looking plastic barrel carried on the back of his truck. Pickerel watches silently from his curtainless window, thankful for stable milk. He has it from a reliable source (local health inspector) that these neighborhood milkmen—known as *lecheros*—adulterate raw milk with a profitable dilution of canal water.

> If no milking stable is at hand and you do not wish to purchase raw milk from the local lechero, buy your clotted cream at a lácteo stall in the nearest market. Ask for natas de leche.

*Ingredientes* (two servings)
- 1 gallon raw milk (1 *galón de leche bronca*)
- 1/4 tsp salt (1/4 *cucharadita de sal*)
- 3 dried chiltepin chilies (3 *chiles chiltepines secos*)
- Dough to make 6 corn tortillas (*masa para hacer 6 tortillas de maíz*)

*Equipo*
- Large saucepot (*cazuela grande*)
- Soup bowl and spoon (*tazón sopera y cuchara*)
- Tortilla press (*prensa de tortilla*)
- 2 small sheets of plastic (2 *hojas chicas de plástico*); cut a bread bag in half
- Griddle (*comal*)

*Preparación*

Boil wild milk in saucepot. Purists (and the daring) merely scald their milk, but Pickerel gives his a rolling 10-minute boil to kill Pasteurian dungcitus and bovine brucellosis. To ensure more clotted cream, his 10-minute boil consists of three surges (raising the heat until the milk almost boils over, lowering the heat to bring boil down, then raising the heat again—three times).

Cool boiled milk overnight in a covered container.

The following day, skim clotted cream and place in a bowl (*tazón*). One gallon of raw milk makes 1/2 cup of thick, spreadable cream. Add salt and mix well.

Place chiltepin chilies in soup bowl and grind with the bottom of a spoon. Pulverize the hard chili skin into tiny pieces. Add to cream and mix well.

Heat griddle. Make dough balls, press out your first tortilla (See *Corn Tortillas*, page 47.), and place on the heated griddle.

After flipping the cooked tortilla, allow it to puff (See *Squash Blossom Quesadillas*, page 68.) and then remove from griddle. Slit the tortilla along its outer edge with a sharp knife. Make the slit wide enough to deposit inside one heaping tablespoon of clotted cream with chili. Fold the fattened tortilla (hence the name, *gorda*), and send it down the hatch.

The combination of warm tortilla, salty cool cream, and chiltepin bite delivers a knockdown punch.

Save boiled milk to drink with Pickerel's *crepas de cerveza* (See *Thin Beer Crêpes*, page 226.) or to make *arroz con leche* (See *Rice in Milk*, page 224.).

# Chili Water
## *Aguachile*

A short recipe for the hungry poor gringo in a hurry.

*Ingredientes* (one serving)
    2 chiltepin chilies, bright red, freshly picked (2 *chile chiltepines*)
    1/2 liter water (1/2 *litro de agua*)
    12 dozen chiltepin leaves, freshly picked (12 *hojas c chile chiltepín*)
    1/2 tsp salt (1/2 *cucharadita de sal*)

*Equipo*
    Saucepan (*cazo*)
    Soup spoon (*cuchara sopera*)

*Preparación*
    Place chilies in saucepan. Using the spoon, grind chilies into the pan bottom until seeds and flesh are mashed. Add water and bring to a boil. Toss in the chiltepin leaves and boil for 5 minutes. Add salt. Cool.
    Chili, water, and leaves—it doesn't get much simpler than that.
    Serve in cup (*taza*) or bowl (*tazón*) with corn tortillas for dipping. You may eat the leaves.

### A Personal Note on *Chile Chiltepín*

Chiltepin chilies are tiny, oval, long-stemmed chili berries—easy to pick out of the chili crowd for there are none smaller. When you find one, you will find a hundred more on the same bush—some dark green, others red or orange. They grow wild on the hot coastal plains of Mexico, and to find them you must simply remain awake, chili vigilant.
    Take Pickerel, for example.
    Next to his weedy front yard plat, on the edge of his neighbor's well-groomed green, there grows a solitary chiltepin bush. On dark evenings, when Pickerel's intestinal engine grumbles like an untuned Ford running on fumes, his pea-picking hand browses over the intervening fence in silent search of chiltepin. Pickerel only borrows. He never takes without returning. After swallowing as many bowls of chili water as his bilges can

hold, Pickerel saunters into the sable night and relieves himself of all guilt, right there on the neighbor's fence and upon the hidden roots of chiltepin.

From chili water to chili water—one of nature's little cycles.

## *Chilies in Cheese*
### Rajas de Chile con Queso

*Ingredientes* (three servings)
- 6 chilies (6 *chiles largo-verde*)
- 1 small onion (1 *cebolla chica*)
- 2 tbsp margarine (2 *cucharadas de margarina*)
- 1 cup sour cream (1 *taza de crema agria*)
- 1 tsp salt (1 *cucharadita de sal*)
- 1/2 tsp ground pepper (1/2 *cucharadita de pimienta molida*)
- 1/2 cup grated Chihuahua cheese (1/2 *taza de queso de Chihuahua rallado*)

*Equipo*
- Small plastic bag (a bread bag will work) for sweating charred chilies (*una bolsa de plástico chica para hacer sudar los chiles tatemados*)
- Deep skillet (*sartén honda*)

*Preparación*

Char chilies, sweat in plastic bag for 10 minutes, and place in water to remove skins. (See *Charring Chili Peppers*, page 30.) Cut each chili lengthways and remove stalk, seed trunk, and veins. (See *Deveining Chili Peppers*, page 30.) Wash out loose seeds. Slice each chili into strips no wider than a lady's watchband. Slice onion into thin rainbows.

Melt margarine in skillet. Stir in chili and onion. When onion softens, add sour cream, salt, and pepper. Cover and simmer over low heat until cream bubbles. Remove from heat, sprinkle on grated cheese, cover, and allow cheese to melt.

Serve with warm corn tortillas (Pickerel likes his crispy for this recipe). You may dip, spoon, shovel, or simply sink into this creamy chili sea.

# Eggs

## Huevos

*"En México, hasta los gallos ponen huevos."*
*"In Mexico, even the roosters lay eggs."*
*Mexican macho*
*(Anonymous, lest his wife find out)*

Ranch-style Eggs

Green Eggs/No Ham

Scrambled Eggs and Tortillas in Red Chili Sauce

Scrambled Eggs with Prickly Pear

Scrambled Eggs with String Beans

Scrambled Eggs with Manola *Machaca*

Slipped Eggs

Scrambled Eggs with Potatoes

Scrambled Eggs with Veggies

Shrimp Head Omelet

When two- and four-legged proteins grow scarce in Pickerel's larder, eggs are his culinary rabbit-out-of-the-hat. All his neighbors have hens, but Pickerel gets their eggs only if a horny rooster chases a demurring pullet onto his weedy plat. When this happens, the rooster crows his last daybreak (See *Run-over Rooster in Greens*, page 142.), and the hen becomes Pickerel's egg slave. Unfortunately, a captive hen nourished on Pickerel's meager feed of tortilla tatters and culled beans does not produce enough eggs to justify the hen's existence. (See *Wandering Neighborhood Chicken Runs into Cabbage*, page 148.)

**Economic note**: Although every poor gringo is welcome to relocate his miserable existence near an egg farm (to connect with his own Benito), he may also purchase culled eggs (small, cracked, and disgustingly stained with hen guano) at a price cheaper than that of washed, graded, and boxed eggs. Ask your market egg vendor for huevos de segunda, and bring a bag to carry them home. No egg carton supplied.

So Pickerel relies on Benito Blanquillo for his eggs. Benito works the night shift at a local hen farm, responsible for the 24,000 incandescent bulbs that simulate daylight and fool stupid poultry into laying more eggs.

Benito Blanquillo does *not* steal eggs to sell to Miles Pickerel. Pickerel would not allow that. If there is something to steal, Pickerel does it himself. Besides, jeopardizing Benito's job would jeopardize Pickerel's supply of low-cost eggs.

Instead, Pickerel and Benito have a deal. As part of his pay at the egg farm, Benito receives one free carton (*cartera*) of eggs (24) each week. (No doubt, the egg farmer has calculated that a worker will steal that many eggs a week—so including them in the worker's wage makes sense as a business deduction.) Benito does not eat twenty-four eggs in a week. His wife works at the hen farm. His son works at the hen farm. With the Blanquillo family rolling in eggs, Benito sells his share to Pickerel at a price cheaper than what Pickerel would pay at the local market or corner grocery. When *Doctor* Pickerel is short of cash, he reimburses Benito with his unpatented formaldehyde treatments for the Blanquillo family's infestation of poultry lice (*Menacanthus stramineus*) and fowl ticks (*Argas persicus*).

Pickerel gets eggs. Benito gets parasite extinction. Everyone is happy.

# Ranch-style Eggs
## Huevos Rancheros

*Ingredientes* (one serving)
- 1/2 cup fired chili sauce (1/2 *taza de salsa tatemada*)
  (See *Fired Chili Sauce*, page 82.)
- 1-1/2 tbsp cooking oil (1-1/2 *cucharadas de aceite para cocinar*)
- 2 corn tortillas (2 *tortillas de maíz*)
- 2 eggs (2 *huevos*)

*Equipo*
Small skillet (*sartén chica*), no smaller than a tortilla

*Preparación*

Warm sauce. Heat oil in skillet. Fry tortillas until crisp and golden. (See *Dangerously Crisp Tortillas with Toppings*, page 56.) Remove and drain excess oil on kitchen towels (*toallas de cocina*) or, Pickerel style, on old newspapers (*papel periódico*) untouched by dog.

Fry eggs in remaining oil. Pickerel prefers his over easy (like his women). Place cooked eggs on tortillas and spoon aboard warm sauce—as much as you dare.

Serve with stir-mashed beans on the side.

# Green Eggs/No Ham
## *Huevos en Salsa Verde*

*Ingredientes* (one serving)
- 1/2 cup green tomato sauce (1/2 *taza de salsa verde*)
  (See *Green Tomato Sauce*, page 76.)
- 1-1/2 tbsp cooking oil (1-1/2 *cucharadas de aceite para cocinar*)
- 2 corn tortillas (2 *tortillas de maíz*)
- 2 eggs (2 *huevos*)
- 1 tbsp grated ranch cheese (1 *cucharada de queso de rancho rallado*)

*Equipo*
Small skillet (*sartén chica*), no smaller than a tortilla

*Preparación*

Warm sauce. Heat oil in skillet. Fry tortillas until crisp and golden. (See *Dangerously Crisp Tortillas with Toppings*, page 56.) Remove and drain excess oil on kitchen towels (*toallas de cocina*) or, Pickerel style, on old newspapers (*papel periódico*) untouched by dog.

Fry eggs in remaining oil. Place cooked eggs on tortillas and spoon on warm sauce. Sprinkle with grated ranch cheese.

Serve with stir-mashed beans on the side.

# Scrambled Eggs and Tortillas in Red Chili Sauce
## Sopitas de Tortilla con Huevo y Chile Colorado

*Ingredientes* (two servings)
- 4 corn tortillas (4 *tortillas de maíz*)
- 1 tbsp margarine (1 *cucharada de margarina*)
- 1 tbsp cooking oil (1 *cucharada de aceite para cocinar*)
- 1/2 cup red chili sauce (1/2 *taza de salsa de chile colorado*) (See *Red Chili Sauce*, page 81.)
- 2 eggs (2 *huevos*)
- 1/4 tsp salt (1/4 *cucharadita de sal*)
- 2 tbsp grated ranch cheese (2 *cucharadas de queso de rancho rallado*)

> Not just for breakfast, this is a Pickerel favorite at any hour.

*Equipo*
Small skillet (*sartén chico*)

*Preparación*

Cut tortillas into bite-size pieces. Melt margarine in skillet. Add oil and mix. When hot, add tortilla pieces and stir until buttery, cooking over low heat. Warm red chili sauce. Beat eggs. Turn up fire. Add eggs to skillet and scramble with tortilla pieces. When eggs cook, remove skillet from heat and add red chili sauce. Mix thoroughly, salt lightly, and serve quickly—before you run out of adverbs.

Sprinkle with grated cheese and serve with enough room on the side for stir-mashed beans. No tortillas needed—unless you live redundantly.

# Scrambled Eggs with Prickly Pear
## Huevos Revueltos con Nopalitos

### Nopales

Armed with Miriam's gardening gloves (left behind during her hasty retreat), a vegetable peeler, and a plastic bag, Pickerel harvests his prickly pear paddles (*hojas de nopal*) from the nearest desert thornscrub—a place that also happens to be his neighborhood park. Abandoned by decent, law-abiding Mexicans and overgrown with weeds, brambles, and cacti, this park is the home to local fugitives, incurable drunks, the mentally marginal, and the simply soulless—a dangerous place for most, but not for Pickerel, who is recognized as a kindred spirit.

In his nopal hunt, Pickerel seeks out the smallest and firmest cacti paddles, pale green preferably, and without bird pecks or wrinkles. Wearing Miriam's gloves, he breaks off three or four pads, scraping each with his peeler to shave off the thorny bumps. Then he places them in the plastic bag for the journey home.

### Preparing nopales

Back in his scullery, Pickerel cuts away the thickest part of the paddle (where it attaches to cactus trunk), washes it well, and dices it into small cubes (the size of peas). These he places in a saucepot with cold water, bringing them to boil with a pinch of salt (boiled *nopalitos* lose the unsavory slipperiness of raw ones). Pickerel boils his cacti until they turn dull green and lose their crunchiness—about 20 minutes for a half kilo—then he drains the hot water, adds cold, and allows them to cool before draining again. Pickerel refrigerates diced and boiled prickly pear for up to two weeks for later use.

*Ingredientes* (one serving)
- 1 tbsp cooking oil (1 *cucharada de aceite para cocinar*)
- 1/4 cup diced and boiled prickly pear pieces (1/4 *taza de nopalitos cocidos*) See above.
- 1/4 tsp salt (1/4 *cucharadita de sal*)
- A pinch of ground pepper (*una pizca de pimienta molida*)
- 2 eggs (2 *huevos*)

*Equipo*
- Small skillet (*sartén chica*)

*Preparación*

Heat oil in skillet. Add boiled nopales, salt, and pepper. Mix well and cook over low heat until nopales sizzle. Crack eggs, scramble, and add to skillet. Stir until eggs cook.

Serve with warm corn or flour tortillas and refried beans. No salsa needed.

> If you do not have an unsafe park overgrown with cacti in your vicinity, go to the local market and buy your nopales. Once, when police chased Pickerel from the park, he purchased his prickly pear already peeled and diced from the Tarahumara ladies who squat on the sidewalks outside local markets selling greens and herbs.

# Scrambled Eggs with String Beans
## Huevos Revueltos con Ejotes

*Ingredientes* (one serving)
   12 string beans (12 *ejotes*)
   1 tbsp cooking oil (1 *cucharada de aceite para cocinar*)
   2 eggs (2 *huevos*)
   1/4 tsp salt (1/4 *cucharadita de sal*)
   A pinch of ground pepper (*una pizca de pimienta molida*)

*Equipo*
   Saucepan (*cazo*), strainer (*colador*), and skillet (*sartén*)

*Preparación*
   Wash beans. Snap off ends, pull away fiber (See *String Beans*, page 25.), split lengthwise, and cut into bite-size pieces. In saucepan with 1 liter of boiling water, parboil beans for 2 minutes. Drain.
   Heat oil in skillet. Crack eggs and scramble. When oil is hot, stir-fry beans with salt and pepper, adding eggs when beans begin to brown. Stir until eggs cook.
   Serve with crisp corn tortillas and a dash of your favorite bottled sauce.

# Scrambled Eggs with Manola Machaca
## Huevos Revueltos con Machaca de Manola

*Ingredientes* (two servings)
- 1 tbsp cooking oil (1 *cucharada de aceite para cocinar*)
- 1/2 serrano chili (1/2 *chile serrano*)
- 4 eggs (4 *huevos*)
- 1/2 cup pounded meat (1/2 *taza de machaca*) (See *Carne machaca*, pages 21/22.)

*Equipo*
- Skillet (*sartén*)

> A recipe dedicated to the memory of Manola—the next-door neighbor's female Chihuahua with a Doberman attitude whose canine soul prematurely departed this world. Her earthly remains received a timely and proper (i.e., culinary) internment—RIP*.
>
> *Rest in Pieces

*Preparación*

Heat oil in skillet. Dice chili finely. Crack and scramble eggs. When oil is hot, add *machaca* and chili. Stir and cook over medium heat until meat fibers darken with oil. Add eggs. Mix well with *machaca*, stirring until eggs cook No salt needed.

Serve with corn or flour tortillas and stir-mashed beans on the side.

# Slipped Eggs
## Huevos Resbalados

*Ingredientes* (one serving)
- 1/2 cup cooked sauce (1/2 *taza de salsa cocida*) (See *Cooked Sauce*, page 73.)
- 2 tbsp cooking oil (2 *cucharadas de aceite para cocinar*)
- 2 eggs (2 *huevos*)
- 2 corn tortillas (2 *tortillas de maíz*)

*Equipo*
- Skillet (*sartén*), large enough to cook two tortillas side by side

*Preparación*

Warm sauce. Heat oil in skillet. Fry eggs. When eggs cook enough to lift with a spatula (*espátula*), slip a corn tortilla under each. Allow eggs to fry on tortillas. If you do not like your eggs sunny-side up, baste yolk with hot oil. Remove tortilla-topped egg, and bathe with cooked sauce. Serve with refried beans on the side.

# Scrambled Eggs with Potatoes
## Huevos Revueltos con Papas

*Ingredientes* (one serving)
 1 large potato (1 *papa grande*)
 1 tbsp cooking oil (1 *cucharada de aceite para cocinar*)
 Salt and ground pepper to taste (*sal y pimienta molida al gusto*)
 2 tbsp tomato puree (2 *cucharadas de puré de tomate*)
 2 eggs (2 *huevos*)

*Equipo*
 Skillet (*sartén*)

*Preparación*

Wash potato, peel, and dice. Heat oil in skillet. Fry potatoes with salt and pepper until golden. Remove potatoes from skillet, and place on an absorbent towel (Pickerel uses old newspapers untouched by dog) to remove excess oil. Drain excess oil from skillet. Return fried potatoes to skillet, add puree, and mix well over low heat.

Crack eggs, scramble, and add to fried potatoes. Stir until eggs cook. Serve with crisp corn tortillas and your favorite cooked sauce on the side. (See *Sauces*, page 71.)

# Scrambled Eggs with Veggies
## Huevos Revueltos con Verduras

*Ingredientes* (one serving)
- 1 medium tomato (1 *tomate mediano*)
- 1 serrano chili (1 *chile serrano*)
- 1/2 small onion (1/2 *cebolla chica*)
- 1 tbsp cooking oil (1 *cucharada de aceite para cocinar*)
- 1/4 tsp salt (1/4 *cucharadita de sal*)
- A pinch of ground pepper (*una pizca de pimienta molida*)
- 2 eggs (2 *huevos*)

*Equipo*
- Skillet (*sartén*)

*Preparación*

Peel tomato and dice. Slice chilies thinly. Dice onion.

Heat oil in skillet and stir-fry veggies with salt and pepper.

Crack eggs, scramble, and add to fried veggies. Mix well, cooking eggs.

Serve with corn tortillas hot off the griddle, or roll inside warm flour tortillas to make egg burritos. Add stir-mashed beans on the side.

# Shrimp Head Omelet
## Omelet de Camarón

> This is the closest Pickerel comes to eating shrimp for breakfast without actually biting into a crustacean. A surprisingly flavorful shellfish illusion well within any poor gringo's budget.

*Ingredientes* (one serving)
1 tbsp cooking oil (1 *cucharada de aceite para cocinar*)
2 eggs (2 *huevos*)
2 tbsp shrimp powder (2 *cucharadas de polvo de camarón*) (See *Shrimp Powder*, page 24.)
1/4 tsp salt (1/4 *cucharadita de sal*)
A pinch of ground pepper (*una pizca de pimienta molida*)

*Equipo*
Skillet (*sartén*)

*Preparación*

Heat oil in skillet. Crack eggs and scramble with shrimp powder, salt, and pepper. When oil is hot, add eggs. Fold cooked egg onto itself, omelet-style, flip, and finish cooking. Serve with warm corn or flour tortillas, stir-mashed beans, and your favorite bottled sauce.

# Potatoes

## Papas

*"All I wanted was to be a Freedom Fry."*
Mexican Mr. Potato Head caught entering United States illegally

Red Chili Potatoes

Tomatoed Potatoes with Veggies

Potato Shrimp Cakes

Potatoes with Manola *Machaca*

In a previous lifetime, Pickerel was related to the spud—not genetically (the tall, willowy figure of Pickerel does not suggest kinship with any tuber except the carrot), rather in a culinary sense. Perhaps Pickerel was a black-soiled Russian peasant distilling homemade Smirnoff on the banks of the Ob. Or he was a rank Dubliner on the lam, with nothing but pockets full of Irish Cobblers for his noonday stew. However, Pickerel prefers to think that his tie to the spud has more distinguished roots than these. Perhaps, once upon a time, he was an Inca noble—yes!—one riding his many-manned litter upon the shores of Lake Titicaca—yes, yes—sipping *chichi* and taking delicate bites of soft white potato bread—definitely so! This is much more in keeping with Pickerel's deformed image of himself. After all, just because Pickerel is poor in this life does not mean that he was so in all others.

As to where Pickerel gets his potatoes, let's just say that sticky-fingered karma has followed him (along with dirty fingernails) to his ignoble present. This does not mean that Pickerel trespasses on private potato property to get his potatoes. No! The inconveniences of barbed-wire fencing, armed night watchmen, and guard dogs oblige him to wait for local potato farmers to harvest their crops first.

Pickerel is not alone. Standing on the edge of a newly dug potato field, he is one among a crowd of women, children, and shameless grown men like himself—all waiting for the farmer to finish his potato harvest. Everyone has an empty pail, sack, or both. Pickerel brings his wheelbarrow (*carretilla*). When the farmer finally opens his fence gates, signaling that his land is free to be picked over by the potato-craving public, the race to find buried spuds begins.

The liberation of a Mexican potato field (*campo de papa*) is an event every poor gringo should take seriously. There are taters hiding in that dirt—culls, minis, bruised potatoes, cut potatoes, and the most prized potato of all: grade A spuds miraculously missed by the farmer's harvesting machines. In his mad rush to reach them, Pickerel runs his wheelbarrow past the young, old, and soon-to-be disabled. Women scream, the elderly curse, children pelt him with dirt clods, but Pickerel is not to be detained. The enticement of free spuds propels his gangly figure across the spaded rows as if he too traveled on wheels. Once on his knees, he is a quick digger, his gimlet eye searching for the pale peekaboo of potatoes left behind. After two hours of grubbing, Pickerel wheels his barrow from the potato-gleaned field with a six-month supply of spuds aboard. Trailed by a throng of urchins, some still tossing clods, others grabbing for a spud, Pickerel plows across the furrowed earth, his wheelbarrow bouncing. He succeeds in leaving his tormentors behind only when the wheelbarrow reaches a paved road.

He remains bedridden the following week, unable to walk, bend over, or peel a spud—exhausted by the effort. But he has potatoes.

For the faint of heart, weak-legged, or arthritic, Pickerel suggests you buy your potatoes. Freed field spuds often make their way to street corners and market stalls, sold cheaply by the same harvest throng who battled Pickerel in the potato trenches.

# Red Chili Potatoes
## Papas Fritas en Chile Colorado

*Ingredientes* (two servings)
- 2 potatoes (2 *papas*)
- 2 tbsp cooking oil (2 *cucharadas de aceite para cocinar*)
- 1/4 tsp salt (1/4 *cucharadita de sal*)
- A pinch of ground pepper (*una pizca de pimienta molida*)
- 1/4 cup of red chili sauce (1/4 *taza de salsa de chile colorado*)
    (See *Red Chili Sauce*, page 81.)

*Equipo*
- Skillet (*sartén*)

*Preparación*

Wash, peel, and dice potatoes. Heat oil in skillet. Fry potatoes with salt and pepper until crisp. Drain oil, stir in red chili sauce, cover, and fry chili potatoes on high heat for 1 minute, stirring often. Serve with corn tortillas.

# *Tomatoed Potatoes with Veggies*
## Papas Fritas con Verdura

*Ingredientes* (two servings)
- 2 potatoes (2 *papas*)
- 2 tbsp cooking oil (2 *cucharadas de aceite para cocinar*)
- 1/2 tsp salt (1/2 *cucharadita de sal*)
- A pinch of ground pepper (*una pizca de pimienta molida*)
- 1 medium tomato (1 *tomate mediano*)
- 1/2 small onion (1/2 *cebolla chica*)
- 1/2 Anaheim chili deveined and seedless (1/2 *chile largo-verde sin venas, ni semillas*) (See *Deveining Chili Peppers*, page 30.)
- 1 serrano chili (1 *chile serrano*)
- 1/4 cup tomato puree (1/4 *taza de puré de tomate*)

*Equipo*
- Skillet (*sartén*)

*Preparación*

Wash potatoes, peel, and dice. Wash tomato, onion, and chilies. Dice finely. Heat oil in skillet and fry potatoes with salt and pepper. When potatoes have browned, add veggies and puree. Mix well and cover. Simmer over medium heat 10 minutes. Remove cover and turn up heat. Cook, stirring often, until the vegetable broth boils off.

Serve with crisp corn tortillas and a splash of your favorite bottled sauce.

# Potato Shrimp Cakes
## Tortitas de Papa con Camarón

### For cakes (makes 12)
*Ingredientes*
- 3 large potatoes (3 *papas grandes*)
- 2 eggs (2 *huevos*)
- 1 tbsp margarine (1 *cucharada de margarina*)
- 1/2 cup shrimp powder (1/2 *taza de polvo de camarón*) (See *Shrimp Powder*, page 24.)
- 1 tsp salt (1 *cucharadita de sal*)
- 1/2 tsp ground pepper (1/2 *cucharadita de pimienta molida*)
- 2 tbsp cooking oil (2 *cucharadas de aceite para cocinar*)

*Equipo*
- Saucepan (*cazo*)
- Bean masher (*moledor de frijol*)
- Skillet (*sartén*)

### For sauce
*Ingredientes*
- 2 tomatoes (2 *tomates*)
- 1/2 onion (1/2 *cebolla*)
- 1/2 garlic clove, peeled (1/2 *diente de ajo, pelado*)
- 1 tsp beef bouillon powder (1 *cucharadita de consomé de res en polvo*)
- 1 cup tomato puree (1 *taza de puré de tomate*)
- 1 tbsp cooking oil (1 *cucharada de aceite para cocinar*)

*Equipo*
- Saucepot (*cazuela*)
- Blender (*licuadora*)

*Preparación*

**Sauce**: Quarter tomatoes, slice onion, and chop garlic. Place in saucepot with 1 liter of water and bring to a boil. Add bouillon powder, cover, and simmer for 5 minutes. Allow to cool. Mash tomatoes with fork (*tenedor*) and remove skins. Pour contents into blender. Add puree and blend until smooth.

Heat cooking oil in empty saucepot. Pour in contents of blender. Fry tomato mixture over low heat until it bubbles and thickens. Tomato sauce is ready.

**Cakes**: Peel potatoes, cut in quarters, and boil in saucepan with 1 liter of water until soft. Drain. Mash potatoes with bean masher. Beat 1 egg. Add to potatoes together with margarine, shrimp powder, salt, and pepper. Mash ingredients until smooth (no lumps). Sometimes Pickerel sets his bean masher aside and uses his hands instead, squeezing fistfuls of shrimp potato mix between his fingers (Pickerel is fifty-six going on six).

Make 12 potato shrimp cakes: coffee-cup diameter and 3/4 inch thick.

Heat oil in skillet. Beat remaining egg in a shallow dish. When oil is hot, place each cake *briefly* in egg—in and out—first one side then the other. One egg ÷ 12 cakes = you do the math.

Place cakes in hot oil and fry each side until crisp and brown. Three minutes per side should do. Drain excess oil from cakes (Pickerel uses old newspapers untouched by dog), and serve with spoonfuls of tomato sauce on each. Enjoy the taste of soft potato with deep-fried shrimp inside.

**Optional**: Serve with white rice on the side. (See *Fried White Rice*, page 124.)

# Potatoes with Manola Machaca
## Papas con Machaca de Manola

See dedication to Manola, page 105.

*Ingredientes* (two servings)
- 3 tbsp cooking oil (3 *cucharadas de aceite para cocinar*)
- 1 large potato (1 *papa grande*)
- 1/4 tsp salt (1/4 *cucharadita de sal*)
- 1 small tomato (1 *tomate chico*)
- 1/4 medium onion (1/4 *cebolla mediano*)
- 1/4 Anaheim chili deveined and seedless (1/4 *chile largo-verde sin venas, ni semillas*) (See *Deveining Chili Peppers*, page 30.)
- 1 cup *machaca* (1 *taza de machaca*) (See *Carne machaca*, pages 21/22.)
- A pinch of ground pepper (*una pizca de pimienta molida*)

*Equipo*
Skillet (*sartén*)

*Preparación*

Heat oil in skillet. Peel potato and dice. Fry potato cubes with salt until crisp and golden.

Peel tomato, squeeze out juice, and chop finely. Slice onion and chili thinly.

Remove fried potatoes from oil. Drain (Pickerel uses old newspapers untouched by dog). Keep oil warm. Add *machaca* to skillet. Using a spatula (*espátula*), mix well with oil. Keep heat low or *machaca* will fry and turn crisp. When *machaca* darkens with oil, push to one side of skillet. Add veggies to empty side and stir-fry on high heat for 1 minute before mixing with *machaca*. Add potatoes plus that pinch of pepper. Mix well. Cover and cook over low heat for 1 minute. Stir, remove from heat, and leave covered until ready to serve.

Spoon inside flour tortillas to make *machaca* burritos or serve with stir-mashed beans and tortillas on the side.

# Rice

## Arroz

*"Man who goes week with no rice has Chinaman for sister."*
Mexfucius
(Mexican half-brother of Confucius)

Pickerel's Rice

Country Rice

Green Rice

Buttered Rice with Cheese and Corn

Fried White Rice

Prior to his poor gringo incarnation and the rise of the Virgin Miriam, Pickerel ate his rice on the side—next to beef tenderloin tips in Cabernet sauce, under paprika pork chops, beside basil chicken Florentine, and spilling off an overcrowded plate of Chinese buffet food. In those days, rice was Pickerel's best grain in a supporting role.

Then Miriam ascended from hell's kitchen to throw converted rice on his plate. Minute Rice, Uncle Ben's Boil-in-Bag, and Rice-A-Roni Pilaf became permanent denizens of their microwave. Pickerel summoned patience. He lobbied for risotto. He gently suggested pasta, then potatoes. Finally, he demanded that instant rice get off his plate.

He might as well have commanded the high, cold stars to dance. Miriam smiled. "I like it," she replied simply, knowing how Pickerel hated that as a reason. "Besides," she added, "it's quick." For Miriam—whose cold Norwegian blood could not have been thinned with a keg of Lao-Lao—cooking rice for Pickerel was not unlike making love to Pickerel: the quicker the better, and no leftovers please.

Now that he is free of Miriam and her microwave settings (both in and out of the bedroom), Pickerel has returned long-grain and unconverted to his plate—to the center of it. Sometimes rice is the only thing there.

# Pickerel's Rice
## *Sopa de Arroz (Literally, Dry Soup)*

*Ingredientes* (four servings)
- 1 cup long-grain, unconverted, white rice (1 *taza de arroz blanco, grano largo y fino*)
- 1/4 Anaheim chili, deveined and seedless (1/4 *chile largo-verde sin venas, ni semillas*) (See *Deveining Chili Peppers*, page 30.)
- 1/4 medium onion (1/4 *cebolla mediano*)
- 2 tbsp chicken bouillon powder (2 *cucharadas de consomé de pollo en polvo*) or 3 cups of chicken stock (3 *tazas de consomé de pollo*) (See *Green Chicken*, page 143, for stock.)
- 2 tbsp cooking oil (2 *cucharadas de aceite para cocinar*)
- 1 garlic clove, peeled (1 *diente de ajo, pelado*)
- 1 cup tomato puree (1 *taza de puré de tomate*)
- 1 tsp salt (1 *cucharadita de sal*)
- 1/4 tsp ground pepper (1/4 *cucharadita de pimienta molida*)

Optional (*opcional*)
- 2 sliced bananas (2 *plátanos rebandados*)
- 2 hardboiled eggs, sliced (2 *huevos bien cocidos, rebandados*)

*Equipo*
- Optional (*opcional*): cafeteria tray (*charola*) or cookie sheet (*bandeja para hornear*)
- Small saucepan (*cazo chico*)
- Deep skillet with cover (*sartén honda con tapadera*)

*Preparación*

Wash rice and drain well. Spread on tray or cookie sheet and set in sun for 30 minutes (Pickerel's precook). If the sun is not out, skip to next step.

Dice chili and onion finely. In saucepan, bring chicken stock (or 3 cups of water with bouillon powder) to a boil. Heat oil in skillet. Cut garlic in half and brown in oil until skillet smells strongly of garlic. Remove garlic. Keep heat low.

Add rice to hot oil and fry (stirring frequently) for 10 minutes or until rice turns a pale gold color. Drain excess oil (tip skillet, hold rice). Add diced onion, chili, puree, salt, and pepper to fried rice. Stir well. Add boiling chicken stock (or bouillon broth). Stir once, cover, and cook over low heat until tomato liquid disappears—about 15 minutes—and vent holes show in rice surface. Your dry soup—tomatoed rice with garlic underflavor—is ready.

To serve as a meal, top with slices of banana and hardboiled egg.

# Country Rice
## *Arroz Campestre*

*Ingredientes* (four servings)
- 1 cup long-grain, unconverted, white rice (1 *taza de arroz blanco, grano largo y fino*)
- 2 tbsp cooking oil (2 *cucharadas de aceite para cocinar*)
- 2 tbsp chicken bouillon powder (2 *cucharadas de consomé de pollo en polvo*) or 3 cups of chicken stock (3 *tazas de consomé de pollo*) (See Green Chicken, page 143, for stock.)
- 1 tbsp mustard (1 *cucharada de mostaza*)
- 1 tsp salt (1 *cucharadita de sal*)
- 1/2 tsp ground pepper (1/2 *cucharadita de pimienta molida*)

*Equipo*
- Optional (*opcional*): cafeteria tray (*charola*) or cookie sheet (*bandeja para hornear*)
- Deep skillet with cover (*sartén honda con tapadera*)
- Saucepan (*cazo*)

*Preparación*

Wash rice and drain well. Spread on tray or cookie sheet and set in sun for 30 minutes (Pickerel's precook). If the sun is not out, skip to next step.

Heat oil in skillet. In saucepan, bring chicken stock (or 3 cups of water with bouillon powder) to a boil, mixing in mustard, salt, and pepper. When oil is hot, fry rice, stirring well to coat grains with oil. Pickerel's brand—San Martín—fries in 10 minutes over medium heat. When rice turns a pale gold color, drain oil (tip skillet, hold rice), add boiling chicken stock (or bouillon broth). Stir only once, cover, and cook over low heat. Liquid will disappear in about 15 minutes, leaving vent holes in rice. Your *arroz campestre* is ready: puffy yellow rice with the faint flavor of mustard.

# Green Rice
## *Arroz Verde*

*Ingredientes* (two servings)
- 2 poblano chilies (2 *chiles poblanos*) Green bell peppers (*chile morrón or pimiento verde*) may be substituted.
- 1 small garlic clove, unpeeled (1 *diente chico de ajo, sin pelar*)
- 2 slices medium onion (2 *rebanadas de una cebolla mediana*)
- 1/2 tbsp chicken bouillon powder (1/2 *cucharada de consomé de pollo en polvo*)
- 1/2 tsp salt (1/2 *cucharadita de sal*)
- 1/2 tsp ground pepper (1/2 *cucharadita de pimienta molida*)
- 1/2 cup long-grain, unconverted, white rice (1/2 *taza de arroz blanco, grano largo y fino*)
- 1 tbsp margarine (1 *cucharada de margarina*)

*Equipo*
- Optional (*opcional*): cafeteria tray (*charola*) or cookie sheet (*bandeja para hornear*)
- Blender (*licuadora*)
- Deep skillet with cover (*sartén honda con tapadera*)

> **Cultural note**: When Pickerel feels a sudden welling of patriotic pride for his adopted land, he spoons some green rice next to some white rice next to some tomato rice to create the colors of the Mexican flag. Pickerel stands at attention when he does this, humming the Mexican national anthem under his breath.

*Preparación*

Wash chilies, remove stems, and seeds. Devein. (See *Deveining Chili Peppers*, page 30.) Chop garlic. Place chilies and garlic in blender with onion, bouillon powder, salt, pepper, and 1-1/4 cups of cold water. Blend until smooth. Your blender will turn forest green.

Wash rice and drain well. Spread on tray or cookie sheet and set in sun for 30 minutes (Pickerel's precook). If the sun is not out, skip to next step.

Melt margarine in skillet and fry rice, mixing well with margarine. When rice turns pale gold (not brown), pour in contents of blender. Stir, cover, and cook 15 minutes or until rice softens and puffs (turning green) and liquid disappears. Do not stir.

Serve immediately or eat right out of the pan.

# Buttered Rice with Cheese and Corn
## Sopa de Arroz a la Mantequilla

*Ingredientes* (two servings)
- 1/2 cup long-grain, unconverted, white rice (1/2 *taza de arroz blanco, grano largo y fino*)
- 1/2 tsp chicken bouillon powder (1/2 *cucharadita de consomé de pollo en polvo*) or 1-1/4 cups of chicken stock (1-1/4 *tazas de consomé de pollo*) (See *Green Chicken*, page 143, for stock.)
- 1/2 garlic clove, peeled (1/2 *diente de ajo, pelado*)
- 2 tbsp margarine (2 *cucharadas de margarina*)
- 1/4 cup canned corn (1/4 *taza de granos de elote enlatado*), the only canned veggie Pickerel buys
- 1/2 tsp salt (1/2 *cucharadita de sal*)
- A pinch of ground pepper (*una pizca de pimienta molida*)
- 1/4 cup grated Chihuahua cheese (1/4 *taza de queso de Chihuahua rallado*)

*Equipo*
- Optional (*opcional*): cafeteria tray (*charola*) or cookie sheet (*bandeja para hornear*)
- Saucepan (*cazo*)
- Deep skillet with cover (*sartén honda con tapadera*)

*Preparación*

Wash rice and drain well. Spread on tray or cookie sheet and set in sun for 30 minutes (Pickerel's precook). If the sun is not out, skip to next step.

In saucepan, bring chicken stock (or 1-1/4 cups of water with bouillon) to a boil.

Dice garlic finely. Melt margarine in skillet. Cook garlic in butter. Do not brown. Add rice to margarine and garlic, keeping skillet over medium heat. Mix well. Add corn, salt, and pepper. Stir.

Fry rice 10 minutes or until it turns a pale gold color, stirring often. Add boiling chicken stock (or bouillon broth). Stir again. Cover and cook over low heat 20 minutes or until liquid is consumed. Do not stir.

When vapor holes appear in rice surface, sprinkle on grated cheese. Cover and finish cooking rice, letting cheese melt.

Serve immediately.

# Fried White Rice
## *Arroz Blanco*

*Ingredientes* (two servings)
- 1/2 cup long-grain, unconverted, white rice (1/2 *taza de arroz blanco, grano largo y fino*)
- 1/2 tsp chicken bouillon powder (1/2 *cucharadita de consomé de pollo en polvo*) or 1-1/4 cups of chicken stock (1-1/4 *tazas de consomé de pollo*) (See *Green Chicken*, page 143, for stock.)
- 1/4 garlic clove, peeled (1/4 *diente de ajo, pelado*)
- 1 tbsp cooking oil (1 *cucharada de aceite para cocinar*)
- A pinch of salt (*una pizca de sal*)
- A pinch of ground pepper (*una pizca de pimienta molida*)

> Along with 4 billion other souls on the planet, Pickerel considers fried white rice a meal in itself.

*Equipo*
- Optional (*opcional*): cafeteria tray (*charola*) or cookie sheet (*bandeja para hornear*)
- Saucepan (*cazo*)
- Deep skillet with cover (*sartén honda con tapadera*)

*Preparación*

Wash rice and drain well. Spread on tray or cookie sheet and set in sun for 30 minutes (Pickerel's precook). If the sun is not out, skip to next step.

In saucepan, bring chicken stock (or 1-1/4 cups of water with bouillon) to a boil.

Dice garlic finely. Heat oil in skillet. When oil is hot, add rice and fry, stirring often. Add garlic, salt, and pepper. Stir-fry rice until it turns a pale gold color.

Add boiling chicken stock (or bouillon broth). Cover and cook over low heat for 20 minutes or until liquid is consumed. Do not stir.

Serve by itself or under *Run-over Rooster in Greens* (page 142), *Chicken in Banana Leaf* (page 146), *Ranch Fish* (page 168), *Papered Fish* (page 167), or *Red Chili Pork with Nopales* (page 187).

# From the Garden

## Del Jardín

*The three biggest lies in Mexico:*
***Un momento, por favor*** *(one moment, please).*
***Mañana te pago*** *(tomorrow I'll pay you).*
***Prohibido de paso*** *(no trespassing).*
*M. S. Pickerel (renowned liar)*

Squash in Melted Cheese

Creamed String Beans

Fried Cauliflower

Cabbage Cakes

String Beans with Cheese

Charcoaled Onions

Roasted Corn on the Cob

Hot Tomato

Greens with Tomatoes and Onions

Greens with Corn

Pickerel first recognized the bartering power of garden vegetables the day a highway traffic cop stopped him for speeding on the Natoches road. Heaped on the backseat of Pickerel's rundown sedan were several bushels of freshly stolen corn—formally field corn; now Pickerel's corn.

As the law enforcement officer approached the driver's window, Pickerel prepared his familiar speech: "Oops—registration lost—license expired—plates stolen. Are my taillights broken too? Must have been kicked out by that road-crossing stampede of cattle back yonder ..."

Pickerel also pretended to reach for his wallet as if to extract payoff pesos—though the only thing of value inside were two condoms: these carried for emergency tire repairs and/or water storage bladders in case of an unexpected desert crossing with damsels in distress (Pickerel always prepared for the best-case scenario).

The officer gave Pickerel's poorly maintained excuse for a speeding sedan the grim once over. His eyebrows lifted slightly at the sight of fresh corn in the backseat.

"*Venía a exceso de velocidad*," he began accusatorily, taking a traffic ticket booklet and pen from his shirt pocket.

Pickerel quickly agreed. Yes, he had been speeding. (Pickerel's number-one rule for a moving violation is no denial with a smile. Pickerel may be a liar and cheat, but he is not a shape-shifter of Newtonian mechanics—not in broad daylight.) He added, by way of parley, that he had been in a hurry to get home and boil corn.

The officer nodded and smiled, as if to say this reason was as good as any to be driving twice the speed limit.

Pickerel saw his opening. "Help yourself," he said to the officer in Spanish, gesturing grandly toward the backseat. "Got plenty. Picked it myself."

Two minutes later, Pickerel was picking up speed on the Natoches road, his backseat a dozen ears lighter but the front seat free of any legal paperwork encumbering his race toward boiling water. He had even provided the officer with a bag to carry his corn home. Pickerel always carries extras.

Though no longer motorized, MSP continues to empower himself with other people's vegetables. Once he filled in as a local deputy inspector of Transporte Federal (the chief inspector is Pickerel's *compadre*) at a roadside weigh station. Inspector Pickerel dutifully required all produce carriers to lighten their loads of garden fresh in exchange for allowing their overweight vehicles to continue unsafely down the road. Outfitted in khaki pants, his tan *guayabera*, and flashing his faded military ID, Pickerel has posed (in the pursuit of putting veggies on his table) as a phytosanitary inspector, a USDA rep attached to the local farm bureau, and an agent from agricultural pest control. Halting vegetable vendors on the street, he checks their legumes for the presence of cabbageworms, squash bugs, bean beetles, and whitefly infestations. Pickerel is sympathetic to violators. He understands that vegetable vendors are only trying to grind out a miserable existence, so he accepts small tokens of seasonal produce in return for casting a blind eye to leguminous plagues. Otherwise, Pickerel is forced to quarantine all violating vegetables—the freshest, of course—in his home.

# Squash in Melted Cheese
## Colache

*Ingredientes* (two servings)
- 1/4 small onion (1/4 *cebolla chica*)
- 2 small zucchinis (2 *calabacitas*)
- 1 tsp salt (1 *cucharadita de sal*)
- 1/2 tsp ground pepper (1/2 *cucharadita de pimienta molida*)
- 2 tbsp margarine (2 *cucharadas de margarina*)
- 1/2 cup grated Chihuahua cheese (1/2 *taza de queso de Chihuahua rallado*)

*Equipo*
Deep skillet with cover (*sartén honda con tapadera*)

*Preparación*

Slice onion thinly. Cut squash into bite-size cubes (2 small zucchinis will make 3 cups of cut squash). Place squash in skillet with 1/2 cup of water for each cup of squash. Add salt, pepper, and onions. Cover and bring water to a boil, stirring occasionally. Boil over medium heat 20 minutes or until squash is tender. When skewered with a fork (*tenedor*), squash should slide off. Drain water (tip skillet, hold squash). Add margarine. Mix until squash and onion are buttery. Add cheese—as much as you can afford but at least 1/2 cup—cover and keep warm over low flame until cheese melts.

Serve inside warm corn tortillas.

# Creamed String Beans
## Ejotes con Crema

*Ingredientes* (three servings)
- 1/2 kg string beans—about 3 dozen beans (1/2 *kilo de ejotes*—3 *docenas de ejotes*)
- 1 small onion (1 *cebolla chica*)
- 2 tbsp margarine (2 *cucharadas de margarina*)
- 1/2 cup grated Chihuahua cheese (1/2 *taza de queso de Chihuahua rallado*)
- 1 cup sour cream (1 *taza de crema agria*)
- 1 tsp salt (1 *cucharadita de sal*)
- 1/2 tsp ground pepper (1/2 *cucharadita de pimienta molida*)

*Equipo*
- Saucepot (*cazuela*)
- Colander (*escurridor*)
- Deep skillet (*sartén honda*)

*Preparación*

Snap off bean ends, pull away fiber (See *String Beans*, page 25.), and cut each bean lengthwise in strips (leave thin beans whole). In saucepot with 2 liters of boiling water and 1/2 teaspoon of salt, parboil bean strips for 3 minutes. Drain.

Slice onion. Melt margarine in skillet. Add onion and parboiled beans. Gently fry without browning (*acitronar*) until onion softens. Add sour cream, 1/2 teaspoon of salt, and pepper. Mix well and cook for 2 minutes over low heat. Sprinkle cheese, cover again, and remove from heat. Allow cheese to melt.

Serve with corn tortillas and refried beans—old beans chumming with young beans.

# *Fried Cauliflower*
## *Coliflor Empanizada*

Cauliflower may be cabbage with a college education, but Pickerel cannot swallow this pretentious crucifer unless it gets lowbrow and pedestrian—that is, deep-fried.

*Ingredientes* (four servings)
- 1 head fresh cauliflower (1 *cabeza fresca de coliflor*)
- 1/4 cup salt (1/4 *taza de sal*)
- 5 dried chiltepin chilies (5 *chiles chiltepines secos*)
- 3 eggs (3 *huevos*)
- 1 cup corn flour (1 *taza de harina de maíz*)
- 1/4 cup cooking oil (1/4 *taza de aceite para cocinar*)
- 3 cups cooked tomato sauce (3 *tazas de salsa de tomate cocido*) (See *Boiled Tomato Sauce*, page 75.)

*Equipo*
- Saucepot (*cazuela*)
- Colander (*escurridor*)
- Mortar and pestle (*molcajete y tejolote*)
- Deep skillet (*sartén honda*)

*Preparación*

Break cauliflower head into bite-size flowerets. To evict arthropodic residents (both larval and adult), soak flowerets in 2 liters of water mixed with 1/4 cup of salt for 10 minutes.

Boil flowerets in saucepot with 3 liters of water until stalks are tender and the flowerets are soft but not mushy (probe with fork). Drain in colander.

Grind chilies to a peppery powder (if a *molcajete* is unavailable, grind chilies in a soup bowl using the back of a spoon). Beat eggs, whites first, and then yolks. Mix flour with beaten eggs (Pickerel's shortcut to normal, two-step breading). Add ground chilies and beat again. Warm tomato sauce. Heat oil in skillet.

Batter cauliflower sprigs and fry in skillet over medium heat until the batter turns crisp and golden.

Spoon warm tomato sauce over fried sprigs, or dip individual sprigs into sauce. Either way, savor the chili flavor of cauliflower slumming it.

# Cabbage Cakes
## *Tortitas de Repollo*

*Ingredientes* (10 cabbage cakes)
- 1/2 small cabbage (1/2 *cabeza chica de repollo*)
- 2 eggs (2 *huevos*)
- 2 tbsp corn flour (2 *cucharadas de harina de maíz*)
- 3 tbsp cooking oil (3 *cucharadas de aceite para cocinar*)
- 1/4 kg melting cheese (1/4 *kilo queso para derretir*) Pickerel prefers Mennonite cheese for this recipe. (See *Cheeses*, page 23.)
- 2 cups cooked tomato sauce (2 *tazas de salsa de tomate cocido*) (See *Boiled Tomato Sauce*, page 75.)

*Equipo*
- Steamer (*olla vaporera*)
- Shallow dish (*plato poco hondo*)
- Deep skillet (*sartén honda*)

*Preparación*

Place whole cabbage in whatever steamer you own, cover, and cook over high heat. While cabbage steams, beat the egg whites, add the yolks, and beat those too. Spread corn flour in a shallow dish.

When cabbage has cooked—about 10 minutes or until the center is tender (press with spatula)—remove and allow to cool. *Carefully* take cabbage apart one leaf at a time. The inside leaves will be crisper than the outer ones.

Stack leaves. Heat oil in skillet. Slice cheese thinly. Warm tomato sauce.

Place 1 slice of cheese in each leaf and fold into a neat cabbage leaf packet. Tuck in loose edges to prevent cheese from falling out. Dip cabbage packets in beaten egg, flour both sides, and slip into hot oil.

Fry, turning once, until golden brown. Cabbage should be crisp. Drain excess oil (Pickerel uses old newspapers untouched by dog). Bathe with cooked tomato sauce, and serve with refried beans on the side.

> Pickerel's steamer consists of a dozen stones (golf ball size) laid in the bottom of a tall pot. He adds enough water to cover the stones, and he positions two circles of mosquito screen (cut to fit the diameter of his pot) over the stones. In the Miriam years, Pickerel's steamer proved a valuable tool in monitoring private postal correspondence. Pickerel regularly steamed (and opened) all envelopes addressed to Miriam from her meddling, stateside mother. Outgoing mail was cooked as well. Did he read the contents? Did he destroy the evidence? To the best of his recollection, Pickerel has no comment.

# String Beans with Cheese
## Ejotes con Queso

*Ingredientes* (three servings)
- 1 tsp salt (1 *cucharadita de sal*)
- 1/2 kg string beans—about 3 dozen beans (1/2 *kilo de ejotes*—3 *docenas de ejotes*)
- 1/4 small onion (1/4 *cebolla chica*)
- 1 small tomato (1 *tomate chico*)
- 1/4 Anaheim chili deveined and seedless (1/4 *chile largo-verde sin venas, ni semillas*) (See *Deveining Chili Peppers*, page 30.)
- 1/4 tsp diced serrano chili (1/4 *cucharadita de chile serrano picado*)
- 1 tsp cooking oil (1 *cucharaditaa de aceite para cocinar*)
- 1/4 tsp ground pepper (1/4 *cucharadita de pimienta molida*)
- 1/8 kilo of fresh ranch cheese (1/8 *kilo de queso fresco de rancho*) (See *Cheeses*, page 23.)

*Equipo*
- Saucepot (*cazuela*)
- Saucepan (*cazo*)
- Strainer (*colador*)
- Large skillet with cover (*sartén grande con tapadera*)

*Preparación*

In a saucepot, heat 2 liters of water with 1/2 tsp of salt. Snap off bean ends, pull away fiber (See *String Beans*, page 25.), cut each bean in half, and then cut lengthwise into strips (leave thin beans whole). Boil beans 6 minutes, stirring occasionally. Drain in colander.

Slice onion into rainbows. Chop tomato, but not too finely. Halve chili lengthwise and slice thinly. In saucepan, boil 1/2 cup of water.

Over low flame, heat oil in skillet. Fry onion, tomato, Anaheim chili, and diced serrano without browning (*acitronar*). Add cooked beans and ground pepper. Stir. Add boiling water and 1/2 tsp of salt. Mix well over high heat. Crumble ranch cheese evenly across the top of beans and vegetables. Cover and remove from heat. Leave covered 2 minutes. Serve with corn tortillas and refried beans on the side.

# Charcoaled Onions
## Cebollas al Carbón

*Ingredientes* (two servings)
- 2 large white onions (2 *cebollas blancas y grandes*)
- 1 tbsp cooking oil (1 *cucharada de aceite para cocinar*)
- 1/2 tsp salt (1/2 *cucharadita de sal*)

*Equipo*
- Charcoal or wood fire (*fuego al carbón o leña*)
- 2 sheets of aluminum foil (2 *hojas de papel aluminio*)
- Tongs (*pinzas*)

*Preparación*

Make a charcoal or wood fire, allowing it to burn down to the coals. Wash onions well. Brush or wipe oil on each. Drop onions into coals. Cook for 20 minutes, turning often, then remove and wrap in tin foil. Cook 20 minutes more on coals. Open tinfoil. Allow to cool. Salt and eat with a spoon.

> Pickerel learned this recipe while loitering near local taco stands, drawing deep breaths of skirt steak grilled over a charcoal fire.

# Roasted Corn on the Cob
## *Elotes Asados*

Forget boiling. Forget butter. When the Aztecs dropped maize into wood ash (to make *nixtamal*), they knew what fire could do for *Zea mays*. This is the cob corn Mexicans eat in the street and off their grills—a green field corn recipe that even poor gringo horses hoof across the border to nibble.

*Ingredientes* (two servings)
- 6 ears green field corn (6 *elotes*)
- 1/2 cup grated ranch cheese (1/2 *taza de queso de rancho rallado*) (See *Cheeses*, page 23.)
- 4 limes (4 *limones*)
- 1/2 tsp salt (1/2 *cucharadita de sal*)
- 1 tbsp Salsa Huichol (1 *cucharada de Salsa Huichol*) (See *Bottled Sauces*, page 29.)

*Equipo*
- Charcoal grill (*parrilla*)
- Dry wood or charcoal (*leña seca o carbón*)
- 6 skewers (6 *brochetas*) Pickerel uses coat hanger wire, cut to 6-inch lengths, bent at the ends.
- Tongs (*pinzas*)
- Lime squeezer (*exprimidor de limón*)
- Basting brush (*brocha para bañar con su jugo*) Pickerel has employed both paint- and toothbrushes.

*Preparación*

Start fire in the grill. Husk corn, remove corn silk, and skewer each ear, pushing the wire into the cob far enough that the corn will not fall off when lifted.

Place grated cheese in a shallow receptacle (a sheet of tinfoil crimped at the edges works). Slice limes and squeeze into a bowl (*tazón*). Add salt and bottled sauce to lime juice. Mix well.

When grill is hot, place corn ears over fire and turn often with tongs until cooked evenly on all sides. The tops of the kernels should blacken. Move to edge of grill (position skewer away from heat). When the skewer is cool enough to

> See Green Corn Tamales (page 232) for Pickerel's tips on picking the right ears from market vegetable stalls and the local farmer's corn patch.

hold, remove corn from grill and brush on seasoned lime juice. Don't be stingy. Let it drip. Place corn ear in receptacle with grated cheese, and roll until covered with cheese. Your *elote asado* is ready.

Start at either end. You may never boil sweet corn again.

# *Hot Tomato*
## *Tomate a las Brasas*

*Ingredientes* (two servings)
- 4 large, ripe tomatoes (4 *tomates, maduros y grandes*)
- 2 dried chiltepines, finely ground with mortar and pestle (2 *chiles chiltepines secos y molidos en el molcajete y tejolote*)
- 1 tsp salt (1 *cucharadita de sal*)
- 8 corn tortillas (8 *tortillas de maíz*)

*Equipo*
- Charcoal or wood fire (*fuego al carbón o leña*)
- Tongs (*pinzas*)

*Preparación*

Make a charcoal or wood fire, allowing it to burn down to coals. Place whole tomatoes on coals, taking care they do not split. Cook on coals, turning occasionally, until tomato is black all over. Remove from coals, peel burnt skin with tongs or fork (*tenedor*), and spoon soft tomato centers onto a plate. Sprinkle with ground chiltepin and salt. Mix well. Spread on warm corn tortillas. Fold tortillas into tomato tacos.

# Greens: Verdura de Hoja Verde

Until Pickerel met Doña Yerba, his knowledgeable guide in the world of potherbs (Doña Yerba is now a *comadre*), he had difficulty telling one green from another. *Quelites* (wild spinach), *acelgas* (Swiss chard), *bledo* (green amaranth), *verdolagas* (purslane), and *chiquelites* (garden huckleberry)—they all looked the same to the deuteranopic Pickerel.

Yet it matters not that our hero is leaf-vegetable blind *and* ignorant. What matters is that the picking of greens in Mexico's public domain is free from police pursuit and misdemeanorly conviction (Pickerel knows his local penal code). Growing prolifically along roadsides, in highway median strips, on the edge of fields, next to fencerows, at parks, on municipal lawns, and even in the acid-rich soil of Pickerel's own weedy plat, these potherbs are a poor gringo's cheapest source of iron, calcium, and dietary fiber (especially during famine conditions).

For those reluctant to test statutory enactments or to handle the common nightshade weeds (fearing an accidental ingestion of poisonous alkaloids), all of the above-mentioned leafy greens are available in most local markets—almost for the taking—if you look poor enough—which Pickerel does.

# Greens with Tomatoes and Onions
## Verdolagas con Tomate y Cebolla

*Ingredientes* (four servings)
- 1 kg freshly pulled purslane (1 *kilo de verdolagas recién cortadas*) Any green may be substituted.
- 1/2 cup corn flour (1/2 *taza de harina de maíz*)
- 1 large tomato (1 *tomate grande*)
- 1 small onion (1 *cebolla chica*)
- 1/2 garlic clove, peeled (1/2 *diente de ajo, pelado*)
- 1 tbsp cooking oil (1 *cucharada de aceite para cocinar*)
- 1/2 tsp salt (1/2 *cucharadita de sal*)
- 1/2 tsp ground pepper (1/2 *cucharadita de pimienta molida*)

*Equipo*
- Saucepot (*cazuela*)
- Colander (*escurridor*)
- Mixing bowl (*tazón para mezclar*)
- Large skillet with cover (*sartén grande con tapadera*)

*Preparación*

Remove taproots and thicker stems (purslane leaves are stalkless). Wash well. In a saucepot with 3 liters of water, boil greens for 10 minutes (until red stems darken). Boiling eliminates purslane's unsavory slipperiness. Drain in colander.

To make thickener, add corn flour to 1 cup of warm water in mixing bowl (*tazón para mezclar*). Mix until smooth (no lumps).

Slice onion, chop tomato, and dice garlic finely. Over low flame, heat oil in skillet. Fry without browning (*acitronar*) onion, tomato, and garlic until onion is soft. Add greens, salt, pepper, and corn flour thickener. Mix well, cover, and simmer over low heat for 5 minutes.

Serve with corn or flour tortillas with stir-mashed beans on the side.

# Greens with Corn
## Quelites con Elote

*Ingredientes* (four servings)
- 6 ears of fresh corn (6 *elotes de maíz*) Lazy gringos may use 5 cups of canned corn (5 *tazas de grano de elote enlatada*)
- 1 kg wild spinach (1 *kilo de quelites*) Any green may be substituted.
- 1/2 cup corn flour (1/2 *taza de harina de maíz*)
- 1 tbsp cooking oil (1 *cucharada de aceite para cocinar*)
- 1/2 small onion (1/2 *cebolla chica*)
- 1/2 garlic clove, peeled (1/2 *diente de ajo, pelado*)
- 1/2 tsp salt (1/2 *cucharadita de sal*)
- 1/2 tsp ground pepper (1/2 *cucharadita de pimienta molida*)

*Equipo*
- Stockpot (*olla*)
- Saucepot (*cazuela*)
- Colander (*escurridor*)
- Mixing bowl (*tazón para mezclar*)
- Skillet with cover (*sartén con tapadera*)

*Preparación*

For this recipe, Pickerel uses green field corn (sweet corn is still undiscovered in his poor gringo neck of the universe). Shuck ears, remove corn silk, and boil corn for 20 minutes in stockpot. Allow ears to cool, and cut kernels from cob (corn comes off in strips, which will then separate into individual grains). Save 1 cup of corn broth.

Stem greens, wash well, and boil in saucepot for 10 minutes. Drain in colander.

To make thickener, add corn flour to the cup of corn broth in mixing bowl (*tazón para mezclar*). Mix until smooth (no lumps).

Heat oil in skillet. Slice onion thinly. Dice garlic. Over low flame, fry without browning (*acitronar*) garlic and onion until soft. Add corn flour thickener, stir, and bring to a low boil.

Add greens, mix well, and simmer under cover for 10 minutes. Add cut corn, salt, and pepper. Mix well.

Serve with corn tortillas and refried beans on the side.

# Poultry

## Aves

*Señor Pollo, Mr. Pollo,
Juan Pollo, Don Pollo,
Pollo Loco, Pollo Pepe,
Pollo Rico, Pollo Feliz,
Pollo Rey, Pollo Boy,
El Pollo Chilango,
El Pollo Valiente,
El Pollo Norteño,
El Pollo Urbano*
Chicken Rotisseries in
Pickerel's Unnamed City

Run-over Rooster in Greens

Green Chicken

Pickerel's Unholy Mole

Suicide Hen in Banana Leaf

Wandering Neighborhood Chicken Runs into Cabbage

Tattered Tortillas with Chicken in Red Chili Sauce

Capon Overboard in Vinegar

When Pickerel counted among his possessions a motorized conveyance, he ran over domestic fowl at least once a week—on country roads, down neighborhood streets, behind speeding poultry trucks (Pickerel pursued these cage-laden vehicles at a close distance, slipstreaming his Chevy Nova in a white wake of chicken feathers). In those days, such culinary concoctions as run-over rooster, suicide hen, capon overboard, and wandering neighborhood chicken were familiar dishes on Pickerel's table. Now that he rides a bicycle, however, the challenge of keeping poultry on the menu requires another skill set. First, Pickerel must pedal like a demonized Yellow Jersey if he is to intercept free-range fowl. Then he must take care that panicked *pollos* do not lodge between his bicycle spokes (turning both poultry and Pickerel into run-over). Finally, Pickerel must deal with the inconveniences of pursuing chickens with a nonmotorized vehicle—bird owners chasing Pickerel, dogs chasing Pickerel, and chickens outrunning Pickerel. Add mechanical failure (a flat tire or a bicycle chain jumping off its sprocket), and suddenly Pickerel finds himself in a pickle—stranded in the middle of a street, surrounded by barking dogs, berated by broom-wielding housewives, and chickenless.

On days such as these, Pickerel prepares pigeon (*pichón;* see *Pickerel's Unholy Mole,* page 144) to satisfy his appetite for something flighty grounded in a pot. Using tortilla tatters for bait, Pickerel lures the world's oldest domesticated bird onto his rooftop, where he entices it into a specially designed trap for disoriented fowl.

**Ecological note**: Out of respect for the universal symbol of peace, Pickerel releases from his rooftop entrapment all doves carrying olive branches. Those caught without branches go into the pot.

In further pursuit of putting something winged on his platter, Pickerel attempted one summer to raise turkeys (*guajolotes*) while gathering recipes for red chili gobbler, turkey in mole, and soused turkey. He purchased three poults from a local grower, allowing them to peck freely on his weedy plat and to fatten at a glacial pace upon vegetable peelings, tortilla scraps, and eggshells. When his gobblers began to wander (in search of more filling pastures), Pickerel cut three short lengths of baling twine and tethered each bird by the leg to his fruitless front yard mango tree. With mango bark and mango leaves to amuse them, turkey life continued copasetic for his rafter of young toms. Then Hurricane Fausto made landfall not far from Pickerel's stretch of coastal plain, bringing his experiment in avian husbandry to a sudden end. One turkey drowned. Another expired under the fallen mango tree. The third died of fright, or so Pickerel suspected, though he was unable to perform a culinary autopsy due to the ripening effects of warm weather on turkey meat (see *No recipes for turkey in these pages*). **Cautionary note**: Never leave a turkey tied to a tree in a hurricane.

> For butchering and dressing poultry, consult a local chicken farmer, your great-grandmother, or the appendix.

# Run-over Rooster in Greens
## Pollo con Acelgas

*Ingredientes* (three servings)

> Best served over arroz blanco. (See Fried White Rice, page 124.)

1/2 freshly dressed rooster (1/2 *pollo fresco*) Hen may be substituted.
1 garlic clove, peeled (1 *diente de ajo, pelado*)
2 tomatoes (2 *tomates*)
1/2 onion (1/2 *cebolla*)
1/2 Anaheim chili, deveined and seedless (1/2 *chile largo-verde sin venas, ni semillas*) (See *Deveining Chili Peppers*, page 30.)
1 kg Swiss chard (1 *kilo de acelgas*) Any fresh green may be substituted.
2 tbsp cooking oil (2 *cucharadas de aceite para cocinar*)
1/2 cup tomato puree (1/2 *taza de puré de tomate*)
1/2 tbsp salt (1/2 *cucharada de sal*)
1/2 tbsp ground pepper (1/2 *cucharada de pimienta molida*)
3 cups fried white rice (3 *tazas de arroz blanco*) (See *Fried White Rice*, page 124.)

*Equipo*
Colander (*escurridor*)
Large saucepot with cover (*cazuela grande con tapadera*)

*Preparación*

Cut chicken into small, serving-size pieces. Dice garlic finely. Chop tomatoes, onions, and chili. Remove thicker stalks from greens and cut leaves into salad-size pieces. Wash well and place in cold water for 10 minutes. Drain in colander.

Heat oil in saucepot. Add garlic and chicken. Fry chicken, turning often, until pieces have browned on the outside. Add veggies. Stir and cook with chicken until onion sizzles. Add tomato puree. Stir and add greens, salt, and pepper. Mix well and add 1 liter of cold water. Stir and cover. Bring to boil and cook over high heat for 20 minutes. Stir and simmer over low heat for 10 minutes.

Serve over fried white rice with a sprinkle of Salsa Huichol (See *Bottled Sauces*, page 29.) across the greens.

# Green Chicken
## Pollo en Salsa Verde

*Ingredientes* (three servings)
- 1/2 freshly dressed chicken, run-over, wandering, or purchased (1/2 *pollo fresco*)
- 1 small onion (1 *cebolla chica*)
- 1 garlic clove, peeled (1 *diente de ajo, pelado*)
- 1/2 tbsp salt (1/2 *cucharada de sal*)
- 1/2 tsp ground pepper (1/2 *cucharadita de pimienta molida*)
- 2 tbsp margarine (2 *cucharadas de margarina*)
- 2 cups green tomato sauce (2 *tazas de salsa verde*) (See *Green Tomato Sauce*, page 76.)
- 3 cups country rice (3 *tazas de arroz campestre*) (See *Country Rice*, page 121.)

> Best served with arroz campestre.
> (See Country Rice, page 121.)

*Equipo*
- Large saucepot (*cazuela grande*)
- Deep skillet with cover (*sartén honda con tapadera*)

*Preparación*

Halve onion, peel garlic, and cut chicken into serving-size pieces.

In saucepot with 2 liters of water, boil chicken pieces with garlic, half the onion, salt, and pepper. When chicken is cooked, drain stock. (Save stock for making *Country Rice*, page 121, or *Cheese Ball Soup*, page 195.)

Slice remaining half onion thinly. Melt butter in skillet and gently fry onion without browning (*acitronar*). Pour in green tomato sauce. Stir. Add cooked chicken. Mix well, cover, boil for 5 minutes, and then simmer over low heat for 10 minutes.

Serve with country rice on the side. (See *Country Rice*, page 121.)

# *Pickerel's Unholy Mole*
## *Pichón en Mole Poblano*

Pickerel does not make his mole sauce from scratch. Instead, he buys Mole Doña María concentrate, and then he tells guests he made his mole sauce from scratch. This deceit—though in accord with Pickerel's inherently dishonest nature and lack of work ethic—is committed with the object of saving himself time (otherwise spent swindling/freebooting natives) and money (a significant sum of poor gringo pesos). Pickerel has done the math. By the time he spends two hundred pesos (twenty dollars) purchasing the necessary mole ingredients—dried chilies (four kinds), seeds (four more), spices (five), nuts (two), chocolate, charcoal, bread, and lard, none of which are easily pilfered from neighbors or nearby fields—Pickerel can take a two-minute stroll to the corner grocery and spend fourteen pesos (one dollar forty cents) for one 8-ounce jar of Doña Maria, which—when water is added—makes mole for six.

And he gets to keep the glass jar—designed as an attractive drinking glass when emptied of mole concentrate. Pickerel uses them to serve his post-mole tequila coolers—a testimony to his fondness for Doña Maria's mole.

Now, a Pickerel pop quiz. True or False:

1. Pickerel's recipe for mole is authentic Mexican cuisine.
2. You are reading *The Poor Gringo Guide to Authentic Mexican Cuisine*.
3. No one makes mole cheaper or faster than Pickerel.*

*Ingredientes* (two servings)
- 4 pigeon breasts (4 *pechugas de pichón*) or 6 dove breasts (6 *pechugas de paloma*). See *Appendix* for dressing fowl.
- 1 garlic clove, peeled (1 *diente de ajo, pelado*)
- 1 tbsp salt (1 *cucharada de sal*)
- 1 tsp ground pepper (1 *cucharadita de pimienta molida*)
- 3 potatoes (3 *papas*)
- 4-oz jar Mole Doña María sauce concentrate (*frasco de 4 onzas de Mole Doña María en pasta*)
- 1/2 bar semisweet chocolate or 1 tbsp of sugar (1/2 *barra de chocolate Abuelita o 1 cucharada de azúcar*)

---

* (1) False   (2) False   (3) Damn right.

1 tbsp cooking oil (1 *cucharada de aceite para cocinar*)
2 cups Pickerel's rice (2 *tazas de sopa de arroz*) (See *Pickerel's Rice*, page 119.)

*Equipo*
2 saucepots (*cazuelas*)
Blender (*licuadora*)

*Preparación*

In a saucepot with 2 liters of water, boil pigeon/dove breasts with garlic, salt, and pepper. When breasts are tender (probe with fork)—about 30 minutes—remove from pot. Save broth.

Peel potatoes and cut into serving-size chunks. In 4 cups of pigeon broth, boil potatoes for 15 minutes.

Allow 1-1/2 cups of broth to cool. Add to blender with Doña María concentrate and chocolate (or sugar). Blend until contents are smooth.

Heat oil in the second saucepot. Add contents of blender. Wash blender with 1/2 cup of warm broth and add to pot. Stir well and cook over low heat until it bubbles. Add breasts, potatoes, and 1 cup of pigeon broth. Stir, cover, and boil over low heat for 20 minutes.

Serve with *sopa de arroz*. (See *Pickerel's Rice*, page 119.) Watch for bones—they are small!

# Suicide Hen in Banana Leaf
## *Pollo en Achiote*

Pickerel gets his banana leaves (*hojas de plátano*) from the same place he gets his bananas (and his cooking plantains, *bocadillo* plantains, and banana shoots)—from a nearby *platanera* or banana grove. Such is the convenience of living on the warm plantain plain where bananas grow long and banana growers sleep late. As for oranges (also needed for this recipe), Pickerel buys these at below-market price from orange-thieving boys who juggle them for tips on busy street corners (juggled oranges—dropped once or twice on asphalt—make for easy hand squeezing).

> **Achiote paste** (recado rojo) is a ground spice blend made from pounded annatto seeds condimented with oregano, cumin, clove, garlic, and salt. Pickerel buys achiote paste at his local markets, where he picks the very reddest from mounds of colored pastes sold in the spice stalls. You may buy it in small, packaged blocks in grocery stores. A 100-gram package will season 5 kilos of meat.

*Ingredientes* (four servings)
6 oranges (6 *naranjas*)
3 garlic cloves, peeled (3 *dientes de ajo, pelados*)
1/2 cup vinegar (1/2 *taza de vinagre*) Pickerel uses white cane vinegar.
1 whole chicken (1 *pollo entero*)
1 freshly cut banana leaf (1 *hoja de plátano recién cortado*) Pick a young leaf that is just opening.
3 tbsp of achiote paste (3 *cucharadas de pasta de achiote*)
1/2 tbsp salt (1/2 *cucharada de sal*)
4 cups fried white rice (4 *tazas de arroz cocido*)
(See *Fried White Rice*, page 124.)

*Equipo*
   Large saucepot (*cazuela grande*)
   Blender (*licuadora*)

For cooked onion garnish (*guarnición de cebolla guisada*)
   1 onion (1 *cebolla*)
   1 tbsp cooking oil (1 *cucharada de aceite para cocinar*)
   1 tbsp vinegar (1 *cucharada de vinagre*) Pickerel uses white cane vinegar.
   A pinch of ground, whole-leaf oregano (*una pizca de hoja de orégano molido*)
   5 peppercorns (5 *pimientas enteras*)

*Equipo*
　Small skillet (*sartén chica*)

*Preparación*
　Squeeze oranges. Place garlic cloves in 1/2 cup of vinegar. Chop chicken into small, serving-size pieces.
　Remove center vein from banana leaf. Do this by placing the leaf on a flat surface and cutting along both edges of the vein with a sharp knife. You will end up with two halves of banana leaf—waxy, waterproof, and green. Wash well—banana weevils (*Cosmopolites sordidus*—those sordid citizens of the banana world and undetectable except when tasted) make their home in a rolled banana leaf.
　Over a stove burner, warm leaf halves one at a time. Hold each leaf by its ends and slide back and forth over flames—not too close, not too slow—burnt holes in banana leaf are unacceptable. When the leaf becomes warm and pliable, lay it in the saucepot (which should be nearby), molding it to the bottom and sides of this receptacle. Allow leaf ends to stick out of pot. These will fold over later. Place second leaf crossways to the first, also fitting it to the inside of the pot.
　Place orange juice, vinegar with garlic, achiote paste, and salt in blender. The color "blood orange" will appear as soon as you push a button (warring Mayan tribes used achiote for body paint). Blend well. Sniff the bitter annatto.
　Place chicken pieces one at a time into leaf-covered saucepot, pouring in blended achiote mix as you do. Coat all pieces with sauce. Fold banana leaves over each other inside pot, cover, and place over low heat. Cook for 1 hour. After 30 minutes, remove cover, unfold leaves with a fork (watch out for hot achiote sauce), and gently stir chicken pieces. Cover and cook 30 minutes more.
　While the essence of plantains, orange groves, and achiote fill your kitchen, prepare the garnish. Slice onion into rainbows, and heat oil in skillet over a low flame. Fry without browning (*acitronar*) onion slices with vinegar, oregano, and peppercorns, stirring often until onion softens. Cover.
　When chicken is cooked, lift leaves from the pot (they will be wilted and shrunken) and dispose. Pickerel has yet to find a use for them.
　Serve achiote chicken over fried white rice. Sprinkle with cooked onions.

> Suicide hen also goes well with mashed potatoes.

# Wandering Neighborhood Chicken Runs into Cabbage
## *Pollo con Repollo*

*Ingredientes* (four servings)
- 1 whole neighborhood chicken (1 *pollo entero*)
- 1 garlic clove, peeled (1 *diente de ajo, pelado*)
- 1 tbsp cooking oil (1 *cucharada de aceite para cocinar*)
- 1 tsp salt (1 *cucharadita de sal*)
- 1/2 tsp ground pepper (1/2 *cucharadita de pimienta molida*)
- 1/2 head of cabbage (1/2 *cabeza de repollo*)
- 2 tomatoes (2 *tomates*)
- 1/2 Anaheim chili, deveined and seedless (1/2 *chile largo-verde sin venas, ni semillas*) (See Deveining Chili Peppers, page 30.)
- 1/2 small onion (1/2 *cebolla chica*)
- 3 tbsp tomato puree (3 *cucharadas de puré de tomate*)
- 4 cups fried white rice (4 *tazas de arroz cocido*) (See Fried White Rice, page 124.)

*Equipo*
- Large saucepot with cover (*cazuela grande con tapadera*)
- Saucepan (*cazo*)

*Preparación*

Cut chicken into small, serving-size pieces. Dice garlic. Heat oil in saucepot. Add chicken, garlic, salt, and pepper. Fry chicken until brown on the outside.

Chop cabbage into salad-size pieces. Dice tomatoes and chili. Slice onion thinly. Heat 2 cups of water in saucepan.

Add veggies (not cabbage) to the chicken in saucepot. Stir, cover, and simmer over low heat until onion softens. Add chopped cabbage. Mix well. Add hot water and puree. Mix again. Cover. Cook cabbage and chicken over high heat, stirring occasionally, until broth boils. Simmer over low heat 20 minutes.

Serve over fried white rice.

# Tattered Tortillas with Chicken in Red Chili Sauce
## Chilaquiles Rojos con Pollo

*Ingredientes* (three servings)
- 10 corn tortillas (10 *tortillas de maíz*)
- 1 cooked chicken breast (*1 pechuga de pollo cocida*)
- 1/2 tsp salt (1/2 *cucharadita de sal*)
- 1/4 tsp ground pepper (1/4 *cucharadita de pimienta molida*)
- 2 cups red chili sauce (2 *tazas de chile colorado*) (See *Red Chili Sauce*, page 81.)
- 1 cup grated ranch cheese (1 *taza de queso de rancho rallado*) (See *Cheeses*, page 23.)
- 3 tbsp cooking oil (3 *cucharadas de aceite para cocinar*)
- 6 rings cut from a medium onion (6 *anillos de una cebolla mediana*)

> Tattered tortillas take a poor gringo leap when chicken comes aboard.

*Equipo*
- Large skillet with cover (*sartén grande con tapadera*)

*Preparación*

Stack tortillas and cut in quarters. Shred chicken breast. (See *Shredding Meat*, page 31.) Salt and pepper the shredded chicken. Warm red chili sauce.

Open each tortilla triangle (separate the two layers, thin from thinner) and fill with cheese and a three-finger pinch of shredded chicken meat.

Heat oil in skillet. Place filled tortilla triangles in oil thin side up. The thick side must fry first; otherwise, the filling will spill. Position as many tortilla triangles as you can fit into the skillet. Flip each at first sign of browning. The thin side will take less time. Fry tortilla triangles until golden and crisp.

Keep flame low. Spoon in red chili sauce. Cover triangles, making sure sauce seeps into all the tortilla spaces. Sprinkle on the remainder of cheese. Place raw onion rings on top. Cover and remove from heat. Let sit 3 minutes. Serve with stir-mashed or refried beans on the side.

**Note**: You may substitute green tomato sauce for the red to prepare *chilaquiles verdes con pollo*. (See *Green Tomato Sauce*, page 76.)

# Capon Overboard in Vinegar
## *Estofado de Pollo*

Best served with *sopa de arroz*. (See *Pickerel's Rice*, page 119.)

*Ingredientes* (four servings)
- 2 carrots (2 *zanahorias*)
- 3 potatoes (3 *papas*)
- 1 garlic clove, peeled (1 *diente de ajo, pelado*)
- 1 Anaheim chili, deveined and seedless (1 *chile largo-verde sin venas, ni semillas*) (See *Deveining Chili Peppers*, page 30.)
- 3 tomatoes (3 *tomates*)
- 1/2 onion (1/2 *cebolla*)
- 1 whole run-over chicken (1 *pollo entero*) Roadkill must not be missing parts.
- 2 tbsp cooking oil (2 *cucharadas de aceite para cocinar*)
- 12 peppercorns (12 *pimientas enteras*)
- 5 bay leaves (5 *hojas de laurel*)
- 1 tbsp salt (1 *cucharada de sal*)
- 1/4 cup vinegar (1/4 *taza de vinagre*) Pickerel uses white cane vinegar.
- 1 cup tomato puree (1 *taza de puré de tomate*)
- 1 tbsp Salsa Ranchera (1 *cucharada de Salsa Ranchera*) (See *Bottled Sauces*, page 29.)

*Equipo*
Large saucepot with cover (*cazuela grande con tapadera*)

*Preparación*
Peel and slice carrots. Peel and cut potatoes into chunks. Chop garlic finely. Slice chili. Cut tomatoes and onion coarsely.

Chop chicken into small, serving-size pieces (running over helps tenderize a bird). Warm oil in saucepot and add chicken, veggies (except potatoes), peppercorns, bay leaves, and salt. Mix well. Pour in vinegar, puree, and ranch sauce. Mix again. You now have a big pot of raw chicken and vegetables smelling strongly of vinegar.

Cover and raise heat to high. Boil 10 minutes, stirring occasionally. Reduce heat to low and simmer 15 minutes. Remove cover and probe a carrot slice with fork (*tenedor*). It should slide south when fork is tilted. Add potatoes, stir, and cover again. Cook over low heat for 30 minutes, stirring occasionally.

Serve with *sopa de arroz*. (See *Pickerel's Rice*, page 119.)

# Fish and More

## Pescados y Más

*"El pez por la boca muere."*
*"A fish dies by its mouth."*
Jonás Pescado
One-armed Mexican fisherman, age 93

Naked Fish

Tuna Turnovers

Dried Carp Egg Cakes

Shrimp Ball Soup

Stingray Stew

Soused Marlin

Marlin Stew

Papered Fish

Ranch Fish

Fish Head Soup

When Pickerel goes fishing, he takes nothing—not hook, not net, not even his shoes. Neither does he get wet, waterborne, or Waltonian. Instead, Pickerel fishes out of the water—dockside, at boat landings and wharves—in places where local fishermen school and the fish have already been caught. (For Pickerel, a fish out of the water is the only fish worth catching.)

Fishermen and Pickerel swim in the same subcultural sea of shamelessness. Like him, they are anglers, liars, and cheats—big fish preying upon small ones, sharks masquerading as smelts. Pickerel is at home in these murky waters. Among local piscators he is known as "*el científico*"—the scientist—or the crazy, barefooted gringo who studies,

collects, and preserves fish in his experimental pursuit of a cure for cancer and the common cold. Pickerel's erudite manner, sturgeon looks, and ample (albeit spurious) knowledge of native fishes, Nobel laureates, and nasal decongestants lure even the most unscrupulous angler to surrender a fish for the rapid advancement of science. Cancer is a killer—one as mysterious as the kraken—and the common cold is a hell of an inconvenience in a choppy sea, so if the gringo needs fish for his experiments, then, by God, give the gringo fish. Pickerel makes a scholarly display of examining any piscine sample donated to his noble cause. He peers cryptically into the eyes of an iced-down mackerel. His finger probes the open mouth of a long-lined puffer fish. He balances flounder on the edge of his hand to test for freshness. And Pickerel tells fish stories while he works. For example, his mother died tragically of cerebral arrest after choking on a crab croquette. His father was lost at sea during liver failure. The horrific teeth of some kingfish carry a rare strain of undersea rabies. And so on.

Actually, Pickerel's whole life is a fish story, now in its culinary installment. His eccentric, one-man mission to discover a medical miracle in the catch of the day keeps dockside skeptics at bay and fresh tilapia on the table—a ruse that leaves Pickerel at peace with himself and with his stomach.

Here are the fish he hooks on a brave day near the sea: *mojarra* (surfperch), *botete* (puffer fish), *roncacho* (grunt), *robalo* (snook), *mero* (grouper), *lenguado* (flounder), *curvina* (croaker), *sierra* (kingfish), *cazón* (dogfish), *marlin* (marlin), *cochito* (triggerfish), *mantarraya* (stingray), *jurel* (mackerel), *huachinango* (red snapper), and *pargo* (any snapper).

For those who prefer to buy their fish, go early to your local market or boat dock, and do not mention that Pickerel sent you.

# Naked Fish
## Cebiche

*Cebiche, ceviche, seviche, sebiche.* This cool and refreshing lime marination of chopped fish with diced chili and veggies has as many spellings as Pickerel has *comadres*. Pickerel's favorite spelling is *sebiche*, derived from when English sailors—new to the Peruvian coast—tasted naked fish mixed with fiery ají chili and started screaming, "Sonofabitch! Sonofabitch!" The natives took this incomprehensible expression as the English name for a spicy fish dish, and soon they began imitating its sound, unsuccessfully—sonofabitch … sonabitch … sebitch … sebiche …

Four hundred years later and four thousand miles up the coast, every Mexican seaside dweller has a recipe for naked fish. Some *cebiche* makers add pickled jalapeños to their marination. Others add fresh serrano chilies. Some like it with finely diced coriander, while a few prefer a pinch of oregano. There are those who add tomato puree, tomato juice, canned V-8, Clamato cocktail, a trickle of beer, or a dash of red wine. Others add none of the above, preferring instead to condiment with their favorite bottled sauce.

Pickerel's recipe comes from the kitchen of Maria Delgado Viuda Del Mar (widow of Del Mar), who Pickerel continues to console whenever he visits Playa Colorado, a fishing village west of Guasave, Sinaloa.

*Ingredientes* (four servings)
- 1/2 kg filleted fish (1/2 *kilo pescado fileteado*) Pickerel prefers surfperch (*mojarra*) or triggerfish (*cochito*) for this recipe.
- 1 tsp salt (1 *cucharadita de sal*)
- 1 tsp ground pepper (1 *cucharadita de pimienta molida*)
- 10 limes (10 *limones*) For extra tanginess, use green limes (i.e., not yellowed).
- 1 cucumber (1 *pepino*)
- 1/2 white onion (1/2 *cebolla blanca*)
- 1 medium tomato (1 *tomate mediano*)
- 1 serrano chili (1 *chile serrano*)
- 3 sprigs coriander (3 *ramitas de cilantro*)
- 1 cup Clamato juice (1 *taza de jugo Clamato*) V-8 juice may be substituted.
- 1 tbsp Salsa Huichol (1 *cucharada de Salsa Huichol*) (See *Bottled Sauces,* page 29.)
- 12 tostadas (12 *tostadas*) (See *Dangerously Crisp Tortillas with Toppings,* page 56.)

*Equipo*
- Lime squeezer (*exprimidor de limón*)
- Mixing bowl (*tazón para mezclar*)
- Colander (*escurridor*)

*Preparación*

Cut fish into dice-size cubes. Remove errant bones. Place fish in bowl and mix with salt and pepper. Squeeze lime juice into a cup. Ten limes = about 1 cup of juice. Pour juice onto fish and mix well. Lime juice should cover fish. Squeeze more limes if necessary. Cover bowl, and allow fish to marinate. Go drink beer, lie on the beach, or spy on female neighbors. When marinated fish turns white—about 20 minutes—it is "cooked." Instead of drinking beer, lying on the beach, or spying on neighbors, you should have been dicing those veggies.

Peel cucumber, remove seeds, and slice. Dice the same size as fish. Next, dice onion, tomato, and chili (remove seeds first). Cut these smaller than cucumber. Remove stems from coriander; mince leaves finely.

Using colander, drain lime juice from fish. Add veggies. Mix well. Add Clamato. Mix again. Add Salsa Huichol. Mix once more. Cover and chill 20 minutes. Your naked fish is ready.

Spoon *cebiche* onto whole tostadas, or break tostada into chips and use to spoon *cebiche*. Either way, enjoy the taste of marinated fish and crunchy cucumber with coriander in the background. Watch for lime juice dribbling down your chin.

# Tuna Turnovers
## Empanadas de Atún

*Ingredientes* (two servings)
- 1 medium tomato (1 *tomate mediano*)
- 1/4 onion (1/4 *cebolla*)
- 1 serrano chili (1 *chile serrano*)
- 1 garlic clove, peeled (1 *diente de ajo, pelado*)
- 2 tbsp margarine (2 *cucharadas de margarina*)
- 1/2 tsp salt (1/2 *cucharadita de sal*)
- 1/2 tsp ground pepper (1/2 *cucharadita de pimienta molida*)
- 1 can tuna fish (1 *lata de atún*)
- 1/2 cup cooked sauce (1/2 *taza de salsa cocida*) (See *Cooked Sauce*, page 73.)
- 1/4 cup cooking oil (1/4 *taza de aceite para cocinar*)
- 1 cup corn tortilla dough—enough to make 6 corn tortillas (1 *taza de masa—suficiente para hacer 6 tortillas de maíz*) (See *Corn Tortillas*, page 47.)
- 1 cup chopped crisphead lettuce—optional (1 *taza de lechuga iceberg picada—opcional*)

> Due to an absence of fresh tuna (or free tuna) in local markets, Pickerel fishes his chicken of the sea out of a 6-ounce can (Dolores brand). Since Mexican commercial tuna fishing is no longer dolphin-safe, Pickerel feels he is doing his small part to ensure the worldwide extinction of this beloved cetacean.

*Equipo*
- 2 skillets, one with cover (2 *sartenes, una con tapadera*)
- Bean masher (*moledor de frijol*)
- Tortilla press (*prensa de tortilla*)
- 2 small sheets of plastic (2 *hojas chicas de plástico*); cut a bread bag in half

*Preparación*

### For tuna fish filling

Dice tomato, onion, and chili. Mince garlic. Melt margarine in skillet and add garlic. Use bean masher (or the bottom of a spoon) to crush garlic into a polyunsaturated internment. Add onion and fry without browning (*acitronar*) until onion is soft. Add tomato and chili. Stir well, cover, and cook 5 minutes over medium heat. Add tuna fish. Stir, add salt and pepper, cover, and simmer over low heat for 5 minutes.

Warm cooked sauce.

### *For turnovers*

Take a *small* pinch of corn dough (half the pinch for a normal-size tortilla) and make a sphere. Press between palms, leaving flat spots on opposite sides. Place one plastic sheet on tortilla press, set dough ball on top of plastic in the middle of press, then cover with the second sheet of plastic. (See *Corn Tortillas*, page 47.) Flatten dough ball in press. Open press and peel off the top piece of plastic. Spoon a heaping tablespoon of prepared tuna filling onto the center of the tortilla. Carefully lift (from press) the bottom sheet of plastic with the tortilla (and tuna). Using the plastic sheet for support, fold the tortilla over tuna filling (as if making a taco) and crimp tortilla edges around filling.

Heat oil in second skillet.

Place turnovers in skillet, frying both sides until tortilla is golden and crisp. Remove and drain excess oil, placing turnovers on absorbent paper (Pickerel uses old newspapers untouched by dog).

Serve with sauce on the side for dipping. Alternatively, open turnovers wide enough to spoon in sauce. Drop chopped lettuce into the turnover at the same time.

# Dried Carp Egg Cakes
## *Tortitas de Hueva de Carpa*

When Pickerel dedicates his day to raping the pristine countryside (at least once a week), he arms himself with dip net, gunnysack, and a plastic pail. Then he heads for the canals that deliver irrigation water from local reservoirs to the farmers' fields. (Remember, Pickerel is an environmentally unfriendly purveyor of biological specimens. He eats axolotl tamales. He is green only with dollar bills in his wallet.) Walking along the canal banks, Pickerel finds treasure for pleasure and profit—frogs, freshwater clams, turtles, snagged fishnets, and abandoned tires. Once he found a 5-ounce bag of Mexican locoweed—abandoned by a police-pursued delinquent, no doubt—that Pickerel gave to his drug-addicted neighborhood thief in exchange for a lawn chaise in mint condition (property of the local country club).

In his wanderings along canal banks, Pickerel also finds another prize—freshly laid carp eggs. During the carp-spawning season, jellied mats of eggs shimmer at the water's edge, where they lie attached to submerged grasses. With his dip net, Pickerel selects the freshest, which he takes home by the pailful. These he spreads across a sheet of plastic on his rooftop to dry in the sun. A single cloudless tropical afternoon turns 2 kilos of eggs into a mass of crisp, black Rice Krispies ready to be ground to powder (which Pickerel does just before he prepares his egg cakes) in a *molcajete*.

*Ingredientes* (two servings/eight cakes)
- 4 cups of dried carp eggs (4 *tazas de huevera de carpa*)
- 1 cup roasted corn flour (1 *taza de pinole de flor*)
- 2 eggs (2 *huevos*)
- 1/4 cup cooking oil (1/4 *taza de aceite para cocinar*)
- 1 cup red chili sauce (1 *taza de salsa de chile colorado*)
    (See *Red Chili Sauce*, page 81.)

*Equipo*
- Mortar and pestle (*molcajete y tejolote*)
- Mixing bowl (*tazón para mezclar*)
- Soup bowl (*tazón*)
- 2 small skillets, one with cover (2 *sartenes chicas, una con tapadera*)

*Preparación*

Grind carp eggs to a fine powder in *molcajete*. In mixing bowl (*tazón para mezclar*), combine ground carp eggs with roasted corn flour. In soup bowl (*tazón*), beat egg whites to froth, add yolks, and continue to beat. Add beaten eggs to mixing bowl. Mix well with flour and carp eggs. Batter should be thick enough to make cakes. Add additional corn flour as needed. Make eight cakes the size of flattened golf balls.

Warm chili sauce in skillet with cover.

Heat oil in second skillet. Fry cakes in oil until crisp and golden on the outside. Place each in the skillet with chili sauce, spooning sauce on top. Cover and cook over low heat for 5 minutes. Serve with warm corn tortillas.

You will never look at a canal bank the same way again.

# Shrimp Ball Soup
## Albóndigas de Camarón

### For shrimp balls (albóndigas)
*Ingredientes* (four servings)
- 1 cup long-grain, unconverted, white rice (1 *taza de arroz blanco, grano largo y fino*)
- 1 egg (1 *huevo*)
- 2 cups shrimp powder (2 *tazas de polvo de camarón*) (See *Shrimp Powder*, page 24.)
- 1 tsp salt (1 *cucharadita de sal*)

*Equipo*
- Small skillet (*sartén chica*)
- Colander (*escurridor*)

> The taste of shrimp without the inconvenience of pricey crustaceans.

*Preparación*

Wash rice. In skillet, boil rice in 2 cups of water until soft (about 10 minutes). Drain in colander, rinse with cold water, and place in mixing bowl (*tazón para mezclar*). Beat egg and add to rice with shrimp powder and salt. Mix well (with hands) until gooey shrimp batter clings to your fingers. Make golf ball-size spheres. Your mix should make about 12 shrimp balls.

### For broth (caldo)
*Ingredientes*
- 1 Anaheim chili, deveined and seedless (1 *chile largo-verde sin venas, ni semillas*) (See *Deveining Chili Peppers*, page 30.)
- 4 medium tomatoes (4 *tomates medianos*)
- 1 large onion (1 *cebolla grande*)
- 5 coriander sprigs with stems (5 *ramitas de cilantro con tallos*)
- 6 large carrots (6 *zanahorias grandes*)
- 4 large potatoes (4 *papas grandes*)
- 1 tbsp cooking oil (1 *cucharada de aceite para cocinar*)
- 1 cup tomato puree (1 *taza de puré de tomate*)
- 2 tbsp shrimp powder (2 *cucharadas de polvo de camarón*) (See *Shrimp Powder*, page 24.)
- 1 tbsp salt (1 *cucharada de sal*)
- 1 tbsp ground pepper (1 *cucharada de pimienta molida*)
- 1 sliced lime (1 *limón partido*)

*Equipo*
- 2 large saucepots (2 *cazuelas grandes*)
- Lime squeezer (*exprimidor de limón*)

*Preparación*

In a saucepot, bring 5 liters of water to a boil.

Chop chili, tomatoes, and onion finely. Cut coriander finger length. Peel carrots, and slice into bite-size pieces. Wash, peel, and cut potatoes into serving-size chunks. Leave potatoes in cold water with a pinch of salt.

Heat oil in second saucepot. Add chili, tomatoes, and onion. Stir. Add puree and shrimp powder. Stir and cook until puree bubbles. Add boiling water from saucepot. Add carrots and cover. When broth boils, add shrimp balls, one at a time. They will sink. Cover and cook over medium heat. After 30 minutes, add potatoes, coriander, salt, and pepper. Shrimp balls have now risen from the brothy deep as pale spheres. Stir and cover. Cook until potatoes are soft—15 to 20 minutes.

Serve with a freshly squeezed lime in the broth and bean tacos on the side. Enjoy the sandy texture of ground carapace with each shrimp ball bite.

# Stingray Stew
## *Caguamanta*

A popular dish with Mexicans who like to pretend they are eating the endangered Pacific sea turtle (*caguama*). When stewed, stingray (*mantarraya de espina*) tastes strikingly like sea turtle, yet can be eaten without risking a felony conviction for harboring a CITES-protected species in the stew pot. Thus the name: *cagua—manta(rraya)*.

The dark-fleshed manta ray (*mantarraya diablo o mantarraya gigante*) has a stronger flavor than the pale-colored meat of the stingray.

Serve with *sopa de arroz*. (See *Pickerel Rice*, page 119.)

> **Salted versus fresh stingray**: Pickerel uses either to make his stew, buying salted only when fresh is unavailable (free). Double boil salted stingray before cooking. Boil 1/2 kilo of dried fish in 1 liter of water for 20 minutes. Discard water and boil a second time for 20 minutes. Allow to cool.

*Ingredientes* (four servings)

1/2 kg stingray, salted or fresh (1/2 *kilo de mantarraya, seca o fresca*)
1 serrano chili (1 *chile serrano*)
1 garlic clove, peeled (1 *diente de ajo, pelado*)
2 large carrots (2 *zanahorias grandes*)
1 Anaheim chili, deveined and seedless (1 *chile largo-verde sin venas, ni semillas*) (See Deveining Chili Peppers, page 30.)
1 small purple onion (1 *cebolla morada chica*)
2 large tomatoes (2 *tomates grandes*)
3 tbsp cooking oil (3 *cucharadas de aceite para cocinar*)
5 bay leaves (5 *hojas de laurel*)
1/2 tsp peppercorns (1/2 *cucharadita de pimiento entera*)
1 tsp ground, whole-leaf oregano (1 *cucharadita de hoja de orégano molido*)
1 cup tomato puree (1 *taza de puré de tomate*)
1/4 cup vinegar (1/4 *taza de vinagre*) Pickerel uses white cane vinegar.
12 green olives (12 *aceitunas verdes*), or as many as you can afford.
1-1/2 tsp salt—for fresh stingray (1-1/2 *cucharadita de sal—para mantarraya fresca*)
1 slice lime (1 *limón partido*)

*Equipo*
   Large saucepot (*cazuela grande*)
   Large saucepan (*cazo grande*)
   Lime squeezer (*exprimidor de limón*)

*Preparación*

**For salted**: Shred fish into small pieces using fork or fingertips. This is *desmenuzar*—to make minute or small. Stingray flesh is conspicuously striated and easy to pick apart.

**For fresh**: Wash well. If "wing" meat is thick, slice into thinner slabs and cut into bite-size pieces.

Dice serrano and garlic finely. Peel and slice carrots, not too thinly. Crosscut Anaheim into rings. Slice onion and chop tomatoes.

Heat oil in saucepot. Add veggies with bay leaves, peppercorns, and oregano. Mix well and fry over high heat, stirring often.

In a saucepan, bring 1 liter of water to a boil.

Add puree and vinegar to veggies in saucepot. Lower heat. Stir well. Add fish, olives, carrots (and salt, if stingray is fresh). Mix thoroughly. Pour in 2-1/2 cups of boiling water from saucepan. Stir and cover. Cook over low heat for 45 minutes. Fresh stingray will fall apart when cooked. Carrots should be tender.

Squeeze aboard a lime, and you are ready to ride a ray. Serve with *sopa de arroz* on the side. (See *Pickerel Rice*, page 119.)

# Soused Marlin
## Marlin en Escabeche

This is another of Pickerel's muggy summer dishes.

*Ingredientes* (four servings)

**On marlin:** Caught by long-liners and drift gill-netters with shark permits, marlin sells in big, fly-happy piles at local fish market stands. Brined and smoked, it sells for about fifty pesos a kilo ($2/lb)—a price even the poorest, peso-pinching gringo can afford.

- 1/2 kg smoked marlin (1/2 *kilo de marlin ahumado*)
- 2 potatoes (2 *papas grandes*)
- 2 carrots (2 *zanahorias*)
- 1 zucchini (1 *calabacita*)
- 1/4 kg string beans—about 18 beans (1/4 *kilo de ejotes*—*aproximadamente* 18 *ejotes*)
- 1 pickled jalapeño (1 *chile jalapeño en escabeche*) (See *Canned Chili Peppers*, page 29.)
- 1/2 cup vinegar (1/2 *taza de vinagre*) Pickerel uses white cane vinegar.
- 1 tsp salt (1 *cucharadita de sal*)
- 1 large onion (1 *cebolla grande*)
- 2 tbsp cooking oil (2 *cucharadas de aceite para cocinar*)
- 1 tsp peppercorns (1 *cucharadita de pimienta entera*)
- A pinch of ground, whole-leaf oregano (*una pizca de hoja de orégano molido*)
- 4 bay leaves (4 *hojas de laurel*)
- 16 tostadas (16 *tostadas*) (See *Dangerously Crisp Tortillas with Toppings*, page 56.)

*Equipo*
- 2 saucepots (2 *cazuelas*)
- Colander (*escurridor*)
- Mixing bowl (*tazón para mezclar*)
- Large skillet (*sartén grande*)
- Covering dish (*tazón con tapadera*)

*Preparación*

Wash marlin and shred into small pieces using fork or fingertips. This is *desmenuzar*—to make minute or small. Peel potatoes and carrots and cut into pencil-wide strips. Cut squash to same size. Snap off bean ends, pull away fiber (See *String Beans*, page 25.), and cut each bean lengthwise in strips. Dice chili finely.

Heat water in saucepots. Parboil potatoes, carrots, beans, and squash separately (first carrots, then potatoes, and so on). Add 1 tablespoon of vinegar and 1/4 teaspoon of salt to each vegetable as it boils. Do not overcook squash. Veggies should end up on the soft side of crunch. Drain in colander and cool.

In mixing bowl (*tazón para mezclar*), combine boiled veggies, diced chili, and shredded marlin. Mix well.

Slice onion into rainbows, and heat oil in large skillet over a low flame. Gently fry without browning (*acitronar*) onion slices with oregano, peppercorns, bay leaves, and remainder of vinegar, stirring until onion is soft. Add marlin and veggies. Mix well. Cover and cook over low heat for 5 minutes.

Allow to cool, and place in a covered dish inside refrigerator. Chill for 1 hour.

Serve atop crisp corn tostadas (See *Dangerously Crisp Tortillas with Toppings*, page 56.), and enjoy the taste of smoked marlin with crunchy vinegar veggies and jalapeño in the background. Poor gringo marlin in the fast lane.

# Marlin Stew
## Marlin Estofado

Serve with *arroz campestre*. (See *Country Rice*, page 121.)

*Ingredientes* (three servings)
- 1/2 kg smoked marlin (1/2 *kilo marlin ahumado*)
- 3 carrots (3 *zanahorias*)
- 1 medium onion (1 *cebolla mediana*)
- 3 tomatoes (3 *tomates*)
- 2 garlic cloves, peeled (2 *dientes de ajo, pelados*)
- A pinch of ground, whole-leaf oregano (*una pizca de hoja de orégano molido*)
- 1-1/2 tsp salt (1-1/2 *cucharadita de sal*)
- 1 tsp peppercorns (1 *cucharadita de pimienta entera*)
- 1 tbsp mayonnaise (1 *cucharada de mayonesa*)
- 2 chipotle peppers (2 *chiles chipotle adobados*) (See *Canned Chili Peppers*, page 29.)
- 2 tbsp margarine (2 *cucharadas de margarina*)
- 12 tostadas (12 *tostadas*) (See *Dangerously Crisp Tortillas with Toppings*, page 56.)

*Equipo*
- Saucepot (*cazuela*)
- Blender (*licuadora*)

*Preparación*

Wash marlin and shred into small pieces using fork or fingertips (*desmenuzar*). Peel carrots and cut into thin strips. Slice 1/2 of onion into rainbows.

In a saucepot with 1 liter of water, boil remainder of onion with whole tomatoes, garlic, oregano, salt, and peppercorns. Cook until tomato and onion are soft. Allow to cool, remove tomato skins with fork, and pour contents of saucepot into blender. Add mayonnaise and chipotle peppers. Blend until smooth.

Melt margarine in same saucepot. Add marlin. Stir and cover. When marlin is warm and steamy, add carrot strips and onion rainbows. Mix well. Pour in contents of blender. Stir and cover. Cook over low heat for 30 minutes, stirring occasionally. When carrot strips are tender, stew is ready.

Spoon on corn tostadas. (See *Dangerously Crisp Tortillas with Toppings*, page 56.)

# *Papered Fish*
## *Pescado Empapelado*

*Ingredientes* (three servings)
- 1/2 kg filleted fish (1/2 *kilo pescado fileteado*) Pickerel prefers puffer fish (*botete*) or flounder (*lenguado*) for this recipe.
- 3 sheets of aluminum foil 12"×12" (3 *hojas de papel aluminio* 12"×12")
- 1 tbsp margarine (1 *cucharada de margarina*)
- 1 tbsp mayonnaise (1 *cucharada de mayonesa*)
- 1 tbsp mustard (1 *cucharada de mostaza*)
- 1 tsp garlic salt (1 *cucharadita de sal de ajo*)
- 1 tsp ground pepper (1 *cucharadita de pimienta molida*)
- 1/2 tsp ground, whole-leaf oregano (1/2 *cucharadita de hoja de orégano molido*)
- 1/2 medium onion (1/2 *cebolla mediana*)
- 1 Anaheim chili, deveined and seedless (1 *chile largo-verde sin venas, ni semillas*) (See *Deveining Chili Peppers*, page 30.)
- 5 small tomatoes (5 *tomates chicos*)
- 2 tbsp cooking oil (2 *cucharadas de aceite para cocinar*)
- 1/4 cup tomato puree (1/4 *taza de puré de tomate*)
- 2 tbsp shrimp powder (2 *cucharadas de polvo de camarón*) (See *Shrimp Powder*, page 24.)

> Serve over arroz blanco. (See Fried White Rice, page 124.)

*Equipo*
- Large skillet (*sartén grande*)
- Steamer (*olla vaporera*)

*Preparación*

Divide fish into three equal portions. Spread a thin layer of margarine on each aluminum foil sheet. Follow with a layer of mayonnaise and then a layer of mustard. Place fish on foil and sprinkle with garlic salt, pepper, and a thin pinch of oregano. Fold up four sides of foil and crimp edges to make an open-topped, aluminum foil boat.

Dice onion, chili, and tomatoes. Heat oil in skillet. Fry veggies, adding tomato puree, shrimp powder, and 1 cup of water. Stir. When mixture boils, remove from heat. Pour into aluminum boats, covering fish portions in equal amounts. Close foil by twisting edges together. No leaks allowed.

Set each papered fish into steamer with enough water to steam 30 minutes (steamer warm-up time does not count).

When fish is cooked, you may eat it right out of the boat or pour onto a bed of white rice. (See *Fried White Rice*, page 124.) Pickerel eats his with corn tortillas, lightly toasted.

# Ranch Fish
## Pescado Ranchero

*Ingredientes* (three servings)
- 3 tomatoes (3 *tomates*)
- 1/4 onion (1/4 *cebolla*)
- 1 Anaheim chili, deveined and seedless (1 *chile largo-verde sin venas, ni semillas*) (See *Deveining Chili Peppers*, page 30.)
- 1 tsp salt (1 *cucharadita de sal*)
- 1/2 tsp ground pepper (1/2 *cucharadita de pimienta molida*)
- 1/2 kg filleted fish (1/2 *kilo pescado fileteado*) Pickerel prefers surfperch (*mojarra*) or triggerfish (*cochito*) for this recipe.
- 1/4 cup cooking oil (1/4 *taza de aceite para cocinar*)
- 1 tbsp margarine (1 *cucharada de margarina*)
- 2 tbsp shrimp powder (2 *cucharadas de polvo de camarón*) (See *Shrimp Powder*, page 24.)
- 1/2 cup tomato puree (1/2 *taza de puré de tomate*)

> Serve over arroz blanco. (See Fried White Rice, page 124.)

*Equipo*
Deep skillet with cover (*sartén honda con tapadera*)

*Preparación*
Dice tomato, onion, and chili. Salt and pepper fish. Heat oil and margarine together in skillet. Give fish fillet(s) a quick fry over high heat, searing both sides. Add veggies and shrimp powder. Stir gently, cover, and cook over low heat for 20 minutes. When fish is cooked (white on the inside), add tomato puree. Stir, cover, and simmer for 10 minutes. Fish should fall apart when probed with a fork (*tenedor*).

# Fish Head Soup
## Caldo de Pescado

Pickerel's savior after excessive but voluntary ethylic toxication—in short, a hangover. Colloquially dubbed "*Levanta muertos,*" or "Raising the dead," Pickerel's fish head soup carries a resurrecting power not seen since Christ tasered Lazarus into the upright position. Fish aren't smart, but something in their tiny brains turns hot water and veggies into a miracle of fish soup. Pickerel personally guarantees that two bowls, sipped slowly, will make you want to drink again by dusk.

As for fish heads, MSP recommends snapper, though in the gut-wrenching, head-hammering throes of katzenjammer, any piscine head will do. Pickerel gets his heads from the same carcinophobic fishermen who donate fish bodies to science. You may get yours at a local market (ask for *cabezas de pescado*), or you may decapitate them yourself.

*Ingredientes* (two servings)
- 4 fish heads (4 *cabezas de pescado*) Pickerel prefers snook (*robalo*), grouper (*mero*), mackerel (*jurel*), or snapper (*pargo*) for this recipe.
- 1 carrot (1 *zanahoria*)
- 2 tomatoes (2 *tomates*)
- 1/2 medium onion (1/2 *cebolla mediana*)
- 1/2 Anaheim chili, deveined and seedless (1/2 *chile largo-verde sin venas, ni semillas*) (See Deveining Chili Peppers, page 30.)
- 1 garlic clove, peeled (1 *diente de ajo, pelado*)
- 4 tbsp cooking oil (4 *cucharadas de aceite para cocinar*)
- A pinch of ground, whole-leaf oregano (*una pizca de hoja de orégano molido*)
- 1 tsp salt (1 *cucharadita de sal*)
- 1/2 tsp ground pepper (1/2 *cucharadita de pimienta molida*)
- 1 sliced lime (1 *limón partido*)

*Equipo*
- 2 large saucepots (2 *cazuelas grandes*)
- Lime squeezer (*exprimidor de limón*)

*Preparación*
Wash fish heads. In saucepot, bring 3 liters of water to a boil.
Peel carrots and slice thinly. Chop tomato, onion, and chili. Dice garlic. In second saucepot, heat oil. Fry tomato, onion, and chili. When chili

and onion soften, add carrots. Pour in boiling water and stir. Add fish heads, oregano, salt, and pepper. Stir, cover, and boil over medium heat for 30 minutes.

Serve with a squeeze of lime—nothing else. Fish heads should be grinning, their white eyes staring at you. Watch for bones and loose teeth.

# Farm, Field, and Front Porch

## Del Granja, Campo y Porche

*Tacos de miztón — $15.00 por orden (en temporada)*
*(It) Walks Softly tacos — $15.00 per order (seasonal)*
*Menu item at Taquería El Árbol Caído*
*Pickerel's favorite cat taco stand*

Pounded Frog Legs Benito Style

Chacha's Pozole for Six

Rabbit Stew

Beefsteak Charlie

Pan-broiled Horse in Tomato Sauce

Cortez-On-Foot Burritos

Red Chili Pork with Nopales

Fired Tequila Goat

Stewed Iguana

When Pickerel brought horse steaks home to grill, Miriam devoured them as if they were choice center cut top sirloins. When he brought rabbit meat to make stew, Miriam assumed it was chicken deboned by the local butcher. Pounded frog legs posed as turkey *machaca* in burritos. Iguana tail impersonated pork in tamales. But the morning Pickerel tried to pass canine for caprine in a plate of *birria*,* Christ's false teeth fell out before the faithful.

Our hero had arrived with takeout—two orders of "goat" stew from his favorite eatery, *El Chivo de Oro* (the Golden Goat), offering a two-for-one special on Tuesdays. Pickerel knew the owner. He knew the recipe. He knew two-for-one was a screaming deal of a meal—even if dog meat was in it.

Miriam probed her plate. "Miles, this isn't goat," she said, sniffing the meat, squinching her nose. She gave Pickerel her thin-eyed, wicked-witch-of-the-west look. "Goat meat doesn't smell like this. And it isn't this greasy. Look at it!"

Pickerel served himself a second helping. There was an explanation, of course. He only had to say it. "Miriam," he intoned gravely, "this poor goat must have been attacked by the chupacabras,** which sucked its blood dry. Goat meat never tastes the same after …"

Miriam threw her spoon at him—hitting the table instead—then fled the room. After a befitting silence, Pickerel rose from his chair and gave Miriam's plate to Ladrón, their dog, who sniffed it—perhaps to make sure this was no canine he knew—and then finished it in a single gobble. Miriam later apologized for missing him with the spoon (she had been aiming for his big mouth, she said). She also refused to eat *birria* or takeout again.

Pickerel, however, continues to takeout whenever the opportunity arises—not from local eateries, which he can no longer afford, but from local fauna, unfenced livestock, and those small, domesticated species wandering the streets in search of a new home.

Here, kitty, kitty … Come to Pickerel.

---

\* Spicy meat stew of lamb, goat, or unidentifiable quadruped, steamed or barbecued.
\*\* A cryptid that drinks the blood of livestock, especially goats. Pickerel has yet to sight one.

# *Pounded Frog Legs Benito Style*
## *Machaca de Ancas de Rana Estilo Benito*

This recipe is named in honor of Benito Batracio—frog fisherman and tequila-toasting *compinche* of Pickerel's—who drowned tragically on a nearby waterway while breaking two state wildlife laws: gigging frogs *and* doing it out of season. Benito, this one is for you.

*Ingredientes* (two servings)
   1/2 kg frog legs, fresh or frozen (1/2 *kilo de ancas de rana, frescas o congeladas*)
   1 garlic clove, peeled (1 *diente de ajo, pelado*)
   1/2 onion (1/2 *cebolla*)
   2 tomatoes (2 *tomates*)
   1 Anaheim chili, deveined and seedless (1 *chile largo-verde sin venas, ni semillas*) (See *Deveining Chili Peppers*, page 30.)
   2 tbsp salt (2 *cucharadas de sal*)
   1 tsp ground pepper (1 *cucharadita de pimienta molida*)
   3 tbsp cooking oil (3 *cucharadas de aceite para cocinar*)
   6 flour tortillas (6 *tortillas de harina*)

> If you do not wish to traverse local canal banks at night, fight mosquitoes, risk snakebite, catch your own frogs, chop their bodies in half, skin the legs, and dispose of frog torsos (with dangling entrails), you may purchase your frog legs fresh each morning at a local fish market—while local frog fishermen sleep.

*Equipo*
   Saucepot (*cazuela*)
   Meat pounder (*machacador de carne*)
   Skillet with cover (*sartén con tapadera*)

*Preparación*
   Wash legs and place in saucepot with 2 liters of cold water. Boil for 30 minutes. Drain, cool, and debone meat (a frog leg has two bones—thigh and leg—both easily stripped when meat is cooked).
   Dice garlic finely. Slice onion and chop tomatoes. Cut chili into thin rings.
   With fingers, shred (*deshebrar*) frog leg meat into fibers. (See *Shredding Meat*, page 31.) Add salt, pepper, and diced garlic. Mix well. Using the *machacador*, pound shredded meat on a solid surface (cutting board, cast-iron skillet, concrete walkway—Pickerel has tried them all). Work to make the salt and garlic disappear. Lift meat and fluff it as you pound—imagine

tossing a salad while hammering—until its texture feels less like rope and more like yarn. (Remember, frog legs are the power behind frog jumping, so meat fibers are wiry.) If you do not have a meat pounder, use any blunt, wife-beating instrument to pound frog legs. Pickerel uses a smooth, flat-bottomed stone the size of his hand. When he mislays it in the clutter of his cave, he substitutes one of the following: a ceramic paperweight, his cast-iron lime squeezer, or the thick glass bottom of a Tecate beer bottle—return/deposit and amazingly shatter resistant. (Don't try this at home!)

Over a low flame, heat oil in the skillet. Add onion and fry without browning until soft (*acitronar*). Add pounded frog meat. Mix with onion and cook, stirring often, until meat browns slightly. Add remaining veggies, mix, cover, and simmer over low heat until tomatoes and chili cook.

Serve inside flour tortillas—rolled in burritos—with fried beans on the side.

A lot of work for a meal you will never eat at Chipotle.

# Chacha's Pozole for Six
## *Pozole para Seis*

Within a week of Miriam's precipitous departure, Pickerel initiated his search for domestic help. The business of exploiting natives and despoiling habitats left Pickerel little time for household chores. And there were simply too many potted plants for one man to water.

So he tacked a handwritten sign to his front door: *Se Solicita Muchacha* (Girl Wanted), resisting the urge to add "*Bonita*"—as in *Pretty* Girl Wanted.

Three weeks (and one massive potted-plant die-off) later, Chacha Machado knocked, the only applicant. When Pickerel opened his door, a dark-skinned, diminutive, but robust woman sporting flip-flops, a field tan, and a baseball cap stood before him. "I work," she announced, no preamble, no smile, voice like a bludgeon. Pickerel nodded, retreating far enough from this heavy-duty, Hackensack mama to observe the unshaved hair on her thick legs. Female? Yes. Girl? When the planet was young. But could Pickerel afford to be age discriminatory? "*Claro*," he replied. Of course she could work—her legs testified to that. He quickly explained the terms of employment, and in a matter of moments, Chacha Machado found herself hired at Pickerel's starting salary of false promises and deceiving smiles.

Chacha hailed from Oaxaca, and straightaway she proved to be a working dervish of a woman. She swept and mopped; she scrubbed and dusted. She weeded the weedy plat, washed the dog, dispatched domiciled rodents, and limed the latrine. With his kingdom shaping up handsomely, Pickerel made the mistake of adding culinary duties to Chacha's work list—his first request, a plate of *burritos de machaca* (meat burritos). He gave her twenty pesos (two dollars) for ingredients, left the house, and, when Pickerel returned later that day, he found approximately one hundred meat burritos piled high on his kitchen table—each one neatly rolled. Pickerel ate ten, refrigerated thirty, and sent Chacha home with the leftovers.

The next day Pickerel gave Chacha Machado ten pesos and requested another favorite: *bistec ranchero*. That evening he found his cast-iron skillet filled with country steak—enough for a hearty bivouac.

Thinking that he may have accidentally set in motion the Mexican miracle of the seven loaves, Pickerel requested no cookery the next day—he would eat *bistek* again, or maybe those burritos—but he did give Chacha five pesos to buy a bar of laundry soap. That night, Pickerel came home to a pot of *cochinita pibil* (barbecued meat) warming on his stove.

By then, Pickerel should have figured it out. He is, after all, intimately familiar with shameless and deceitful behavior—being shameless and deceitful himself. However, it was around this time that Chacha Machado began making romantic advances toward her employer.

First came a suggestive coyness not becoming in a woman who caught and killed rodents with her bare hands. Then followed her culinary conversation laced with innuendo—Did Señor Pickerel like his eggs hard? Did Señor Pickerel prefer small melons to large ones? Finally, came the bare flesh—a glimpse of bristly thighs, a flash of unwashed bosom–enough to make Pickerel check his door locks at night. (Pickerel is not made of wood, but he would have preferred to undress a warthog than view any acreage on Chacha Machado where the sun had not hit).

Meanwhile, the elusive meat dishes continued to set his table. *Birria.* Tamales. Pork in adobo sauce. Within days, Pickerel began to feel strange after meals—flushed following a plate of mole, nauseous after meatballs in chipotle, itchy in bed. He began to suspect that Chacha was experimenting darkly with his victuals—adding love potion number nine.

Then Ladrón, the dog, disappeared the day before Chacha prepared pozole for a dinner party of six. The next night, as Pickerel ate in mixed company, he discretely examined the bones on his spoon for genus and species. When he found a vestigial dewclaw hiding amid the hominy, his suspicions were confirmed. Ladrón had become pozole.

The next morning, Pickerel turned Chacha Machada away at his door. But not before extracting the details of a confession he already knew: she had pocketed money for menu ingredients while feeding her employer no-cost dog and cat, and lately she had chemically shamanized his food with the purpose of making him sick enough to embrace—literally—any attempt to nurse his ailing digestive system back to health. (Frankly, Pickerel objected more to a loose bowel than to thievery or fraud.)

She returned his accusatory glare with an insouciant shrug, as if to say Pickerel had no reason to complain. He was alive. He had benefited from artful cooking at bargain prices. And his house was clean and rodent-free.

She left without looking back (Pickerel watching from his window). The last news he had of her was that she had returned to Oaxaca where she opened a *birriaría* on Highway 190—serving truck drivers and adventurous gringo tourists.

## *For soup* (*caldo*)
*Ingredientes* (six servings)
- 2 onions (2 *cebollas*)
- 6 garlic cloves, peeled (6 *dientes de ajo, pelados*)
- 2 tbsp beef bouillon powder (2 *cucharadas de consomé de res en polvo*)
- 1 kg white hominy (1 *kilo de nixtamal*) (See Hominy, page 24.)
- 1 kg sectioned pork spine (1 *kilo de espinazo de cerdo, seccionado*)
- 1 kg sliced pork hock (1 *kilo de codillo de cerdo, en rabanadas*)
- 2 tsp salt (2 *cucharaditas de sal*)
- 5 ancho chilies (5 *chiles anchos*) (See Chilies, pages 87/88.)
- 4 guajillo chilies (4 *chiles guajillos*) (See Chilies, pages 87/88.)
- 2 tomatoes (2 *tomates*)
- 1 tsp ground, whole-leaf oregano (1 *cucharadita de hoja de orégano molido*)
- 1 tsp ground pepper (1 *cucharadita de pimienta molida*)
- 5 bay leaves (5 *hojas de laurel*)

*Equipo*
- Stockpot (*olla*)
- Large bowl (*tazón grande*)
- Saucepan (*cazo*)
- Blender (*licuadora*)
- Lime squeezer (*exprimidor de limón*)

## *For garnish* (*guarnición*)
*Ingredientes* (six servings)
- 1 small white onion (1 *cebolla blanca chica*)
- 4 small shallots (4 *chalotes*)
- 1/4 crisphead lettuce (1/4 *lechuga iceberg*)
- Fistful of coriander sprigs (*un racimito de cilantro*)
- Limes (*limones*)
- Ground dried chiltepin chilies (*chiles chiltepines secos y molidos*)

> **On pozole meat**: The cheapest and most flavorful pozole is made with pork spine (espinazo de cerdo). Ask the market butcher to joint it (cortar en trozos). Pickerel also adds hock (codillo de cerdo) to his pozole. This should be sliced.

*Preparación*

Fill stockpot with 6 liters of water. Halve onion and add to water with 4 garlic cloves. Cover and bring water to boil. Add bouillon powder.

Place hominy in a large bowl with cold water. Rub kernels briskly between hands to shed their glassy sheaths. Remove dark "eye" at the base of each kernel.

When pot water boils, add hominy, cover, and cook over low heat for 1 hour.

Place meat in cold water with 2 tablespoons of salt and soak for 1 hour.

Halve tomatoes. Open chilies, remove seed trunks, and wash out loose seeds. Place tomatoes, chilies, and remaining garlic cloves in saucepan with 3 cups of water. Cover and cook over low heat, stirring occasionally, until chilies are soft—about 30 minutes. Drain water. Remove tomato skins. Pour contents of saucepan into blender. Add 2 cups of cold water, oregano, pepper, and bay leaves (after washing). Blend until smooth.

Check hominy by spooning a few kernels from pot and pressing each between thumb and forefinger (after cooling). If kernels are soft enough to squash, add meat. If kernels resist, boil another 15 minutes and try again.

Remove meat from saltwater and place in the pot with hominy. Add contents of blender. Stir. Remove from pot 2 cups of hominy and broth (more hominy than broth). Cool and place in blender. Add salt and blend until smooth. Return this mixture to the pot (as a thickener). Mix well, cover, and boil pozole over low heat for 2 hours. When meat is tender enough to fall off the bones, pozole is ready.

For garnish, dice onion and shallots (including stems) and mix. Chop lettuce and coriander finely. Place in separate bowls (*tazones*). Slice limes.

When preparing his bowl of pozole, Pickerel first squeezes a lime—both halves—into his empty bowl. Then he spoons in pozole—meat, hominy, and broth—mixing it well with the lime juice. Next, he sprinkles in a pinch of coriander, and then he comes with the onion and lettuce, a spoonful each. Finally, he adds a sprinkle of dried chiltepin chili ground finely in his *molcajete*. (See *Essentials & Utensils*, page 17.)

Serve with crisp corn tostadas fresh off the clothesline. (See *Dangerously Crisp Tortillas with Toppings*, page 56.)

# *Rabbit Stew*
## *Estofado de Conejo*

One Easter morning, when the twins were still toddlers and Miriam was still sane, Pickerel surprised the family by bringing home their first pet—a baby rabbit. (Yes, Pickerel celebrates major Christian holidays in typical pagan fashion.) The twins danced with delight. Miriam beamed her approval. Pickerel gloried in his resurrection (albeit short-lived). That afternoon, he set up a hutch (old tomato crate) for their bunny—baptized "Connie Joe" by the twins—after *conejo* (the Spanish word for "rabbit") and because Connie Joe's gender remained unknown, in spite of Pickerel's persistent fondling.

Wishing to instill in his young progeny the old man's work ethic and high standards of pet care, Pickerel taught his daughters the rigorous routine of rabbit husbandry—feed and water rabbit, chase rabbit to give it exercise (for muscle buildup), and clean up rabbit turds.

Connie Joe responded in characteristic leporine fashion. He grew, becoming a Joe rather than a Connie, and before Christmas, CJ—as the twins fondly called him—turned into a heavyweight chinchilla packing a dozen pounds of chilies, mangos, and leftover tortillas. Pickerel did his part too. He found CJ a bigger tomato crate. He made sure CJ ate before the dog. And he blocked all rabbit escape routes from his weedy plat. Except one.

It was in Pickerel's car (trunk of) that CJ finally made his escape early one morning while the family slept—only to return Christmas Eve inside "turkey" tamales prepared by a local butcher and his tamale-making wife.

CJ's sudden disappearance left the twins teary-eyed, but their little hearts were cheered Christmas morning when Santa left them a pair of lucky rabbit's feet (fur bleached, of course) under their tree.

Pickerel was quick to blame CJ's departure on a large hawk spotted flying low in the neighborhood on the fatal evening. He decried birds of prey in general, and rabbit hawks in particular. Miriam poised her fork over a "turkey" tamale long enough to remark—in a low voice—that the hawk must have been pretty big to have carried away CJ. As Pickerel removed the

cornhusk from his fourth tamale, he agreed. "A big one it must have been, Miriam," he said.

*Ingredientes* (three servings)
- 2 carrots (2 *zanahorias*)
- 1/2 onion (1/2 *cebolla*)
- 1 Anaheim chili, deveined and seedless (1 *chile largo-verde sin venas, ni semillas*)
    (See *Deveining Chili Peppers*, page 30.)
- 1 garlic clove, peeled (1 *diente de ajo, pelado*)
- 3 large potatoes (3 *papas grandes*)
- 3 tomatoes (3 *tomates*)
- 1/2 kg rabbit meat (1/2 *kilo carne de conejo*)
- 2 tbsp cooking oil (2 *cucharadas de aceite para cocinar*)
- 1/2 tsp peppercorns (1/2 *cucharadita de pimientas enteras*)
- 5 bay leaves (5 *hojas de laurel*)
- 1 tbsp salt (1 *cucharada de sal*)
- 1/4 cup vinegar (1/4 *taza de vinagre*) Pickerel uses white cane vinegar.
- 1 cup tomato puree (1 *taza de puré de tomate*)
- 1 tbsp Salsa Ranchera (1 *cucharada de Salsa Ranchera*)
    (See *Bottled Sauces*, page 29.)

> For those who do not raise rabbits (or hunt them), many Mexican markets offer freshly butchered animals—skinned and jointed. Ask for conejo de rancho (ranch-raised). It is more flavorful than the farm-grown (conejo de granja) variety.

*Equipo*
Saucepot with cover (*cazuela con tapadera*)

*Preparación*
Peel carrots and slice—not too thinly. Slice onion and chili to same thickness. Dice garlic. Peel potatoes and chop with tomatoes into bite-size chunks.

If not jointed, cut rabbit into serving-size pieces (1/2 kg makes about six pieces). Heat oil in saucepot. Add rabbit, veggies (except potatoes), peppercorns, bay leaves, and salt. Mix well. Pour in vinegar, puree, and ranch sauce. Mix again. You now have a pot of raw rabbit smelling strongly of vinegar.

Cover and boil 10 minutes. Lower heat and cook 15 minutes more, stirring occasionally. Add potatoes. Mix, cover, and cook 30 minutes over low heat.

Serve with *sopa de arroz*. (See *Pickerel's Rice*, page 119.)

# Beefsteak Charlie
## *Bistec Carlos*

Deterred by the lengthy prison terms imposed on Mexican cattle rustlers, Pickerel offers only two beef dishes (cow stomach aside) in this compendium of culinary madness. Beefsteak Charlie is one of these, named in honor of Carlos El Carnicero (Charlie the Butcher)—stunner, sticker, skinner, eviscerator, and meat cutter at his own clandestine, itinerant, one-man slaughterhouse that only Pickerel and the police know the multiple locations of. In exchange for his vow of silence, Pickerel gets free bovine parasites (tapeworms and liver flukes)* and a screaming deal on shank, plate or flank. The police get tenderloin.

*Ingredientes* (three servings)
- 1 garlic clove, peeled (1 *diente de ajo, pelado*)
- 3 medium potatoes (3 *papas medianas*)
- 1/2 small onion (1/2 *cebolla chica*)
- 1/2 Anaheim chili, deveined and seedless (1/2 *chile largo-verde sin venas, ni semillas*) (See Deveining Chili Peppers, page 30.)
- 3 tomatoes (3 *tomates*)
- 1/2 kg flank or hanger steak, thinly sliced (1/2 *kilo de carne para asar—falda o espaldillo de res—en corte delgado*)
- 1 tbsp salt (1 *cucharada de sal*)
- 1 tsp ground pepper (1 *cucharadita de pimienta molida*)
- 3 tbsp cooking oil (3 *cucharadas de aceite para cocinar*)
- 1 cup tomato puree (1 *taza de puré de tomate*)
- 1 coriander sprig (1 *ramita de cilantro*)

*Equipo*
- 2 skillets with covers (2 *sartenes con tapaderas*);
- Bean masher (*moledor de frijol*)

*Preparación*

Halve garlic clove. Dice one-half finely; leave the other half uncut. Peel potatoes and cut thinly. Slice onion and chili in rings. Chop tomatoes.

Cut meat into serving-size pieces. Salt and pepper lightly on both sides. In skillet, heat 1 tablespoon of oil with uncut garlic clove. Quickly fry meat

---

\* The parasites go to veterinary school.

over high heat, searing both sides (leave pink in center). Remove meat from skillet. Drain on absorbent paper (Pickerel uses old newspapers untouched by dog). Discard garlic.

Heat 2 tablespoons of oil in the second skillet. Fry potatoes until golden and crisp. Drain on absorbent paper (Pickerel uses old newspapers untouched by dog). Salt lightly.

In the empty meat skillet, fry tomatoes, onions, chili, and diced garlic over low heat. Mix well. Using bean masher, grind veggies inside heated skillet. Add remaining salt and pepper. Stir and continue to mash until veggies become a roughly textured sauce. Add puree and 2 cups of water. Stir. Add meat, making sure tomato sauce covers each strip. Cover and cook over medium heat for 5 minutes. Remove cover and lay potato slices on meat, spooning sauce over potatoes. Place coriander sprig on top, cover, and cook over medium heat for 10 minutes. Potatoes will soften. Meat will finish cooking. Flavor of coriander will spread. Remove sprig before serving.

Warm flour tortillas are mandatory for mopping *bistec* sauce off your plate. Serve with refried beans on the side.

# *Pan-broiled Horse in Tomato Sauce*
## Asado de Caballo en Salsa de Tomate

Other than the time Pickerel hit a horse on the San Blas road (and filled his freezer with equine for a month), he has purchased his horsemeat exclusively from reputable vendors—of which there are several in his city. In Mexico, the slaughter of horses for human consumption is legal and licensed; otherwise, Pickerel would object to the practice on ethical grounds (as a child, his favorite book was *Black Beauty*).

Pickerel's equinophilic sentiments aside, cheap is what matters to poor gringos pinching pesos in the meat market, and among the edible ungulates grazing upon Mexico's rocky hillsides, horse is the cheapest, hoofs down (less than half the price of beef). As to flavor, there is no confusion with beef. Horsemeat has its own taste—best described as woodsy (but not wild) and faintly sweet—which is why it is often prepared as *machaca* or in spicy barbeque.

> **Recommendations**: Horsemeat (carne de caballo) is not sold at butcheries (or market stalls) where other meats are sold. Look for shops that advertise Carnicería de Caballo Para Consumo Humano—Horse Butchery for Human Consumption (the best translation with the oddest suggestion: that there are horse butcheries for nonhuman consumption, perhaps where canines and aliens buy their meat).
>
> Horse fat is yellow, not white (like beef), so be not alarmed by the strange look of marbling in the meat. Like beef, you may order cuts—T-bone, rib roast, boneless shoulder—none of which Pickerel buys (he is too poor to eat off the top of a horse). Avoid dark meat, the kind that is almost black. This comes from an old horse. Instead, ask for potrillo (young horse). The meat is pinkish, like pork, with a distant taste of venison.
>
> If you find more fat than fiber in your meat, chances are you bought donkey (burro), not horse. Donkeys stand around more than horses do, which is why they have more fat.* Likewise, if your meat has a musky flavor and balks when you chew it, you are eating mule (mula). To local butchers (and taxonomists), equines are one big family.
>
> \* According to local equine experts, donkeys spend more time than horses standing under trees, waiting to fornicate.

*Ingredientes* (three servings)
- 1/2 kg eye of round or bottom round of horse (1/2 *kilo de cuete* or *gusano de caballo*)
- 2 garlic cloves, unpeeled (2 *dientes de ajo, sin pelar*)
- 2 tomatoes (2 *tomates*)
- 1 small onion (1 *cebolla chica*)
- 1 Anaheim chili, deveined and seedless (1 *chile largo-verde sin venas, ni semillas*) (See *Deveining Chili Peppers*, page 30.)

3 tbsp salt (3 *cucharadas de sal*)
1 tsp peppercorns (1 *cucharadita de pimientas enteras*)
1/2 tsp ground pepper (1/2 *cucharadita de pimienta molida*)
2 large potatoes (2 *papas grandes*)
3 tbsp cooking oil (3 *cucharadas de aceite para cocinar*)
1/4 cup tomato puree (1/4 *taza de pure de tomate*)
1/4 crisphead lettuce—enough to make 3 cups when chopped (1/4 *lechuga iceberg—suficiente para hacer 3 tazas después de picada*)

*Equipo*
Large saucepot *(cazuela grande)*
Large skillet with cover *(sartén grande con tapadera)*

*Preparación*
In a saucepot with 3 liters of water, place meat (whole) with garlic, 1 tomato (whole), 1/2 onion, 1/2 chili, 2 tablespoons of salt, and peppercorns. Cover and bring to a boil. A half kilo of heel of round will take about 1 hour to cook. Test with fork for tenderness. Save stock to make *caldo de caballo*. (See Horse Broth Soup, page 199.)

Pickerel does not peel his potatoes for this recipe—unpeeled spuds befit horse. Dice potatoes. Heat oil in skillet, and fry potatoes until golden. Remove potatoes and drain on absorbent paper (Pickerel uses old newspapers untouched by dog). Leave oil in skillet.

Slice remaining halves of onion and chili thinly. Cut tomatoes. Chop lettuce finely. Cut meat into cubes, the same size as potatoes. Add ground pepper and 1 tablespoon of salt. Mix well with meat.

Reheat potato oil, and fry cubed meat, stirring frequently until lightly browned. Push meat to one side of skillet. Add tomatoes, onion, and chili. Stir-fry over high heat for 1 minute and then mix with meat. Add potatoes and tomato puree. Mix well, cover, and cook over low heat for 15 minutes.

Serve with corn tortillas, refried beans, and a thick slice of freshly fallen avocado (*aguacate*) or a wedge of basket cheese (*panela*). (See Cheeses, page 23.) Top with chopped lettuce.

# Cortez-On-Foot Burritos
## Burritos de Carne Deshebrada en Chile Colorado

*Ingredientes* (four servings)
- 1/2 kg flank steak of horse (1/2 *kilo de falda de caballo para fajitas*)
- 2 garlic cloves, unpeeled (2 *dientes de ajo, sin pelar*)
- 3 tomatoes (3 *tomates*)
- 1 onion (1 *cebolla*)
- 1 Anaheim chili, deveined and seedless (1 *chile largo-verde sin venas, ni semillas*) (See *Deveining Chili Peppers*, page 30.)
- 3 tbsp salt (3 *cucharadas de sal*)
- 1 tsp peppercorns (1 *cucharadita de pimientas enteras*)
- 1/2 tsp ground pepper (1/2 *cucharadita de pimienta molida*)
- 2-1/2 tbsp cooking oil (2-1/2 *cucharadas de aceite para cocinar*)
- 1/2 cup red chili sauce (1/2 *taza de salsa de chile colorado*) (See *Red Chili Sauce*, page 81.)
- 12 flour tortillas (12 *tortillas de harina*) (See *Flour Tortillas*, page 49.)

*Equipo*
- Large saucepot *(cazuela grande)*
- Meat pounder *(machacador)*
- Skillet with cover *(sartén con tapadera)*

*Preparación*

In 3 liters of water, place meat (whole) with 1 garlic clove, 1 tomato (whole), 1/2 onion, 1/2 chili, 2 tablespoons of salt, and peppercorns. Cover and bring to a boil. A half kilo of flank steak will take about 1 hour to cook. When tender, remove meat from broth and cool. Save stock to make *caldo de caballo*. (See *Horse Broth Soup*, page 199.)

Shred meat into stringy fibers no thicker than a toothpick. Use fingertips and fork to pick meat apart. (See *Shredding Meat*, page 31.) Remove fatty globs. A half kilo of *fajita* (though shrunk after boiling) makes a mound of shredded meat.

Combine meat with 1 tablespoon of salt, the remaining garlic clove, and ground pepper. Mix well. Using the *machacador*, pound shredded meat on a solid surface until meat fibers soften and the salt and garlic disappear.

Lift meat and fluff it as you pound, keeping in mind the meaning of the word *horsepower*.

Slice remaining halves of onion and chili thinly. Dice tomatoes.

Heat oil in skillet. Add meat. Brown lightly. Push meat to one side of skillet, making room for veggies. Add veggies, stir-fry briefly over high heat, and then mix with meat. Add 1/4 cup of broth and red chili sauce. Mix well. Cover and cook over low heat for 10 minutes.

Warm tortillas on griddle. Spoon 2 heaping tablespoons of cooked meat onto the middle of each tortilla, fold ends, and roll into burritos. Serve with refried beans on the side.

# Red Chili Pork with Nopales
## Carne de Puerco con Nopales en Chile Colorado

Pickerel eats pork only when his stars align with the northwest corner of oblivion (aka his outhouse). Such was their position one foggy morning when Pickerel motored breezily on Highway 15, south of Navojoa, Sonora. Ahead he spied a roadside crowd. Then Pickerel saw through the fog a sight that made his tilted can of Tecate suddenly resume an upright position. He saw pigs on the road. Running on the road. A mad dash of pigs. Swine in the hundreds. Pickerel immediately brought his conveyance to a stop and joined the throng.

A pig truck had run off the highway, overturned, its pig cages busting open, releasing discounted pork by the ton. It was a porcine jailbreak. Pickerel saw men carrying away casualties. He saw women toting off pork by the part. He saw boys chasing pigs. He saw pigs hoofing for the hills. Then Pickerel saw himself tackle a passing porker—a medium-size top hog, a real squirmer—but small enough to wrestle into his parked conveyance, where rope and a tranquilizing whack on the head waited. (Pickerel never travels without a stretch of hawser and a tire iron.)

A week later, Pickerel and his neighbors were still eating pork.

Since that day, Pickerel's stars have refused to realign themselves in the pork-producing position. In spite of this unobliging astrology, he has benefited on occasion from other roadside windfalls: two crates of honeydew melons fallen from a passing produce truck (Pickerel had to fight a fellow plunderer for the second); a pail of unrefined sugar spilled off a cane wagon; and a 50-kilo sack of potatoes that fell from a speeding tractor trailer. Fortunately, Pickerel was not tailgating at the time. Otherwise, he might have been killed by flying spuds.

*Ingredientes* (four servings)
- 2 cups cooked and cut nopales (2 *tazas de nopalitos cocidos*) (See *Preparing Nopales*, page 102.)
- 1 cup long-grain, unconverted, white rice (1 *taza de arroz blanco, grano largo y fino*)
- 2 cups red chili sauce (2 *tazas de salsa de chile Colorado*) (See *Red Chili Sauce*, page 81.)
- 1/2 kg pork meat, any cut (1/2 *kilo de carne de puerco, cualquer corte*)
- 1 tbsp salt (1 *cucharada de sal*)

*Equipo*
Large saucepot with cover (*cazuela grande con tapadera*)

*Preparación*
Cook nopales. (See *Nopales*, page 102.)

Cook rice. (See *Fried White Rice*, page 124.) Warm red chili sauce. Pretty easy so far, huh?

Cut pork into serving-size pieces (with or without bone) and place in saucepot with 2 cups of water and salt. Cover and boil until water is gone and pork chunks are cooked white. When pork starts to sizzle in a waterless saucepot, stir and allow pieces to brown lightly. Keep heat high. Add cooked nopales, mix well, and then add chili sauce. Stir, cover, and lower heat. Cook until sauce boils, stirring occasionally. Remove from heat and keep covered. Serve over white rice.

# Fired Tequila Goat
## Chivo Tatemado

When Pickerel not-so-accidentally ran over a young goat grazing too close to a country roadside (and out ran the old goatkeeper to claim it), he cooked his prize *tatemado* style that very afternoon. Using the backyard pit (*hoyo*) originally dug as a shallow grave for Miriam, Pickerel filled it with mesquite firewood (supplied by Pablo Quemado, local charcoal burner) and started a roaring fire that sent arsonphobic neighbors fleeing from their houses. While the fire burned, Pickerel enlisted their help in skinning, gutting, and preparing the goat. Pickerel provided potatoes, chilies, herbs, and knowledgeable supervision. For example, never add carrots to your *tatemado*—they rob flavor from goat meat. When Pickerel's pit fire had burnt to embers, he lowered his pot full of chili-basted goat meat into the hole, placing it directly on the coals. Next, he covered the pit with an Oldsmobile hood (1979 Delta 88). Then he shoveled loose dirt on top (grave-dug soil), and he took his water hose and sprinkled the dirt until it was moist (not soggy). For the next 30 minutes, Pickerel monitored the wet dirt for escaping vapor plumes—a sign of heat leaking from the pit. These leaks he immediately plugged by shoveling more dirt on the Oldsmobile hood.

Four hours later, Pickerel's goat pot was ready to be hoisted and shared with cooperative neighbors.

> For those without a backyard pit or a run-over goat, use your stove burner for fire and purchase your goat meat at the local market (ask for carne de chivo or carne de cabra). Lamb (carne de borrego) may be substituted.

*Ingredientes* (serves five)
- 2 guajillo chilies (2 *chiles guajillos*)
- 4 ancho chilies (2 *chiles anchos*)
- 1/2 tsp cumin seeds (1/2 *cucharadita de semillas de comino*)
- 3 garlic cloves, unpeeled (3 *dientes de ajo, sin pelar*)
- 1 tsp peppercorns (1 *cucharadita de pimientas enteras*)
- 3 tomatoes (3 *tomates*)
- 1 cup tequila (1 *taza de tequila*) Pickerel uses El Jimador Blanco, saving his aged reserves for nonculinary occasions.
- 1 cup vinegar (1 *taza de vinagre*) Pickerel uses white cane vinegar.
- 1 tsp ground, whole-leaf oregano (1 *cucharadita de hoja de orégano molido*)
- 2 tbsp salt (2 *cucharadas de sal*)
- 2 bay leaves (2 *hojas de laurel*)

5 large potatoes (5 *papas grandes*)
1 large onion (1 *cebolla grande*)
1/4 cup cooking oil (1/4 *taza de aceite para cocinar*)
1 kg goat meat, cut into serving-size pieces (1 *kilo carne de cabra, cortada en pedazos para servir*)

*Equipo*

Saucepan (*cazo*)
Mortar and pestle (*molcajete y tejolote*)
Blender (*licuadora*)
Large stewpot with cover (*olla grande con tapadera*)
Aluminum foil (*papel aluminio*)

*Preparación*

To prepare chili marinade (*marinada de chile*), open guajillo and ancho chilies, remove seed trunks, and wash out loose seeds. Place in saucepan with 3 cups of water. Crush garlic with cumin seeds and peppercorns in *molcajete*. Halve tomatoes. Add tomatoes and contents of *molcajete* to the saucepan with chilies. Cover and cook over low heat, stirring occasionally until chilies are soft, about 30 minutes. Drain chili water. Pour contents of saucepan into blender. Add tequila, vinegar, oregano, salt, bay leaves (after washing), and 2 cups of cold water. Blend marinade until smooth.

Peel potatoes and cut into serving-size chunks. Slice onion into rings.

Cover bottom of stewpot with cooking oil. Place the first layer of goat meat, using the boniest pieces first. Cover with marinade. Add a few potatoes and onion rings. Add another layer of meat, cover with marinade, then more potatoes and onion. Meat again, marinade, potatoes, onions, and so on.

Pour 2 cups of cold water into blender (empty or not of marinade), blend to a red froth, and add to meat. Cover pot with aluminum foil. Cover with lid. Weigh down with rock. No chili goat vapors should escape. Set stove burner to low and cook for 3-1/2 hours. No more. No less. Goat meat should fall off bones into warm, waiting tortillas.

# Stewed Iguana
## *Estofado de Iguana*

Doña Cuca—a local purveyor of cold-blooded vertebrates—gave Pickerel her recipe for iguana stew the day he threatened to release her sack of captive iguanas onto his tree-lined street (this, after she permanently plugged the front left burner on his Mabe gas stove with kiln-blackened reptile glue while cauterizing broken iguana tails.)

For poor gringos who consider themselves lucky *not* have a Doña Cuca delivering iguanas to their doorstep, you may trap your own in the nearest tropical woodland. Use ripe mangos for bait and a snare pole to catch it. Bring gloves (they bite) and go late in the afternoon. Alternatively, you may purchase your iguana from one of the itinerant reptile vendors who circulate in local markets. Some will even butcher it for you.

**Dressing and preparing iguana:** Pickerel uses only black iguanas (*garrabos*) to make his stew (unfortunately, the green ones are protected by animal cruelty laws and listed in CITES Appendix II as an animal whose trade must be controlled), and he employs only blunt trauma to dispatch them (no spearing, no birdshot, no drowning). Once night has fallen (permanently) upon Pickerel's iguana, he uses his sharpest bladed knife (*cuchillo filoso*) to remove head, tail, and claws. Next, he opens the underside lengthwise and removes entrails (including rectum), and then he dismembers the carcass, amputating legs and cutting the body in half down the spine. Pickerel skins each piece by making a starter cut between flesh and skin and then pulling the hide off the meat (comparable to peeling duct tape from a hairy leg). Finally, he divides the body halves into four pieces, and the legs he cuts in two.

Before iguana meat can be stewed, it must boil first—to tenderize and to dilute its reptilian flavor. Pickerel places his meat in 1 liter of water, to which he adds 1/2 cup of salt (1/2 *taza de sal*—mix well), 2 unpeeled garlic cloves (2 *dientes de ajo, sin pelar*), 1/4 sliced small onion (1/4 *cebolla chica en rabandadas*), and 1 teaspoon of peppercorns (1 *cucharadita de pimientas enteras*). Pickerel boils his iguana for 20 minutes in this salty garlic sea.

*Ingredientes* (two servings)
- 2 carrots (2 *zanahorias*)
- 2 potatoes (2 *papas*)
- 1 garlic clove, peeled (1 *diente de ajo, pelado*)
- 3 tomatoes (3 *tomates*)
- 1 Anaheim chili, deveined and seedless (1 *chile largo-verde sin venas, ni semillas*) (See *Deveining Chili Peppers*, page 30.)
- 1/2 onion (1/2 *cebolla*)
- 2 tbsp cooking oil (2 *cucharadas de aceite para cocinar*)
- Serving-size pieces of parboiled meat from 1 iguana (*piezas para servir de carne hervida de una iguana*)
- 12 peppercorns (12 *pimientas enteras*)
- 5 bay leaves (5 *hojas de laurel*)
- 1/2 tsp ground, whole-leaf oregano (1/2 *cucharadita de hoja de orégano molido*)
- 1 tbsp salt (1 *cucharada de sal*)
- 1/4 cup vinegar (1/4 *taza de vinagre*) Pickerel uses white cane vinegar.
- 1 cup tomato puree (1 *taza de puré de tomate*)
- 1 tbsp Salsa Ranchera (1 *cucharada de Salsa Ranchera*) (See *Bottled Sauces*, page 29.)

*Equipo*
Saucepot with cover (*cazuela con tapadera*)

*Preparación*

Peel and slice carrots, not too thinly. Peel and cut potatoes into bite-size chunks. Chop garlic finely. Dice tomatoes, chili, and onion.

Heat oil in saucepot. Add iguana meat, veggies (except potatoes), peppercorns, bay leaves, oregano, and salt. Mix well. Add vinegar, puree, and ranch sauce. Mix again. Cover and boil 10 minutes over high heat, stirring occasionally. Lower heat to medium, and cook another 15 minutes. Add potatoes, stir, and cover. Cook 30 minutes, stirring occasionally.

Serve with warm corn tortillas and enjoy the flavor of what fish would taste like if they swam in trees.

# Soups and Broths

## Sopas y Caldos

*"Gallina vieja, hace buen caldo."*
*"Old hen makes good soup."*
Mario Moreno (Cantinflas)
Referring to a former first lady of Mexico

Cheese Ball Soup

Bean Bone Soup

Tripe Soup

Horse Broth Soup

Cream of Chayote

Poor Gringo Soup

Chewy Cheese Soup

Ranch Lentil Soup

Aztec Soup

In his pre-gringo life, Pickerel ate soup only when he was sick, cold, or queue-jumping a crowded buffet line. His mother cooked homemade chicken soup when Pickerel got the flu. She served him turkey curry bisque on rain-chilled December afternoons. Miriam—newly swept off her feet by Pickerel's charismatic mendacity—routinely nursed her husband's cold symptoms with Campbell's Condensed Minestrone. And when winter's windchill numbed Pickerel's private parts, she warmed them from the inside out with microwave-heated Lipton Instant Cup-a-Noodle-Soup (purchased by the case).

Today, Pickerel eats soup not because he is sick or cold but because he is poor and living in a land where *caldo* is king—culinarily speaking. No Mexican goes more than a week without getting a soup fix—even in the hottest weeks of summer when houseflies cling to ice trucks to escape the heat.

> Pickerel gathered his soup recipes from local soup makers gracious enough to spend quality soup-making time in his unlit galley—first, by allowing Pickerel to look over their shoulders (at an ear-whispering distance) and then by accepting Pickerel's invitation to look over his (while guiding his long-handled soup spoon). At this time, the author wishes to acknowledge these fearless contributors. They shall remain nameless out of respect for their prior and present conjugal commitments and/or matrimonial bliss.

# Cheese Ball Soup
## Caldo con Albóndigas de Requesón

*Ingredientes*
- 1 Anaheim chili (1 *chile largo-verde*)
- 2 large potatoes (2 *papas grandes*)
- 2 carrots (2 *zanahorias*)
- 1 tomato (1 *tomate*)
- 1/2 onion (1/2 *cebolla*)
- 1 stalk celery (1 *varita de apio*)
- 1 tbsp cooking oil (1 *cucharada de aceite para cocinar*)
- 1/2 cup tomato puree (1/2 *taza de puré de tomate*)
- 4 cups chicken stock (4 *tazas de consomé de pollo*) (See Green Chicken, page 143, for stock or use 1 tbsp chicken bouillon powder [1 *cucharada de consomé de pollo en polvo*].)
- 1-1/2 tbsp salt (1-1/2 *cucharadas de sal*)
- 1-1/2 tsp ground pepper (1-1/2 *cucharadita de pimienta molida*)
- 1/2 kg *requesón* (1/2 *kilo de requesón*) (See Cheeses, page 23.)
- 1 egg (1 *huevo*)
- 1 cup wheat flour (1 *taza de harina de trigo*)

*Equipo*
- Small plastic bag (a bread bag will work) for sweating charred chilies (*una bolsa de plástico chica para hacer sudar los chiles tatemados*)
- Saucepot with cover (*cazuela con tapadera*)
- Mixing bowl (*tazón para mezclar*)

*Preparación*

Char chili and peel skin. (See *Charring Chili Peppers*, page 30.) Remove stalk, seed trunk, and veins. (See *Deveining Chili Peppers*, page 30.) Wash out loose seeds. Cut chili in half and slice into finger-wide strips.

Peel potatoes and carrots. Cut into bite-size pieces. Dice tomato, onion, and celery. Heat oil in saucepot, and fry tomato, onion, and celery until bubbly. Add puree, chicken stock, and 1/2 liter of water (add bouillon powder and 1-1/2 liters of water if chicken stock is unavailable). Mix well. Add potatoes, carrots, chili strips, 1 tablespoon of salt, and 1 teaspoon of pepper. Cover and boil over low heat until potatoes cook. Test with fork.

In mixing bowl, combine *requesón*, egg, flour, 1/2 tablespoon of salt, and 1/2 teaspoon of pepper. Knead mixture until pasty. Take three-fingered pinches of cheese dough and roll into balls—ping-pong ball size. Wet hands to keep cheese from sticking.

When soup is cooked, add cheese balls. Stir, cover, and simmer over low heat 5 minutes. Cheese balls will lose ball shape, becoming cumulus cheese clouds. Serve with corn tortillas.

# Bean Bone Soup
## Wakabaki

This recipe comes from the rocky, grassless highlands of Jalisco where cattle grow thin and cattlemen thinner. You have two options for beef bones (besides foraging in a dumpster behind your local steakhouse). If you ask your market butcher for *retazos con hueso* (soup bones), you will get the lowest part of the short loin, mostly bone. If you ask for *huesos de tuétano* (marrow bones), you will get bone-in shanks. Either works for *wakabaki*.

*Ingredientes* (five servings)
- 1 kg beef bones (1 *kilo de retazos de res con hueso o huesos con tuétano*)
- 1/2 onion (1/2 *cebolla*)
- 1/2 tsp peppercorns (1/2 *cucharadita de pimienta entera*)
- 2 tbsp salt (2 *cucharadas de sal*)
- 1/2 kg beans (1/2 *kilo de frijol*) (See *Beans*, page 34.)
- 1 Anaheim chili, deveined and seedless (1 *chile largo-verde sin venas, ni semillas*) (See *Deveining Chili Peppers*, page 30.)
- 2 coriander sprigs (2 *ramitas de cilantro*)

*Equipo*
Large saucepot with cover (*cazuela grande con tapadera*)

*Preparación*
In saucepot with 4 liters of water, boil bones, onion, peppercorns, and salt. When pot foams, add beans, and continue to boil—about 1-1/2 hours. When beans pass tongue test (firm but chewable—without teeth. See *Beans Cooked in Pot*, page 36.), add chili and coriander. Cover and cook 20 minutes.

Serve with flour tortillas.

# Tripe Soup
## *Menudo*

Pickerel makes *menudo* three mornings a year: New Year's Eve day, Mexican Mother's Day (May 10—in memory of his dearly departed *madre*), and his birthday. Approximately eight hours after preparing *menudo* on these mornings, Pickerel heads to the Spotted Bull, where he enters the ring with Don Julio González Añejo—the aged distiller—determined to go the distance with 750 ml of amber liquid in a short decanter (designed by DJ himself so his guests could talk across a table without looking around a bottle). Ultimately, Pickerel loses in the fifteenth round by TKO (Tequila knock out), but he still manages to stumble home in a celebratory state.

Not surprisingly, the next day Pickerel needs tripe soup to face the light. He reheats his saucepot, slices limes, and grinds chiltepin. Bringing them together in a steaming bowl, Pickerel sips the broth (*menudo's* curative power lies in its broth), and almost at once, he feels that life is worth the hangover.

*Ingredientes* (five servings—Pickerel never cures a hangover once)
    1/2 kg white hominy (1/2 *kilo de nixtamal*) (See Hominy, page 24.)
    1 onion (1 *cebolla*)
    Dried chiltepin chilies—optional (*chiles chiltepines secos—opcional*)
    1/2 kg honeycomb tripe (1/2 *kilo de pancita de res*)
    1 cow foot (1 *pata de res*)
    3 garlic cloves, peeled (3 *dientes de ajo, pelados*)
    3 tbsp salt (3 *cucharadas de sal*)
    3 coriander sprigs (3 *ramitas de cilantro*)
    1 serrano chili (1 *chile serrano*)
    3 limes (3 *limones*)

*Equipo*
    Large bowl (*tazón grande*)
    Saucepot with cover (*cazuela con tapadera*)
    Lime squeezer (*exprimidor de limón*)

*Preparación*
    Place hominy in bowl with cold water. Rub kernels briskly between hands to shed their glassy sheaths. Remove dark "eye" at the base

> **On tripe**: Purchase only beef tripe (pancita de res). Butchers at local market stalls will substitute sheep stomach (pancita de borrego) if you don't speak up. Pickerel prefers the honeycomb tripe (second cow stomach) in his menudo. It makes a fuller broth.

of each kernel. Rinse well. Cut onion in half. Grind chiltepines. Wash tripe thoroughly and cut into bite-size squares. Cut cow's foot in half. You will need a thick-bladed knife to work through the knuckles. Watch fingers.

In a saucepot with 3 liters of water, add tripe, hominy, cow's foot, garlic cloves, and half of the onion. Hominy sinks. Tripe floats. Foot lurks in the middle. It's a density thing.

Cover and boil over medium heat for 3 hours, stirring every 30 minutes. At the 1-hour mark, *menudo* should resemble dishwater with a dirty sweatsock froth. During the second hour—after hominy has flowered—add salt. When tripe is tender enough to slide off a fork, your *menudo* is ready.

Dice remaining onion half, coriander sprigs, and chili (this one very fine). Separate into tiny piles. Slice limes.

Into your steaming bowl of *menudo*, add a pinch of coriander, a spoonful of onions, and as much serrano chili and/or ground chiltepin as you dare. Squeeze in lime. Stir, sip, and feel that hangover head for the hills.

# Horse Broth Soup
## Caldo de Caballo

When Pickerel cooks horse (See *Pan-broiled Horse in Tomato Sauce*, page 183, or *Cortez-On-Foot Burritos*, page 185.), he saves the broth for soup. A squeeze of lime and a dash of hot sauce give this poor gringo consomme a gallop (no saddle needed).

*Ingredientes* (four servings)
- 1/2 kg flank steak or heel of round horse (1/2 *kilo de falda o cuete de caballo*)
- 2 garlic cloves, unpeeled (2 *dientes de ajo, sin pelar*)
- 1 large tomato (1 *tomate grande*)
- 1/2 medium onion (1/2 *cebolla mediana*)
- 1/2 Anaheim chili, deveined and seedless (1/2 *chile largo-verde sin venas, ni semillas*) (See *Deveining Chili Peppers*, page 30.)
- 2 tbsp salt (2 *cucharadas de sal*)
- 1 tsp peppercorns (1 *cucharadita de pimienta entera*)
- Salsa Huichol (*Salsa Huichol*) (See *Bottled Sauces*, page 29.)
- Sliced limes (*limones partidos*)

*Equipo*
- Large saucepot with cover (*cazuela grande con tapadera*)
- Bean masher (*moledor de frijol*)
- Lime squeezer (*exprimidor de limón*)

*Preparación*

In a saucepot with 3 liters of water, place meat (whole) with garlic, uncut tomato, onion, chili, salt, and peppercorns. Cover and boil 1 hour or until meat is cooked. Remove meat for shredding. (See *Pan-broiled Horse in Tomato Sauce*, page 183, or *Cortez-On-Foot-Burritos*, page 185.) With bean masher, mash tomatoes. Remove skins.

Ladle warm broth into a soup bowl (leaving garlic cloves behind). Pump in two shots of Salsa Huichol. Squeeze in lime (two halves at least). Stir and sip.

Serve with bean tacos on the side.

# Cream of Chayote (Merliton)
## Crema de Chayote

A staple starch of the Aztecs and reportedly one of only two foods Hernán Cortés refused to eat. The other was roasted hedgehog (*erizo*).

This smooth, pear-shaped member of the gourd family is a cheap poor gringo substitute for squash or cucumbers, which reside, culinarily speaking, on the better side of the vine. Strongly seasoned, *chayote* can hold its own with zucchini on a bad day.

Pickerel brought this recipe from Veracruz, the *chayote*-producing capital of Mexico—where pear-shaped women and their pear-shaped breasts have also borrowed this vegetable name.

*Ingredientes* (three servings)
3 merliton (3 *chayotes*)
1 small garlic clove, peeled (1 *diente chico de ajo, pelado*)
1/2 serrano chili (1/2 *chile serrano*)
1 small onion (1 *cebolla chica*)
3 coriander sprigs (3 *ramitas de cilantro*)
1 tbsp margarine (1 *cucharada de margarina*)
1 tsp salt (1 *cucharadita de sal*)
1/2 tsp ground pepper (1/2 *cucharadita de pimienta molida*)

*Equipo*
Vegetable peeler (*pelador de verdura*)
Saucepot with cover (*cazuela con tapadera*)
Blender (*licuadora*)

*Preparación*
Peel *chayotes* with vegetable peeler (careful!—slippery when peeled), trim ends, and cut in half lengthwise. Remove soft pip from center, and slice halves into finger-wide strips. Cut crossways into bite-size pieces. Dice garlic and onion. Mince chili. Finely chop coriander leaves and thinnest stems—enough to fill 2 teaspoons.

Melt margarine in saucepot, and fry without browning (*acitronar*) onion, garlic, and chili until onion softens. Add *chayote* and coriander. Mix well and fry 5 minutes, stirring often. Add 2 cups of water, stir, and simmer under cover over low heat 30 minutes or until *chayote* cooks (tender when probed with a fork).

Remove from heat and cool. Pour saucepot contents into blender. Add salt and pepper. Blend until smooth.

Serve in soup bowls (*tazones*) with corn tortillas on the side.

# Poor Gringo Soup
## Caldillo

*Ingredientes* (two servings)
- 2 small tomatoes (2 *tomates chicos*)
- 1 potato (1 *papa*)
- 1/2 small onion (1/2 *cebolla chica*)
- 1/2 Anaheim chili, deveined and seedless (1/2 *chile largo-verde sin venas, ni semillas*) (See Deveining Chili Peppers, page 30.)
- 2 tbsp cooking oil (2 *cucharadas de aceite para cocinar*)
- 1 cup *machaca* (1 *taza de machaca*) (See Carne machaca, pages 21/22.)
- 1/2 tsp salt (1/2 *cucharadita de sal*)
- 1/4 tsp ground pepper (1/4 *cucharadita de pimienta molida*)
- 2 eggs (2 *huevos*)

*Equipo*
- Saucepan (*cazo*)
- Saucepot with cover (*cazuela con tapadera*)

*Preparación*

Peel potato and cut into dice-size cubes. Chop tomatoes, onion, and chili finely. In saucepan, heat 1 liter of water. In saucepot, heat oil.

Add veggies (except potatoes) to hot oil. Stir. When onion cooks, sprinkle in *machaca*. Mix well. *Machaca* sucks up the hot veggie juice. Add potatoes and stir.

When water boils in saucepan, add to saucepot with veggies and *machaca*. Add salt and pepper. Stir and cover. Cook over high heat for 10 minutes.

Crack eggs and drop each into boiling broth. Cover and cook until the eggs poach, their yolks turning hard.

Serve with warm tortillas.

# Chewy Cheese Soup
## Caldo de Papas con Panela

*Ingredientes* (three servings)
- 3 Anaheim chilies (3 *chiles largos-verdes*)
- 3 potatoes (3 *papas*)
- 2 tomatoes (2 *tomates*)
- 1/4 onion (1/4 *cebolla*)
- 1 tbsp cooking oil (1 *cucharada de aceite para cocinar*)
- 3 tbsp tomato puree (3 *cucharadas de puré de tomate*)
- 4 cups chicken stock (4 *tazas de consomé de pollo*) (See Green Chicken, page 143, for stock or use 1 tbsp chicken bouillon powder [1 *cucharada de consomé de pollo en polvo*].)
- 1 basket cheese (1 *panela*) (See Cheeses, page 23.)
- 1 tbsp salt (1 *cucharada de sal*)
- 1 tsp ground pepper (1 *cucharadita de pimienta molida*)
- 4 tbsp sour cream (4 *cucharadas de crema agria*)

*Equipo*
- Small plastic bag (a bread bag will work) for sweating charred chilies (*una bolsa de plástico chica para hacer sudar los chiles tatemados*)
- Saucepot with cover (*cazuela con tapadera*)

*Preparación*

Char chili and peel skin. (See *Charring Chili Peppers*, page 30.) Remove stalk, seed trunk, and veins. (See *Deveining Chili Peppers*, page 30.) Wash out loose seeds. Cut chili in half and slice into finger-wide strips. Peel potatoes and cut into bite-size pieces. Dice tomato and onion. Heat oil in saucepot and fry tomato and onion with puree. When bubbly, add chicken stock and 1/2 liter of water (add bouillon powder and 1-1/2 liters of water if chicken stock is unavailable).

Bring to a boil. Add potatoes, chili strips, salt, and pepper. Cover and boil until potatoes cook (use fork to test for softness). Stir in sour cream. Cut *panela* into serving-size pieces and add to broth.

Serve with warm corn tortillas. Soft potatoes and chewy cheese make a savory couple.

# Ranch Lentil Soup
## Lentejas con Arroz y Queso

When Pickerel tires of beans but still hankers for the earthy taste of a cheap legume (to folate his vascular erectility), he goes lentil with fresh sauce and cheese. Lentils are the reason the long-lived Hunzakuts fornicate into their nineties.

*Ingredientes* (four servings)
- 1/4 small onion (1/4 *cebolla chica*)
- 1/2 cup lentils (1/2 *taza de lentejas*) Pickerel buys Verde Valle brand, a medium green lentil.
- 1 tbsp salt (1 *cucharada de sal*)
- 2 cups cooked white rice (2 *tazas de arroz blanco cocido*) (See *Fried White Rice*, page 124.)
- 1 cup fresh sauce *without lime* (1 *taza de salsa fresca sin limón*) (See *Fresh Sauce with Lime*, page 72.)
- 1/4 kg fresh ranch cheese (1/4 *kg de queso fresco de rancho*) (See *Cheeses*, page 23.)

*Equipo*
Saucepot with cover (*cazuela con tapadera*)

*Preparación*

Slice onion. Wash lentils, place in saucepot with 8 cups of cold water, and heat over high flame. When lentils boil, add onion and salt. Lower heat to medium and cover. In 20 minutes, add 1/2 cup of water. Cover and boil 10 minutes more. Lentils will darken and become tender.

Cook rice and make fresh sauce (if neither is ready). Remember, no lime.

In a large soup bowl (*tazón*), combine 1 cup of cooked lentils (with broth), 1/2 cup of cooked rice, and 4 tablespoons of fresh sauce. Mix well. Crumble fingerfuls of cheese on top.

# Aztec Soup
## Sopa Azteca/Sopa de Tortilla

*Ingredientes* (eight servings)
- 1/2 kg eye of round or bottom round—horse or beef (1/2 *kilo de cuete o gusano—carne de caballo o de res*)
- 3 garlic cloves, peeled (3 *dientes de ajo, pelados*)
- 1 Anaheim chili, deveined and seedless (1 *chile largo-verde sin venas, ni semillas*) (See *Deveining Chili Peppers*, page 30.)
- 1/2 onion (1/2 *cebolla*)
- 2 tbsp salt (2 *cucharadas de sal*)
- 1 tsp peppercorns (1 *cucharadita de pimienta entera*)
- 3 tomatoes (3 *tomates*)
- 1/4 tsp ground, whole-leaf oregano (1/4 *cucharadita de hoja de orégano molido*)
- 1/2 cup cooking oil (1/2 *taza de aceite para cocinar*)
- 16 corn tortillas (16 *tortillas de maíz*) (See *Corn Tortillas*, page 47.)
- 1 avocado (1 *aguacate*)
- 1/2 fresh basket cheese (1/2 *panela fresca*) (See *Cheeses*, page 23.)
- 1/2 cup sour cream (1/2 *taza de crema agria*)
- 7 oz. can chipotle peppers (1 *lata de 7 onzas de chiles chipotles*)

*Equipo*
- Large saucepot with cover (*cazuela grande con tapadera*)
- Blender (*licuadora*)
- Strainer (*colador*)
- Skillet (*sartén*)

*Preparación*

In a saucepot with 4 liters of water, place meat (whole) with garlic, Anaheim chili, onion, salt, and peppercorns. Cover and bring to a boil. A half kilo of meat will take about 1 hour to cook. When tender, remove meat from broth and cool. Shred meat into stringy fibers no thicker than a toothpick. Use fingertips and fork to pick meat apart. (See *Shredding Meat*, page 31.)

Halve tomatoes and add to broth with oregano. Boil tomatoes in broth. When tomatoes have boiled, remove, cool, and place in blender with 3 tablespoons of broth. Remove chili, onion, and garlic cloves from broth (you may have to do some fishing) and discard. Blend tomatoes until smooth. Return blended tomato mixture to broth, straining out skins and seeds first. Simmer broth over low heat.

Heat oil in skillet. Roll tortillas (cigar shape) and cut crossways, finger wide. You now have tortilla curls. Fry curls in oil until golden and crispy. Remove from oil and drain on absorbent paper. Pickerel uses old newspapers untouched by dog.

Cut avocado and *panela* into bite-size cubes. Place sour cream and chipotle peppers in separate dishes.

You are now ready to build your soup.

In a large soup bowl (*tazón*), add 3 cups of broth, 3 forkfuls of shredded meat (shredded chicken or lard-fried pork meat—*chicharrones*—may be substituted), and 2 tablespoons each of avocado and *panela* cubes. Add 1 tablespoon of sour cream, stir, and add as many chipotle peppers as you dare (Pickerel recommends one for beginners). Sprinkle tortilla crisps on top—enough to cover broth.

Serve with absolutely nothing.

# Deep-Fried

## *Fritangas*

| Nutrition Facts |  |
|---|---|
| Serving Size 342 g | |
| **Amount Per Serving** | |
| Calories 1730 | Calories from Fat 761 |
| | % Daily Value* |
| Total Fat 82 g | 126% |
|   Saturated Fat 63g | 315% |
|   Trans Fat 29g | Way Too Much |
| Cholesterol 400 g | 133% |
| Sodium 3720mg | 155% |
| Total Carbohydrate 310g | 103% |
|   Dietary Fiber 0g | 0% |
|   Sugars 10g | |
| Protein 1g | |
| Vitamin A   0%  •  Vitamin C   0% | |
| Calcium   0%  •  Iron   0% | |
| *Percent Daily Values are based on a 2,000 calorie diet. Your daily values may be higher or lower depending on your calorie needs. | |
| NutritionData.com | |

*Nutritional Value of One Fried Dough Boat*
*with Lard Renderings*

Dough Boats with Pork Renderings

Cheese Flutes

Little Fat Ones

So what if deep-fried means dripping with poly-Pickerel saturated fat? Pickerel loudly disclaims any suggestion that his poor gringo cuisine is healthy, much less dietetic. *Al contrario*. It is loaded with salt, full of calories, and awash in trans fat. *Oilé!*

**The benefits:** Eating fatty foods is a poor gringo's dissimulation of affluence, providing him with the illusion that he can afford to gain weight. (Remember, most poor gringos become thin by calamity—economic, not dietary—rather than by choice.)

**The hazards:** Pickerel can only speak for himself when it comes to the dangers of heart disease and high cholesterol. First, he refuses to recognize that he has a heart (not human, anyway). Second, the cold, liquid cornstarch running through his veins is cholesterol soluble. What's more, the willowy Pickerel needs all the body fat his adipose tissue can store just to plow his way through market crowds in the pursuit of a larcenous deal.

So bring on those lard-soaked *sopes*!

# *Dough Boats with Pork Renderings*
## *Sopes con Asientos*

*Ingredientes* (for eight sopes)
- 2-1/2 cups corn flour (2-1/2 *tazas de harina de maíz*)
- 1/4 kg Chihuahua cheese (1/4 *kilo de queso de Chihuahua*) (See *Cheeses*, page 23.)
- 1/4 kg ranch cheese for grating (1/4 *kilo de queso de rancho para rallar*) (See *Cheeses*, page 23.)
- 1/4 kg pork renderings (1/4 *kilo de asientos de puerco*) For pork renderings, see below.
- 1/4 crisphead lettuce (1/4 *lechuga iceberg*)
- 1 small onion (1 *cebolla chica*)
- 2 limes (2 *limones*)
- 1 tsp salt (1 *cucharadita de sal*)
- 2 tbsp vinegar (2 *cucharadas de vinagre*) Pickerel uses white cane vinegar.
- 1 cup roasted tomato sauce (1 *taza de salsa de tomate asado*) (See *Roasted Tomato Sauce*, page 74.)
- 1 cup guacamole (1 *taza de guacamole*) (See *Guacamole*, page 78.)

*Equipo*
- Saucepan (*cazo*)
- Cheese grater (*raspador de queso*)
- Mixing bowl (*tazón para mezclar*)
- Lime squeezer (*exprimidor de limón*)
- Griddle—if using gas stove (*comal—con estufa de gas*)

*Preparación*

Because Pickerel's griddle can accommodate no more than two *sopes* at once, he fires up his charcoal grill for this recipe. For those without a grill, use a griddle (and live with cooking only two *sopes* at a time).

In saucepan, warm 2-1/2 cups of water. Add warmed water to mixing bowl (*tazón para mezclar*) or dishpan (*bandeja*) with corn flour. Mix well and make dough. (See *Corn Tortillas*, page 47.)

Grate cheeses. Warm *asientos* (if not fresh).

> **Pickerel's Pork Rendering Dictionary**
> From most to least expensive:
> **Carnitas**: lard-fried pork meat
> **Chicharrones**: lard-fried pork skins/stomach/intestinal linings
> **Asientos**: leftover, burnt pork bits strained from lard after rendering

Chop lettuce finely.

Halve onion, slice into rainbows, and place in bowl (*tazón*). Slice limes and squeeze onto onions. Add salt, vinegar, and 1/3 cup of warm water (*agua tibia*). Mix, cover, and marinate 15 minutes.

Take a large, five-fingered pinch of dough and make a thick tortilla. Do this by rolling dough into a ball and then flattening the ball between your palms. Clap it back and forth (patty-cake) until you have a smooth, flat circle of dough about 1/4 inch thick and 5 inches in diameter. Wet hands to keep dough moist. Mend cracks around dough edges.

Place each dough circle on the grill (or griddle) over high heat. Cook 2 minutes, rotating 180 degrees once. Flip, cooking 2-1/2 minutes, pressing edges and center of circle occasionally with spatula (*espátula*) or fingers to prevent dough from inflating.

Remove from heat, but do not allow to cool. With fingertips, pinch the edges (circumference) of the hot dough into a ridge. Pinch quickly; dough is hot. You are making a dike around the corn fritter, turning it into a shallow *sope* crater to be filled with *asientos*.

> **Sopes** come with an assortment of toppings—shredded beef, shredded chicken, sausage, and shrimp, to name a few. Pickerel tops his with asientos—literally, the dregs of porcine demise—and the cheapest fat burned off a pig's soul. Sold by the kilo at outdoor rendering stands in local markets (usually on Saturdays and Sundays), lard-strained pork bits refrigerate (and freeze) well.

Return *sope* to the grill (or griddle). Spoon 3 tablespoons of warmed *asientos* into the crater. Spread evenly. Add 3 tablespoons of grated Chihuahua cheese.

Cook until cheese starts to melt, then move *sope* to the edge (of grill or griddle) to keep the bottom from burning. Allow cheese to finish melting.

Warm roasted tomato sauce (if refrigerated). Place guacamole in a bowl.

When *sopes* are cooked, top with shredded lettuce and a forkful of marinated onions. Add a liberal sprinkle of ranch cheese and bathe with spoonfuls of roasted tomato sauce and guacamole. The soul of pork never tasted so divine.

# Cheese Flutes
## *Flautas de Requesón*

*Ingredientes* (two servings)
- 1/2 crisphead lettuce (1/2 *lechuga iceberg*)
- 1 serrano chili (1 *chile serrano*)
- 2 tbsp minced coriander (2 *cucharadas de cilantro picado*)
- 1/4 tsp salt (1/4 *cucharadita de sal*)
- 2 pinches of ground pepper (2 *pizcas de pimienta molida*)
- 1 cup *requesón* (1 *taza de requesón*) (See *Cheeses*, page 23.)
- 8 flute tortillas (8 *tortillas para flautas*) See *Flute tortillas* below.
- 16 toothpicks (16 *palillos*)
- 4 tbsp cooking oil (4 *cucharadas de aceite para cocinar*)
- 1 cup cooked sauce or boiled tomato sauce (1 *taza de salsa cocida o salsa de tomate*) (See *Sauces*, pages 73/75.)

*Equipo*
- Mixing bowl (*tazón para mezclar*)
- Large skillet (*sartén grande*)

*Preparación*

Wash lettuce and cut finely. Wash chili and mince with seeds. In mixing bowl (*tazón para mezclar*), combine chili, minced coriander, salt, pepper, and *requesón*. Mix well.

Place 2 tablespoons of *requesón* mix onto each tortilla—not too close to edge or *requesón* will spill out when the tortilla is fried. Spread cheese mixture evenly toward the center. Roll each tortilla into the shape of a flute and secure with a toothpick. You may use two.

Heat oil in skillet and fry flutes, turning often, until they are golden crisp on the outside. Remove and drain excess oil (Pickerel uses old newspapers untouched by dog). Warm sauce if refrigerated.

Top with shredded lettuce. Spoon on sauce. Watch for toothpicks.

> **Flute tortillas**: Half the thickness of a normal tortilla and shaped in an elongated oval (which, when rolled, resembles a flute—actually a piccolo), a flute tortilla is made especially for deep-frying. Pickerel attempted once to make his own flute tortillas, but these fell apart as he worked for the requisite thinness. Now he buys tortillas para flautas at his local tortillería. He recommends you do the same.

# Little Fat Ones
## Gorditas

Pickerel likes his gorditas—small, thick, deep-fried tortillas—the way he likes his women: petite, curvaceous, and heavy-set (Pickerel diets neither in kitchen nor in bed).

Gorditas may be filled with shredded beef (See *Aztec Soup*, page 204.), shredded horse (See *Cortez-on-Foot Burritos*, page 185.), or shredded chicken (See *Tattered Tortillas with Chicken in Red Chili Sauce*, page 149.), as well as with goat meat, roasted pork, or any other species not outside the chordate phylum. Choose a meat that shreds easily when cooked. (See *Shredding Meat*, page 31.)

### Deep-fried tortillas
*Ingredientes* (for making eight gorditas)
- 1-1/4 cups corn flour (1-1/4 *tazas de harina de maíz*)
- 1 cup cooking oil (1 *taza de aceite para cocinar*)

*Equipo*
- Saucepan (*cazo*)
- Mixing bowl (*tazón para mezclar*)
- Deep skillet (*sartén honda*)

*Preparación*

In saucepan, warm 1-1/4 cups of water. Add warmed water to mixing bowl (*tazón para mezclar*) or dishpan (*bandeja*) with corn flour. Mix well and make dough. (See *Corn Tortillas*, page 47.)

Make 8 dough spheres the size of ping-pong balls. Roll each between palms and flatten into small tortilla paddies the diameter of a coffee mug and 1/4 inch thick. Wet hands to keep dough moist. Mend cracks around dough edges.

With fingertips, pinch the circumference of each fat tortilla into a ridge—making a shallow crater in the center of the dough.

Heat oil in skillet. When hot, fry gorditas, four at a time. Do not turn. Fry until crisp. Remove and stand upright to drain excess oil on kitchen towels (*toallas de cocina*) or, Pickerel style, on old newspapers (*papel periódico*) untouched by dog.

## Bean filling
*Ingredientes* (for filling eight gorditas)
> 1 cup stir-mashed beans (1 *taza de frijoles guisados*)
> (See *Stir-mashed Beans*, page 38.)

## Meat filling
*Ingredientes* (for filling eight gorditas)
> 1 cup shredded meat (1 *taza de carne deshebrada*) from refrigerated leftovers or pick your bird/quadruped and prepare with following ingredients:
> 1/4 kg meat (1/4 *kilo de carne*)
> 1/4 small onion (1/4 de una *cebolla chica*)
> 1 garlic clove, unpeeled (1 *diente de ajo, sin pelar*)
> 1 tsp salt (1 *cucharadita de sal*)
> 1/4 tsp peppercorns (1/4 *cucharadita de pimienta entera*)

*Equipo*
> Large saucepot (*cazuela grande*)

*Preparación*
    Place meat (whole or chopped in large pieces) in 1-1/2 liters of water with onion (unsliced), garlic, salt, and peppercorns. Cover and boil over low heat for 30 minutes (an hour if meat is untamed). Test with fork. When tender, remove from broth and let cool. Using a fork and/or your fingers, shred meat into fibers no thicker than a toothpick. (See *Shredding Meat*, page 31.) Set shredded meat aside. Save stock to make broth (see below).

## Broth
*Ingredientes* (for broth for eight gorditas)
> 1 large tomato (1 *tomate grande*)
> 3 cups of leftover meat stock (3 *tazas de caldo de carne*)
> 1 tsp cooking oil (1 *cucharadita de aceite para cocinar*)

*Equipo*
> Large saucepot (*cazuela grande*)
> Blender (*licuadora*)
> Strainer (*colador*) Pickerel uses mosquito screen.

*Preparación*
    Add uncut tomato to meat stock. Cover and cook 10 minutes over low flame. Have blender washed and ready. Pluck tomatoes from stock,

remove skins, and drop into blender with 2 tablespoons of stock. Blend until smooth.

In saucepot, heat oil. Add blended tomato and fry over low flame until it bubbles and thickens. Pour meat stock into the saucepot with fried tomato, using strainer to remove garlic and onion. Careful—hot stock hitting hot tomato! Stir, cover, and simmer over low heat for 30 minutes. Leave covered. Broth is ready.

## *Sauce*

*Ingredientes* (for sauce for eight gorditas)
- 1 cup prepared broth—see above (1 *taza de caldo ya preparada—ve nota arriba*)
- 1 large tomato (1 *tomate grande*)
- 1 serrano chili (1 *chile serrano*)
- 1/4 small onion (1/4 *cebolla chica*)
- 1/4 garlic clove, peeled (1/4 *diente de ajo, pelado*)
- 1/4 tsp salt (1/4 *cucharadita de sal*)
- A pinch of ground pepper (*una pizca de pimienta molida*)
- A pinch of ground, whole-leaf oregano (*una pizca de hoja de orégano molido*)

*Equipo*
- Saucepan (*cazo*)
- Blender (*licuadora*)

*Preparación*

> After making Little Fat Ones, use leftover beans, broth, meat, sauce, and veggies to make tostadas. (See *Dangerously Crisp Tortilla with Toppings*, page 56.)

In a saucepan with broth, add 1 cup of water, tomato, chili, onion, garlic, salt, pepper, and oregano. Cover and bring to a boil. Lower heat, remove cover, and cook until the chilies soften (test with fork) and half the broth is left. Cool. Remove chili stems and tomato skins with fork. Add contents of saucepan to blender and blend until smooth.

## *Veggie and cheese topping*

*Ingredientes* (for veggie and cheese toppings for eight gorditas*)*
- 1 medium cucumber (1 *pepino mediano*)
- 1/4 crisphead lettuce (1/4 *lechuga iceberg*)
- 3 radishes (3 *rábanos*)
- 1/8 kg hard white cheese for grating (1/8 *kilo de queso blanco duro para rallar*) (See *Cheeses*, page 23.)
- 2 small onions (2 *cebollas chicas*) Pickerel prefers red onion (*cebolla morada*)

on his gorditas.
2 limes (2 *limones*)
1/2 tsp salt (1/2 *cucharadita de sal*)
2 tbsp vinegar (2 *cucharadas de vinagre*) Pickerel uses white cane vinegar.

*Equipo*
Cheese grater (*raspador de queso*)
Lime squeezer (*exprimidor de limón*)

*Preparación*

Peel and slice cucumbers thinly. Chop lettuce finely. Slice radishes. Grate cheese. Place all of the above in separate bowls (*tazones*).

Halve onions, slice into rainbows, and place in bowl (*tazón*). Slice limes and squeeze onto onions. Add salt, vinegar, and 1/4 cup of warm water (*agua tibia*). Mix, cover, and marinate 15 minutes.

### Preparing your gorditas

Spoon a thin layer of warm beans onto each gordita. Follow with a spoonful of shredded meat. Add veggies next—lettuce first, cucumber, then radish. Layer carefully. Add a forkful of onions, spreading them evenly across the gordita. Sprinkle grated cheese on top and spoon on sauce—as much as you dare.

Pour a cupful of broth. Squeeze in half a lime. Stir.

Option #1: Spoon broth on gordita and take a bite, grabbing a little of everything.

Option #2: Do not spoon on broth. Instead, take a bite, grab a little of everything, and then wash it down with a sip of broth.

# Lime Recipes

## Recetas con Limón

*Lima boba* (Daft lime)
*Lima ácida* (Acid lime)
*Limón criollo* (Creole lime)
*Limón chico* (Small lime)
*Limón chiquito* (Smallest lime)
*Limón de Colima* (Coliman lime)
*Limón corriente* (Ordinary lime)
*Limón agrio* (Bitter lime)
*Limón sutil* (Subtle lime)
*Mexican Names for a Sour Lime*


Mexican Potato

Green Tomatoes and Cucumber

Rooster's Beak Fruit Cocktail

Spiny, aromatic, and urine-resistant, Pickerel's solitary lime tree is a tribute to botanical survival. It is also a lime tree waiting for a miracle—the miracle of Pickerel choking on a lime slice with no one nearby to perform the Heimlich. Dog-dug, unfertilized, and watered only when Pickerel drinks excessively (or when the latrine is occupied), its heroic lime legacy has yet to propagate, in spite of Pickerel spitting lime seeds into every corner of his weedy plat.

While he expects his lime tree to wither and die any day, Pickerel savors its fruit in the meantime. When his fanless abode becomes a summer sauna and his pantry boasts tubers, tomatoes, and tropical fruit, he refreshes himself (and tames his foul mood) with one of his favorite lime concoctions described below.

Emerging sudoriferous and half-naked into his weedy plat, he retrieves any yellow, fully ripened limes that have fallen to the ground. Next, he picks from his tree the limes that are light green and soft to the touch. Finally, Pickerel examines his handful harvest, looking for the heaviest lime. This he saves for a special duty—the duty of battling flies that try to get into the bottled beer Pickerel opens every afternoon as he languishes in the heat. One lime alone wins the battle—perched strategically atop the drinking end of his bottle—and not even the large, turd-fed flies visiting from Pickerel's latrine are strong enough to roll it off.

Lime over flies—one of nature's small victories.

# Mexican Potato
## *Jícama*

Pronounced: HEE-kah-mah. The Aztecs called it *xícamatl*. Modern colloquialists know it as the Mexican potato, the Mexican yambean, the Mexican turnip, or south-of-the-border sweet p'tater.

This humble vegetable and member of the vine-creeping, legume family (distant cousin to the bean) is a welcome, though transient, visitor to Pickerel's fruit cellar (aka the coolest corner of his dirt-floor abode). Radish-shaped, this bulbous root has a thin, light brown skin covering a white, crispy, succulent flesh that Pickerel eats raw and with his mouth open—producing an offensively loud crunching noise.

Unfortunately, no jicamas grow within walking distance of Pickerel's unnamed and tomato-crazed city. So when our hero hankers for jicama, he must head to his local market. Cheaply priced (3 pesos or 30 pennies each) and available year-round, these globulous tubers rise above every other vegetable in the market stalls—piled on top of one another like turnips at a legume orgy. Pickerel is particular about picking his jicama. He avoids large ones, which have a woody taste, selecting instead firm, medium (1 to 2 lb) tubers, which are the most flavorful (sweet *and* nutty). His tubers must also have dry roots and show no cracks, bruises, or abrasions. When jicama vendors see Pickerel approaching, they cross themselves and cry "*Dios mío!*" hoping he will suddenly veer off toward the potatoes.

*Ingredientes* (makes 4–5 cups of chopped jicama)
- 1 medium jicama (1 *jícama mediana*)
- 1 tbsp salt (1 *cucharada de sal*)
- 3 limes (3 *limones*)
- 2 tsp Salsa Huichol or Salsa en Polvo Tajín (2 *cucharaditas de Salsa Huichol o Salsa en Polvo Tajín*) (See Bottled Sauces, page 29.)

*Equipo*
- Sharp kitchen knife (*cuchillo filoso*)
- Vegetable peeler (*pelador de verdura*)
- Large bowl (*tazón grande*)
- Lime squeezer (*exprimidor de limón*)
- Toothpicks (*palillos*)

*Preparación*

Wash jicama. Using a sharp knife, remove root. With same knife, lift the brown periderm (jicama skin) at the edge of the root cut. Peel the skin by pulling it back from rootstalk. It will come off in strips. You are "skinning" a jicama.

With vegetable peeler, peel the coarse, fibrous layer beneath the skin until you reach the ivory-white vegetable flesh. Wash again.

Halve jicama from top to bottom. Cut halves into pencil-thick slices. Lay each slice flat and cut into sticks (again, pencil-thick). Cut sticks into bite-size lengths. Place in bowl (*tazón*) and chill for 30 minutes. Add salt. Mix well. Slice limes and squeeze juice. Add salsa or chili powder. Mix again. Use toothpicks as forks.

# Green Tomatoes and Cucumber
## Tomate Verde y Pepino

Pickerel picks his green tomatoes from the same place he picks his red ones—the unguarded fields of local tomato farmers. If trespassing on private property goes against your upbringing or runs counter to sound legal counsel, purchase your ripe and unripe tomatoes at a local market or visit the nearest tomato-packing shed. These *empaques de tomate* offer green tomato culls at below-market prices (just bring a pail). In the days when Pickerel was motorized, he often filled the trunk of his Chevy Nova with culled green tomatoes offered freely by women working on the cullying conveyors. Terrified by Pickerel's lecherous grin and recurrent winking, they wanted him to be gone as soon as possible. With too many green tomatoes to eat, Pickerel gave the surplus to a neighbor, who fed them to his pig.

*Ingredientes* (one serving)
- 1 cucumber (1 *pepino*)
- 2 green tomatoes (2 *tomates verdes*)
- 1 tsp salt (1 *cucharadita de sal*)
- 2 limes (2 *limones*)
- Bottled sauce—optional (*Salsa in botella—optional*)

*Equipo*
- Large bowl (*tazón grande*)
- Lime squeezer (*exprimidor de limón*)

*Preparación*

Peel cucumber, quarter lengthwise, and slice into bite-size portions. Core tomatoes and chop into the same size pieces as cucumber. Add salt. Squeeze limes over ingredients. Mix well. Add bottled sauce to taste.

# *Rooster's Beak Fruit Cocktail*
## Pico de Gallo

Vacationing gringos and clueless Canadian tourists often confuse *salsa fresca* (fresh sauce) for *pico de gallo*. While Pickerel habitually shuns the former and yawnfully dismisses the latter, he invites everyone else to sample his authentic, fruit-concocted rooster beak—sour, salty, and spicy. Also color-coded for those who eat with their eyes.

*Ingredientes* (makes 8 cups)
- 1 cucumber (1 *pepino*)
- 1/2 small jicama (1/2 *jícama chica*)
- 2 oranges (2 *naranjas*)
- 1 medium-size watermelon wedge (1 *trozo mediano de sandia*)
- 1 mango (1 *mango*)
- 3 limes (3 *limones*)
- 5 chiltepin or piquín chilies (5 *chiles chiltepín o piquín*) *Tajin* chili powder may be substituted. (See *Bottled Salsas*, page 29.)
- 2 tsp salt (2 *cucharaditas de sal*)

*Equipo*
- Mixing bowl (*tazón para mezclar*)
- Mortar and pestle (*molcajete y tejolote*)
- Lime squeezer (*exprimidor de limón*)
- Toothpicks (*palillos*)

*Preparación*

Wash fruit well. Peel cucumber, quarter lengthwise, and slice into bite-size portions. Peel jicama (See *Mexican Potato*, page 219.) and halve from top to bottom. Cut halves into pencil-thick slices. Lay each slice flat and cut into sticks (again, pencil-thick). Cut sticks into bite-size lengths.

Peel oranges and divide into sections (Pickerel buys his oranges from orange-thieving boys who juggle them for tips on busy street corners). Cut watermelon flesh from rind, remove seeds, and cube. Peel mango and chop into bite-size pieces.

Place fruit with jicama and cucumber in mixing bowl (*tazón para mezclar*) and chill for 30 minutes.

Slice limes. Grind chilies in *molcajete*. When fruit has chilled, squeeze in lime. Add salt and ground chili. Mix well. Use toothpicks as forks.

# Desserts

## Postres

*Pícaro* (ˈpē-kä-ˌrō); *Sp. n., pl.* –ros (-rōz′):
1. rogue, thief, vagabond, adventurer
2. a warm, often spicy dessert (*mex.*)
3. "Pickerel" pronounced in Spanish

Rice in Milk

Thin Beer Crêpes

Cold Coconut

Mango

Green Corn Tamales

Pickerel's dessert menu offers something for every poor gringo taste—sweet or sour, warm or cool, starchy or fruity, with alcohol or without—while keeping in mind the poor gringo's peso-impoverished pocketbook. As for Pickerel *making* desserts, he does so when (a) the main ingredient is either free or easily pilfered, (b) company is arriving and Pickerel needs to borrow money from one of his satiated and/or intoxicated guests, (c) he has nothing to do, is bored with life, wallowing in self-pity, craving his mother's Boston cream pie, and he is holding enough pesos (fleeced from some innocent native) to make dessert.

# Rice in Milk
## Arroz con Leche

Pickerel has not enjoyed rice this much since he ate bowlfuls of Snap, Crackle and Pop to get the free Mini Frisbee inside the box. Pickerel collected them all. Box tops and proofs of purchase paved his dear mother's road to ruin. The cost of envelopes and postage alone were enough to make her threaten to feed Pickerel oatmeal.

Today, he is too poor to hobnob with Kellogg's or any other of the big guns from Battle Creek. Still, he likes his rice in milk.

*Ingredientes* (serves five)
- 1 vanilla bean (1 *vaina de vainilla*) or 1 tbsp vanilla extract (1 *cucharada de extracto de vainilla*) (See *Vanilla*, page 27, for comments on vanilla extracts.)
- 1 cup long-grain, unconverted, white rice (1 *taza de arroz blanco, grano largo y fino*)
- 2 cups raw milk (2 *tazas de leche bronca*) (See *Gordas con Natas y Chile Chiltepín*, page 93.), or use 1-1/2 cups evaporated milk (1-1/2 *tazas de leche evaporada*—Carnation brand called Clavel).
- 3 orange leaves or 3 slices of orange peel (3 *hojas de árbol de naranja o 3 rebanadas de cascara de naranja*)
- 1 large (2") piece of cinnamon bark (1 *pieza grande de cáscara de canela*) (See *Cinnamon*, page 24.)
- 1/3 cup brown sugar (1/3 *taza de azúcar mascabada*—a moist, dark brown sugar with the molasses flavor of sugarcane juice; cheaper than refined sugar)

*Equipo*
- Large saucepan with cover (*cazuela grande con tapadera*)
- Serving bowl (*tazón hondo*)
- Mortar and pestle (*molcajete y tejolote*)

*Preparación*

Split vanilla bean lengthwise, scraping the seeds free from both sides with the edge of a knife. The seeds of 1 bean equal 2 teaspoons of vanilla extract.

Wash rice. In saucepan, bring rice to a boil in 2 cups of water. Lower heat and cover. Cook until water is gone and rice is tender (about 10 minutes).

Keeping saucepan over low heat, add milk, orange leaves (or rinds), and cinnamon (break into small pieces first). Stir. Add brown sugar and vanilla seeds. Mix well. Cook over low heat, stirring often to keep rice from sticking to the pan bottom. Before bubble holes appear in rice surface, remove from heat and cover. Cool before placing in a serving bowl (*tazón hondo*). Chill for 3 hours and serve with a sprinkle of ground cinnamon bark on top (poor gringos grind with *molcajete*; everyone else use a coffee grinder or spice mill). Watch for the vanilla seeds.

# Thin Beer Crêpes
## *Crepas de Cerveza*

To avoid opening a fresh bottle of beer for this recipe, Pickerel first gathers beer from bottles opened the evening before. If he entertained the previous evening, he collects the requisite 8 fluid ounces in short order, mixing labels as needed (the day-old flavor of dead yeast and esters is not a problem). If Pickerel partied alone, however, he must shake his empty beer bottles with a dancing-for-rain desperation to extract even a few drops. In the end, he grabs a cold one from the fridge, measures 1 cup, and resigns himself to drinking the rest—while he crêpes.

> Serve for breakfast, dessert, or when you run over a jaywalking French tourist—as Pickerel did—and you are obliged to bring him home and feed him until he recovers his bad attitude.

*Ingredientes* (makes twelve)
1 cup wheat flour (1 *taza de harina de trigo*)
2 eggs (2 *huevos*)
1/4 cup milk (1/4 *taza de leche*)
1 cup beer (1 *taza de cerveza*)
2 tbsp melted margarine (2 *cucharadas de margarina derretida*)
1/2 cup grated Chihuahua cheese (1/2 *taza de queso de Chihuahua rallado*) (See *Cheeses*, page 23.)

*Equipo*
   Mixing bowl (*tazón para mezclar*)
   Whisk (*varilla*)
   Large skillet (*sartén grande*)

*Preparación*
   Combine all ingredients except cheese in mixing bowl. Beat with a whisk if you have one (Pickerel does not, so he uses a spoon) until batter is smooth. Add cheese. Batter (with flecks of cheese) should be runny. Add beer (not milk) to achieve the desired consistency. Let mixture sit for 1 hour. Beer needs time to become acquainted with its strange bedfellows. Heat skillet.
   Pour batter onto hot skillet, making flapjack circles the size of compact disks. If the consistency is right, the crêpe should be thin enough to flip after cooking 30 seconds. Another 30 on the backside, and *listo*—light brown on both sides.
   Top with your favorite affordable fruit topping. Pickerel tops his thin beer crêpes with a trickle of mango liqueur—if he has any left to trickle.

# Cold Coconut
## Coco Helado

Pickerel knows a prepubescent boy who, for one peso (a dime), will climb any coconut palm in the public domain. No matter if the tree is lining a busy boulevard, standing in a botanical park, or adorning a government building, he will shimmy skyward, twist off a ripe drupe, hold its fibrous husk with his teeth, and then descend with it—all with simian quickness and pesos chinking in his pocket. Customers know this wiry, streetwise youngster with a felonious lexicon as El Changuito—the little monkey. Pickerel has considered adopting him—to facilitate a steady supply of coconuts—but now has thought better of it. Recently, El Changuito was apprehended descending a local church steeple with a bronze bell clapper tied to his waist (to sell to a crooked metal merchant). Though Pickerel admires the boy's temerity and his good taste in scrap metal, he has no room for another thief in his house. With Pickerel at home, one is enough.

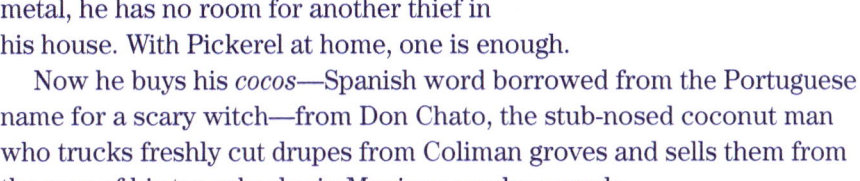

Now he buys his *cocos*—Spanish word borrowed from the Portuguese name for a scary witch—from Don Chato, the stub-nosed coconut man who trucks freshly cut drupes from Coliman groves and sells them from the rear of his ten-wheeler in Mexican produce yards.

Produce yards (*yardas*) are the best places to buy green, freshly cut coconuts. While the drupes sold in city markets are adequate for coconut meat, they are usually too old or too ripe to have coconut water. (Drinking coconut water is half the pleasure of eating a cold coconut.) Unlike Mexican *mercados*, which are congested and centrally located, Mexican produce yards are sprawling, fairground markets found on the outskirts of a city. Every *yarda* has its Don Chato (though not necessarily one with a nose shortened by a coconut machete). Ask for a tender coconut (*coco tiernito*). Its fibrous husk should be rock hard; its color, bright green. Shake it. You should hear (and feel) the heavy sloshing of coconut water inside. If not, you are holding a *coco sazón*—a mature coconut—one with more meat than water. Ask for another, and get your machete ready.

*Ingredientes*
- 1 green coconut (1 *coco tiernito*)
- Straw (1 *popote*)
- Spoon (1 *cuchara*)
- 1/2 tsp salt (1/2 *cucharadita de sal*)
- 1 tsp Salsa Huichol (1 *cucharadita de Salsa Huichol Salsa*) (See *Bottled Sauces*, page 29.)
- 2 limes (2 *limones*)

*Equipo*
- Machete (1 *machete*)
- Chopping block (*un tronco de madera donde cortar cocos*) Pickerel uses a cottonwood stump for his chopping.
- Lime squeezer (*exprimidor de limón*)
- Toothpicks (*palillos*)

> **Safety note**: If unfamiliar with the wielding of a machete or if you have axed your leg while splitting firewood, stop here! Get hammer and a 6-inch nail. Make hole in coconut with nail and pour out water. (You will have to shake coconut.) Use hammer to break apart coconut husk. Peel it from the hard coconut nut. Wrap nut in cloth or towel and break open with hammer. Eat meat with a spoon.

*Preparación*

Chill coconut for 2 hours. Pickerel uses a 5-gallon pail with ice (*hielo*). Those residing near a body of fresh water—river, lake, pond, or neighborhood pool—may cool coconuts (and watermelons) by immersion. Dry-landers use a refrigerator.

Lay your coconut crossways on a chopping block and begin whacking at the pointed end (the one attached to tree). Your task is to whittle off the upper third of the husk until you reach the top of the nut. This will take several whacks. Keep your cut flat (perpendicular to the coconut axis), trimming away an inch or two of husk with each slice. In a green coconut, the nut is soft and easily cut. Do not cut off too much husk or you will section the nut, spilling the coconut water. Ideally, you want to nick the nut, making a small hole in which to insert a straw. When the coconut starts to leak, stop trimming—the nut is cut. Quickly lay down machete. Hold coconut upright. Poke straw into leaking hole. And sip.

For Pickerel, a sip of cold coconut water is Frost in a Frigidaire. Frost, as in Robert Lee Frost—fellow New Englander and Pickerel's chilly worded muse in hot weather. (If the old poet had lived in the tropics, he would have been a climber of *cocos*, not a swinger of birches.)

You may also pour coconut water into a glass, plastic bag, or pitcher to save for later.

With coconut water drained, take machete and chop the coconut nut in half. Using a spoon, scrape the layer of coconut meat loose from inside both halves of the nut. (In a tender coconut, this layer of milky endosperm is thin, soft as gelatin, and easy to scoop.) Combine meat from both halves into the half without the straw hole. Cut meat into bite-size pieces with spoon. Add salt and salsa. Cut limes and squeeze. Mix well, and use toothpicks as forks to eat the soft, sweet coconut meat bathed in spicy, salty lime juice.

Whoever said a world of relief lies in one cold coconut knew there was life before the coconut daiquiri.

# Mango
## Mango

Not just a dessert fruit, a mango is an everymexican fruit—a lush, tropical fix even the poor can afford. Eaten ripe, green, on a stick, in a cup, chopped, whole, limed, salted, with chili or without, Mexico has a mango for every desire, every taste. There are pineapple mangos the shape of kidneys with yellow centers flavored of pineapple. There are parrot mangos, long and lean, their pulp bright orange. There are papaya mangos, pearl mangos, and mangos with proper names like Diplomat, Kate, Kent, and Hayden. There are the tiny lemon mangos (six can fit in one hand) and the smooth, thin-skinned mango *zapote*, big as a softball—a mango to bury your face in. Then there is the Manila mango, whose small, flat seed, thin as a coin, was accidentally introduced in the pocket of a man from Manila, dropped into Mexican dirt the first time he got rolled. Sweetest of the heirloom mangos, the Manila is Pickerel's favorite—for practical and poetic reasons. Not as stringy as other mangos, its pulp does not cling to Pickerel's unflossed teeth. And its long and tapering shape reminds him of a perfect tear—the icon of Pickerelian life.

As for green mangos, Pickerel eats these too. Their pulp is white and dense like a turnip; the seeds are soft and chewable. Pickerel considers himself a green mango expert due to the number of stomachaches he has endured after eating too many of them. He digestively aggravates their bittersweet flavor with a squeeze of lime juice, a dash of powdered chili pepper, and a heavy dose of salt.

When Pickerel tires of green mangos, he turns his thieving eyes (and prehensile organs) to *popozahui* mangos. Pronounced POPO-SAW-WEE, this Indian word with a delicious sound means "place of swelling"—the name given to a mango balanced between green and ripe, one swelling with color, wetness, and sweetness. All mangos are *popozahui* for a short time (a matter of days) before their little engines of starch race to become sugar, giving them the red and orange glow of ripeness.

Once ripe, a mango stops being a polite fruit, and eating it becomes a self-proclaiming and scandalous affair. Instead of getting smaller with each bite, a ripe mango spreads. When Pickerel eats a ripe mango, orange strings hang from his chin and nose. Mango juice stains his shirtfront. Mango strings wedge between his incisors, adding a pumpkin-ravaged ghoulishness to his bright orange smile.

There are many ways to eat a mango. Some Mexicans eat it skin and all, others only the pulp. Still others linger on the seed, while a few attempt not to get wet. They spear their mango onto a pointed stick (making it a big lollipop) and peel the skin back carefully with their teeth, trying to eat it delicately. Carefree souls, on the other hand, dive nose first into their mangos, not stopping until they emerge on the other side. The thorough and thrifty turn their mangos inside out, leaving the skin clean and shiny, while the patient and palsied squeeze their fruit between both hands, massaging the leathery skin with manipulative pressure until the succulent pulp turns liquid and can be sucked out through a tiny, tooth-torn hole.

Pickerel recommends all of the above, as well as any other mango-eating techniques you may wish to invent. His simple recipe leaves the barn door open.

*Ingredientes*
   1 mango (1 *mango*)

*Preparación*
   Wash it.

# Green Corn Tamales
## *Tamales de Elote*

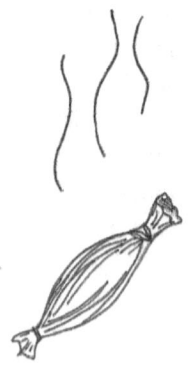

Pickerel and cornfields go back to the days when a younger but still shameless Pickerel escaped the burbs of Beantown on summer evenings, racing his Willy's jeep north on I-93 to prowl the hillside corn patches of taciturn (and early-to-bed) New Hampshire farmers. Always successful in his furtive harvests, only once did Pickerel have Christ's teeth scared out his head by a rampaging raccoon.

To this day, green fields of corn continue to welcome Pickerel between their dense, shadowy rows. They embrace him with their sharp-edged leaves, dropping aphids down his neck and whispering dried-tassel songs of corn lonesomeness in his ear. In deference to falling farm subsidies (no ethanol production in Mexico yet) and the ridiculously low price of silage, Pickerel picks only what he can eat—never leaving a cornfield with more ears (*elotes*) than he can carry.

---

For those who pick their corn from market stalls, choose only tender ears (elotes tiernitos). Overripened ears (elotes sazones ó pasados) require more shortening and butter to make the loose, pasty dough needed for tamales—and more ingredients mean a poorer gringo. Ears with dark, deep green husks (no yellowing near the tips) have the softest white corn (cacahuazintle) underneath. Test for tenderness by pressing corn kernels (with fingernail) until they pop and exude kernel "milk"—the starchy liquid inside the maturing grain. Tender corn will leave your fingertips wet.

While most market vendors loudly object to a customer husking unpaid corn and poking a fingernail into the kernels, poor gringos may get away with this. Corn vendors figure that most gringos in Mexican markets are lost, clueless, or stupid. Why hassle them over poked corn in a foreign language? Just overcharge and be done with the transaction. Then everyone is happy. So peel and poke away.

---

*Ingredientes* (makes about two dozen tamales)
12 ears green field corn (12 *elotes tiernitos*)
1/2 cup (1 stick) margarine (1/2 *taza o una barra de margarina*)
1/4 kg (1-1/3 cups) vegetable shortening or lard (1/4 *kilo o 1-1/3 tazas de manteca vegetal o manteca de puerco*)
2-1/2 tsp salt (2-1/2 *cucharaditas de sal*)
1/2 tsp baking powder (1/2 *cucharadita de polvo para hornear*) Pickerel uses Mexico's Royal brand—*Royal Polvo para Hornear*)
3/4 cup sugar (3/4 *taza de azúcar*)

*Equipo*
  1 machete or wide-bladed kitchen knife (cleaver) (1 *machete*)
  Sharp kitchen knife (*cuchillo filoso*)
  Corn mill (*molino de maíz*)
  Saucepan (*cazo*)
  2 mixing bowls (2 *tazones para mezclar*) or 2 dishpans (2 *bandejas*)
  Steamer (*olla vaporera*)

*Preparación*

With machete, chop off the stalk end of each ear. Chop flush at the base of the husks about 1 inch above where the stalk attaches. Unwrap and discard outer husk (*hojas*). Carefully unfurl each inner leaf, unraveling it without tearing or folding. Two to five leaves will unwrap cleanly. Save these. The leaves nearest the ear will be too thin to peel or too small to use. Remove and discard these. Clean the husked ears of corn silk. Set clean leaves aside. You will soon select the largest for filling.

With a sharp knife, remove any rotten, blackened, or corn-bore-residing patches from corncob. Next, shave kernels off cob and into a large bowl or dishpan. Cut vertically, holding the thick end of the ear near you. Take care not to add your blood to the shaved kernels. As you cut, keep the angle of the knife blade parallel to the corn. If the cutting angle is too steep, you will cut into the cob. If it is too shallow, only the tops of kernels will shave off. Twelve ears will make about 8 cups of shaved corn.

Using corn mill, grind the shaved kernels into a milky paste. This is the real work in making tamales—turning the grinder handle around and around, up then down. As Pickerel grinds, he allows his thoughts to drift to synonymous but more agreeable gyrations, sometimes enlisting the coordination of his pelvic muscles. Adjust corn mill so that corn kernel's waxy sheaths are finely ground.

Melt butter and shortening together in a saucepan over low heat. Butter will melt first. Saucepan should not get hot enough for shortening to smoke.

**Health note**: Since Pickerel has evolved a chemical immunity to most agricultural pesticides, herbicides, and fungicides—due to overexposure while thieving from local fields—he does not worry about washing his corn leaves. Besides, Pickerel picked the ears himself. He knows if he peed before picking or not. If you are not privy to this information or are unsure of your resistance to crop chemicals, Pickerel recommends that you rinse your corn leaves and let them drain before proceeding.

Combine in a second mixing bowl (*tazón para mezclar*) or dishpan (*bandeja*) the melted better and shortening with baking powder, 1 teaspoon of salt, and the ground corn. Mix into a loose, pasty dough. Add sugar. Stir and taste. The mixture should be sweet, with chewy corn in the background. Add sugar to taste.

Select the largest cornhusks for filling—no tears, no holes, no corn-bore stains. Purists trim the pointed ends with a knife. Pickerel doesn't bother. Holding an open husk in one hand, fill with one serving spoon (*cuchara de guisa*)—about 4 tablespoons—of corn dough. Place in the middle of leaf (slightly nearer to the wide end). Cover filling by first folding one side of the cornhusk over the dough, then folding the other side of the cornhusk across the top, making a snug overlap. Fold down the pointed end of husk, covering the leaf seam as far as the middle of the tamale. You now have an open-ended tamale package. Place in a pan with folds facing down.

In steamer, heat 2 liters of water with 1-1/2 teaspoons of salt.

When the water begins to boil, place tamales in steamer. Position horizontally, elevating the open end of each to prevent dough from sliding out. Place crossways, one on top of the other, building a tamale tower. Cover and steam for 1 hour 15 minutes. Keep heat low (no rolling boil) to prevent steamer from running out of water. Meanwhile, clean up mess and wash grinder.

When tamales are cooked, remove from steamer, and serve warm. Pickerel eats his green corn tamales straight from the husks (no fork needed), accompanied by a tall glass of cold milk.

Refrigerate leftover tamales in a sealed plastic bag—no longer than a week. They also freeze well.

---

**Reheating (two options)**

1. Fill a wide pot with 1 inch of water. Place an inverted bowl on the bottom of the pot. Lay tamales (inside their husks) on top of the inverted bowl. Cover pot, bring water to a boil, and steam tamales for 10 minutes. This is a baño maría.
2. Carefully remove tamale from husk and fry in skillet with 1 teaspoon of butter over low heat. Turn once, frying both sides until tamale is golden brown.

# Beverages

## Bebidas Refrescantes

**Aguas Frescas Ponce de León**
(Ponce de León's Fresh Waters)
The name of a beverage stand popular
with the Mexican gray-haired crowd
Los Mochis, Sinaloa

Steeped Rice Water

Hibiscus Cooler

Tamarindade

Barley Water

Plum Water

There are so many beverages Pickerel would love to include—his coconut *pulque* cocktail, his vanilla maguey milkshake, the tamarind tequila sunstroke, a mango mezcal fizz, the Bacanora mama, or just plain *tepache* (made from fermented pineapple rinds and garbanzo—this recipe courtesy of an ex-con who, while in Mexican prison, perfected forty-eight-hour, ready-to-drink alcohol from prison kitchen scraps).

But Pickerel has promised his publisher, parole officer, and AA group sponsor (Mexican chapter) that he would not include alcoholic beverages in these recipes. And Pickerel keeps his promises.

# Steeped Rice Water
## *Horchata de Arroz*

Until Pickerel discovered the *michelada*,* steeped rice water was his preferred beverage for hangover rehydration.

Now he makes *horchata* when he wants to sip rice, not chew it. Pickerel uses vanilla beans, not vanilla extract, in his recipe. (See *Vanilla*, page 27.) He splits 1 bean, scraping the seeds free from both sides of the pod with the edge of his knife. The seeds from 1 bean equal 2 teaspoons of vanilla extract.

As for the cinnamon in this recipe, Pickerel uses the loose bark variety sold as *canela*—long, fragrant quills stealing the show at market spice stalls.

When he can afford evaporated milk and almonds, Pickerel adds both to his steeped rice water. Otherwise, he substitutes water for the first, nothing for the second.

> Vanilla pods may be dried, cut finger-length, and buried in your sugar pot to sweeten coffee that you pretend to be sipping at Starbucks.

*Ingredientes* (makes 3.5 liters)
- 1 cup long-grain, unconverted, white rice (1 *taza de arroz blanco, grano largo y fino*)
- 1/4 cup raw almonds (1/4 *taza de almendras crudas*)
- Seeds scraped from 1 vanilla bean (*semillas de una vaina de vainilla*) See above.
- 2 large pieces (2") of cinnamon bark (2 *piezas grandes de cáscara de canela*) (See *Cinnamon*, page 24.)
- 1 cup evaporated milk (1 *taza de leche evaporada*) The Carnation brand is called Clavel.
- 1 cup sugar (1 *taza de azúcar*)

*Equipo*
- Mortar and pestle (*molcajete y tejolote*)
- Small saucepan (*cazo chico*)
- Mixing bowl (*tazón para mezclar*)
- Blender (*licuadora*)
- Strainer (*colador*)
- Large saucepan with cover (*cazo grande con tapadera*)
- 4-liter pitcher (*una jarra de 4 litros*)

---

* A beer cocktail made with salt, lime juice, Tabasco, and Worcestershire sauces.

*Preparación*

Grind rice in *molcajete* until powdery. (Not a poor gringo? Use your coffee grinder.)

If adding almonds to the recipe, blanch and peel as follows: boil 2 cups of water in saucepan, add almonds, wait 60 ticks, remove almonds, cool, then press each nut between thumb and forefinger, squirting almond from skin.

In mixing bowl, add 4 cups of cold water, ground rice, peeled almonds, vanilla seeds, and cinnamon (break into small pieces first). Stir well, cover, and refrigerate overnight.

The next morning, pour rice mixture into blender with evaporated milk (or 1 cup of cold water). Blend until smooth. The cinnamon should mulch into brown specks.

Strain contents of blender into a large pitcher (purists use cheesecloth; Pickerel uses mosquito screen). This is your *horchata* concentrate. Add sugar and 8 cups of cold water. Stir well before serving over ice (*hielo*). In fact, always stir before serving. Otherwise, the chalky rice grounds settle to the bottom and your *horchata* tastes like skimmed milk from a rice cow.

# Hibiscus Cooler
## *Aqua de Jamaica*

If Pickerel lived near a hibiscus plantation, he would visit its herbaceous shrubbery as soon as the flowers fell. He would handpick the bright red, swollen calyces, and he would sun dry them on his rooftop.

And if Pickerel lived on the moon, he would make cheese.

Instead, he buys his hibiscus flowers (*flor de Jamaica*)—dried, packaged, and ready to boil—at the local market. Resembling withered red arachnids and smelling pungently of a damp cellar, *flor de jamaica* stores best inside a double plastic bag, knotted tightly.

*Ingredientes* (makes 3 liters)
- 3 cups dried hibiscus sepals (3 *tazas de flor de jamaica*)
- 1/4 tsp salt (1/4 *cucharadita de sal*)
- 3 limes (3 *limones*)
- 1/2 cup sugar (1/2 *taza de azúcar*)

*Equipo*
- Large saucepot (*cazuela grande*)
- Strainer (*colador*)
- 4-liter pitcher (*una jarra de 4 litros*)

*Preparación*

In a saucepot with 1 liter of cold water, boil sepals 15 minutes. Water will turn the color of boiled beets. Keep covered.

When cool, strain hibiscus liquid into an empty pitcher (Pickerel uses mosquito screen). Add salt and squeeze in limes. Stir well. Add 2 liters of cold water and stir in sugar. Chill.

> The sweet, tart, cranberry-tasting drink that comes from boiling dried hibiscus sepals is a natural diuretic. Pickerel mentions this not because he has a personal issue with water retention (other than his cirrhotic liver turning tawny), rather for the benefit of poor gringos who—due to the frustrations of living like a Mexican by necessity, not choice—suffer from high blood pressure.

# Tamarindade
## Agua de Tamarindo

> What a fruit! What a tree!
> The Egyptians knew it.
> The Greeks grew it.
> In Burma, the Rain God lives in its shade.
> Tamarind wood fashions into furniture and floors.
> The leaves make poultices, its charcoal, gunpowder.
> Seeds grind into coffee; the bark tans hides.
> Roots whittle into walking sticks.
> Twigs turn into chewsticks; the branches into switches (for birching Jamaicans and bare-bottomed children).
> The pulp cleans brass, flavors Worcestershire sauce, relieves sunstroke, and is a laxative for elephants.
> What a tree! What a fruit!
>
> End of Pickerel's prosaic Ode to Tamarind

Tamarind trees (*árboles de tamarindo*) flourish in Pickerel's poor gringo corner of the planet—in front yards, on city streets, in parks—and along country roads (though he has yet to see one with a horse tied beneath it). Pickerel waits until the gray-green, tender-skinned pods ripen to a cinnamon brown (hollow-sounding when shaken) before he picks them (with the owner's consent, of course). The skins (*cáscaras*) of ripened pods are brittle and easy to shell. The soft, acidic pulp (*pulpa*) is both sweet and tart. On hot days, Pickerel has lost himself for hours sitting under a tamarind tree with ripe pods heaped upon his lap, sucking the tart pulp and dreaming of Burma.

Dried and ready-to-shell tamarind pods (*vainas de tamardindo*) are available year-round in Mexican markets, sold by the kilo. Store in a cool place, sealed in a plastic bag.

*Ingredientes* (makes 3 liters)
8 tamarind pods (8 *vainas de tamarindo*)
1/4 tsp salt (1/4 *cucharadita de sal*)
1 cup sugar (1 *taza de azúcar*)

*Equipo*
Large saucepot (*cazuela grande*)
Strainer (*colador*)
4-liter pitcher (*una jarra de 4 litros*)

*Preparación*
Remove the brittle outer skin (*cáscara*) and the coarse fiber strands (*fibras*) extending the length of each pod. The reddish-brown pulp of the tamarind will be sticky to touch.

Place shelled pulp in a saucepot with 1-1/2 liters

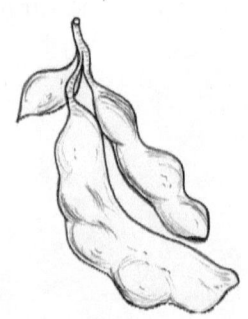

of cold water. Boil 15 minutes. Tamarind pulp will swell and soften. Keep pot covered.

When liquid cools, use fingers (wash hands first) to squeeze the tamarind seeds from the softened pulp. The hard, square-shaped seeds easily separate from boiled tamarind. You do not need to remove seeds, only loosen them from the pulp.

Strain contents of saucepot into pitcher, using a spoon to push pulp through stainer (Pickerel uses mosquito screen). Discard seeds and strained fibers.

To this tamarind concentrate, add salt, sugar, and 1-1/2 liters of cold water. Mix well and chill.

Pickerel drinks tamarindade while he sits in the thin shade of his wash line, wishing he had a tamarind tree in his dooryard but convinced there is order in a universe in which Worcestershire sauce and elephant laxative share what he sips from his glass.

# Barley Water
## Agua de Cebada

Though no stranger to malted barley, Pickerel had yet to discover the enzyme-repressed, sugar-free variety of this cereal grain until he came to Mexico. One heat-soaked summer afternoon as he ambled the unpaved margins of his unnamed city, he came to a shaded street corner where a fat man sat on a stool before a huge glass keg. The keg rested on a tiny table. Its glass sparkled with beaded moisture. Inside the keg was a coffee-brown beverage chilled with glacial chunks of ice. A handwritten sign taped to the table read: *Cebada El Indiote*. The Big Barley Indian. Pickerel stepped to the table and ordered a glass.

Without rising from his stool, the fat man—who was, in fact, the Big Barley Indian—sank a ladle into the depths of the coffee-brown liquid. He pumped the dipper twice, swirled the ice, then lifted the ladle and filled a tall kitchen glass to the brim. His chubby fingertips pulled a straw from a box and poked it into the beverage. "*Un peso*," he grunted, handing over the glass.

Pickerel sipped, digging into his pocket for a peso. Then, as the cool, sweet, grainy flavor of a malthouse floor filled his mouth (shadowed somewhere by chilly vanilla) he dug deeper, deciding to grab two pesos instead of one—for a refill.

Cebada had suddenly taken Pickerel to the North Pole on horseback.

The Big Barley Indian took payment humorlessly, unwilling to engage in Pickerel's exuberant reaction to a refreshing discovery. At a peso a glass, no stupid gringo getting excited about barely water was worth the laugh.

The next day, Pickerel went to the market and bought barley—*cebada*—ready (ground to a powder) and ridiculously cheap. Adding to the ridiculous was the recipe—ridiculously simple, as Pickerel was to find out when he consulted the Big Barley Indian's daughter. A pretty, giggly, underage girl, she detailed both ingredients and proportions (in exchange for Pickerel translating a *Backstreet Boys* song blasting on her radio) while her fat father took a bathroom break. Timing is everything in recipe theft.

*Ingredientes* (makes 1-1/4 liters)
- 1/2 cup barley powder (1/2 *taza de cebada en polvo*—Pickerel buys Siglo XX brand)
- 1/2 cup sugar (1/2 *taza de azúcar*)
- 1/4 tsp salt (1/4 *cucharadita de sal*)

1 cup evaporated milk (1 *taza de leche evaporada*—Carnation brand called Clavel)

Seeds scraped from 1 vanilla bean (*semillas de una vaina de vainilla*) (See Vanilla, page 27.)

*Equipo*

2-liter pitcher (*una jarra de 2 litros*)

*Preparación*

Combine barely powder, sugar, salt, and milk in a pitcher with 1 liter of cold water. Add vanilla seeds. Stir and refrigerate 1 hour. Serve over ice (*hielo*). Stir before refills. Don't swallow vanilla seeds.

# Plum Water
## Agua de Ciruela

The summer before Miriam made her hasty escape, she put the twins to work selling plum-flavored snowcones in front of their house—a little business to supplement her husband's lack of perceivable income. Pickerel had introduced Miriam to the Mexican *raspado*—a naturally flavored, shaved-ice, street corner treat—back in the days when he could still safely be seen with his spouse in the public domain. Soon after this introduction, Miriam became a *raspado* junkie—slurping snowcones every evening, craving snowcones when she was pregnant—plum, her favorite flavor. So that summer, when a neighbor with a prolific plum tree gave Miriam two heaping pails of ripe fruit, the making of plum-flavored snowcones naturally followed. **Side note**: Miriam's little business failed in a matter of days, due mostly to Pickerel draining plum water reserves from their refrigerator after proprietress and employees went to bed.

And now, Pickerel's final testament to Miriam.

To make a plum-flavored snowcone, first you must make plum-flavored water—the recipe for which Pickerel learned, yes, from Miriam. Not only is this her sole contribution to these pages—and fittingly, the last—but it also holds the distinction of being the only recipe in Pickerel's *The Poor Gringo Guide to Mexican Cooking* that never fails to give him diarrhea. Only Pickerel. No one else. Montezuma's revenge renamed. And let it be known that Pickerel boasts a stout bowel—even after he drinks a dozen glasses of plum water.

So Miriam, this one's for you. May life after Pickerel be a Thorazine trip.

### *For ripe plums (ciruela fresca)*
*Ingredientes* (makes 4 liters)
- 1 kg of ripe plums (1 *kilo de ciruelas maduras*), abundantly available when in season. Mexicans give them away!
- 1 cup sugar (1 *taza de azúcar*)
- 1/2 tsp salt (1/2 *cucharadita de sal*)

*Equipo*
- Large saucepot with cover (*cazuela grande con tapadera*)
- Blender (*licuadora*)
- 5-liter pitcher (*una jarra de 5 litros*)

*Preparación*

Wash plums. Place in saucepot with 4 liters of cold water, sugar, and salt. Bring to a rolling boil and cook fruit 20 minutes, stirring occasionally. Plums swell then burst, skins peeling open, exposing pulp. Orange foam rides the boil.

Remove from heat and cool. Pour liquid into a pitcher. Leave cooked fruit in the saucepot. After washing hands, remove plum seeds from cooked fruit. You will have to fish for them, running your fingers through the pulp to find seeds. Pickerel sucks on each before throwing it away.

Place seedless pulp into blender and blend until fruit skins turn to tatters. Add contents of blender to plum liquid in pitcher. Stir well. Chill and serve in tall glass with no straw (plum pieces plug flow). With each sip, soft, sweet plum skins will melt in your mouth.

### *For dried plums* (*ciruela seca*)

*Ingredientes* (makes 4 liters)
- 1 kg of dried plums (1 *kilo de ciruelas secas*), found year-round in Mexican markets
- 1 cup sugar (1 *taza de azúcar*)
- 1/2 tsp salt (1/2 *cucharadita de sal*)

*Equipo*
- Large saucepot with cover (*cazuela grande con tapadera*)
- 5-liter pitcher (*una jarra de 5 litros*)

*Preparación*

Wash plums well. You never know where they have been drying. Place in saucepot with 4 liters of cold water, sugar, and salt. Bring water to a rolling boil and cook fruit 40 minutes, stirring occasionally. Dried plums take twice as long to cook as ripe ones. Plums will swell and turn brown.

Remove from heat and cool. With dried fruit, the flavor of plum water lies *in* the seeds, so do not remove from liquid. Besides, dried plums have twice the number of seeds per kilo as ripe plums, which means you need more time to remove them—time better spent sucking on plum seeds that make it to your mouth.

Pour the entire contents of saucepot into a pitcher. Chill (no ice—*sin hielo*) and serve. Have a spoon handy to fish plums from your glass.

# Appendix

## Killing and Dressing Fowl

**For preparing chicken and squab used in recipes, you will need:**
Short length of rope or cord
Large pot for hot water (stockpot ideal)
Stove (or fire) to heat water and singe feathers
Sharp knife
Cutting board or block
Cold water
Dishpan

Because Pickerel does not raise domestic fowl (he only traps, steals, or runs down wayward birds), he sees no need to feed them or to concern himself with worrisome issues of avian health. For poor gringos who raise their fowl and for those who prefer their chickens and pigeons going to slaughter with clean pipes, purge your bird's digestive tract by taking the animal off its food eight hours before sacrifice. Poor gringos worried about avian flue, bird fever, bruised meat, or abnormal body enlargements should purchase their chicken and squab at a local market.

**Step one—Preparation**: Heat 3 gallons of water in a large pot. The recommended temperature for scalding birds is 140° F. Since Pickerel owns only a rectal thermometer, he waits for the first wisps of steam to rise from his pot. This is his cue that the water is ready for scalding. Do not boil water. Fowl skin tears easily if scalded in water that is too hot.

**Step two—Sacrifice**: Using the short length of cord, hang the bird upside down by its legs. Bind above the feet and use a knot that can be easily undone. Hang the bird from a tree branch, fence post, chair back, table leg, or window awning. Pickerel uses his clothesline. Once upside down, the bird will become still. Take the head in one hand (comb in palm), and place the knife on the *side* of the bird's neck (not its throat) below the ear lobe. Draw knife across the jugular vein until there is a gush of blood. To avoid cutting the animal's windpipe or esophagus, do not press the knife too hard into the neck. Do not decapitate. Avoid blood splattering by holding the bird's head firmly with one hand while restraining its wings loosely with the other. Use dishpan to catch blood. Bleeding takes about 3 minutes. Just before death, the bird will flap its wings in a final struggle.

**Step three—Scalding**: After bird movements stop, scald immediately. Once the carcass cools, picking feathers becomes more difficult. Hold the bird by its feet (or by the cord, which should remain in place), and immerse in the hot water for about 40 seconds (30 seconds for young birds, 50 seconds for an old rooster). Move the bird up and down vigorously in the water so that all feathers are soaked. Hot water also relaxes the muscles holding to feathers. This makes for easier plucking.

**Step four—Plucking**: Hang the bird by one foot after scalding. Remove the feathers by rubbing the carcass against the way the feathers lay. Pluck long wing feathers first, then tail feathers, followed by feathers on legs, breast, neck, and back. Pull wing and tail feathers straight out to avoid skin tears. For difficult-to-remove feathers, use the blunt edge of a knife to grasp and pull feathers from the direction they have grown. Dip bird in hot water again—quickly—to keep carcass from drying. Work around the bird until all feathers are plucked. Older birds will cling to a few hair-like feathers even after scalding. Singe these by rotating the carcass over a low stove flame. Do not catch bird on fire, as Pickerel once did.

**Step five—Evisceration**: Remove the trussing cord from legs and place the plucked carcass on your cutting board or block. Using the knife, remove bird's head. After cutting, you may have to twist it. Next, cut off the feet at the hock joint (upper end of scaly shank of leg) and lop off its preen gland. This is the lobe at the base of the bird's tail. With carcass lying on its back, slit the skin at the bottom of the neck and remove the windpipe, esophagus, and crop. All are connected to the inside of the neck skin. The final step is to open the body cavity. With the carcass still on its back, carefully make a vertical incision from the breastbone down to the anal vent. Take care not to cut into the intestines. Insert your hand into this opening, and gently pull the viscera (intestines, gizzard, heart, reproductive organs, and connective tissue) toward you. The kidneys are close to the backbone. The lungs are embedded in the ribs. Remove both by scraping with fingertips (the lungs are the hardest to remove). With the body cavity eviscerated, rinse carcass in the dishpan with cold water.

**Step six—Dressing**: Since Pickerel immediately reduces his fowl to serving-size pieces and cooks it forthwith (lest its owner suddenly appear and demand that the bird be returned), he does not worry about chilling or storing the carcass. Neither does Pickerel save edible viscera (neck, heart, liver, and gizzard) to prepare as a culinary delight. Instead, he sets them out to attract local felines, which, in turn, become culinary delights themselves—ones not included in this cooking compendium of poor gringo madness.

# Glossary

## A
*aceite de canola:* canola oil
*aceite de maíz:* corn oil
*aceite de cártamo:* safflower oil
*aceite para cocinar:* cooking oil
*acelgas:* Swiss chard
*aceitunas:* olives
*achiote:* a ground spice blend made from pounded annatto seeds
*acitronar:* to fry gently without browning (usually onion or garlic or both)
*adobo:* a sour vinegar paste of ground chilies and herbs
*agrio:* sour or bitter
*aguacate:* avocado
*agua chile (aguachile):* a spicy broth made from boiled chiltepin leaves and chilies
*agua fresca:* a cold drink made from fruits or grains
*agua fria:* cold water
*agua tibia:* warm water
*ahumado:* smoked
*ajo:* garlic
*albóndigas:* meatballs
*almendras:* almonds
*amasar :* to knead
*añejo:* aged
*antojito:* a whim snack to satisfy a food craving
*apio:* celery
*arroz blanco:* white rice
*arroz con leche:* a dessert of rice with milk
*asadera:* unmolded, air-seasoned, fresh cheese
*asado:* roasted
*asientos:* burnt pork bits strained from lard after rendering
*atún enlatado:* canned tuna fish
*aves:* poultry
*azúcar mascabada:* brown sugar
*azúcar refinada:* refined sugar

## B
*bandeja:* dishpan
*bebida refrescante:* a refreshing beverage
*birria:* a spicy meat stew of lamb or goat, steamed or barbecued
*bledo:* green amaranth
*bocadillo:* bite size
*bolsas de plástico:* plastic bag
*borracho:* drunk (Pickerel)
*botana:* snack or appetizer
*burrito:* a folded flour tortilla taco

## C
*caballo:* horse
*cacahuazintle:* a white corn with large kernels
*caguamanta:* a spicy stew made with stingray
*calabaza:* squash
*calabcita:* a small squash, usually zucchini
*cabezas de camarón:* shrimp heads
*caldillo:* an economical soup made with potatoes, machaca, and eggs

*caldo:* broth
*camarón:* shrimp
*canela:* cinnamon
*carbón:* charcoal
*carne:* meat
*carne machaca:* salted, pounded, dried, and shredded meat
*carnitas:* lard-fried pork meat
*carrizo:* a perennial reed whose culm is made into primitive tongs
*cáscara:* skin, rind, or outer shell of a fruit; also tree bark
*cazo:* saucepan
*cazuela:* saucepot
*cebada:* barley; a refreshing drink made from powdered barley
*cebiche:* chopped fish marinated in lime juice
*cebolla blanca:* white onion
*cena:* dinner
*cerdo:* pig or pork
*cilantro:* coriander
*ciruela seca:* dried plum
*ciruela fresca:* fresh plum
*cochinita pibil :* slow-roasted, marinated pork
*cochino:* dirty or messy (Pickerel)
*cocido:* cooked or boiled
*cocina:* kitchen
*coco helado :* cold coconut
*coco tiernito:* a tender coconut, one with more water than meat
*coco sazón:* a mature coconut, one with more meat than water
*codillo de cerdo :* pig hock
*colache:* a combination of unlike ingredients; a dish of squash and cheese
*colador:* strainer
*coliflor:* cauliflower
*comal:* griddle

*comino:* cumin
*comida:* food; the main, midday meal
*conejo:* rabbit
*consomé en polvo:* bouillon powder
*crema:* cream
*cucharada (cuchara sopera):* tablespoon
*cucharadita (cucharita):* teaspoon
*cuchara de guisar:* serving spoon
*cucharón:* ladle
*cuchillo:* knife
*cuete or gusano:* eye of round, heel of round, or bottom of round of beef or horse
*chamuscar:* to scorch (meat)
*charro:* horseman
*chayote:* a pear-shaped, edible gourd; sometimes called vegetable pear
*chicharrón:* lard-fried pork skins
*chilaquiles:* a casserole dish made with tortillas, cheese, and salsa
*chilaquiles rojos:* a casserole dish made with tortillas, cheese, and red salsa
*chilaquiles verdes:* a casserole dish made with tortillas, cheese, and green salsa
*chile ancho:* a dried poblano chili used to make red chili sauce
*chiltepín:* a tiny, oval, long-stemmed chili
*chiles curtidos:* chilies pickled in vinegar
*chiles en escabeche:* sectioned chilies mixed with sliced carrots and onions
*chiles enlatados:* canned chilies
*chiles rellenos:* stuffed chilies

**chipotle:** ripened red jalapeño peppers, dried, smoked, and seasoned
**chiquelites:** garden huckleberry
**chiquihuite:** a woven basket to keep tortillas warm
**chorizo:** pork sausage

## D
**desayuno:** breakfast
**deshebrar:** shred (meat) into fibers
**deshuesar:** to debone
**derretir:** to melt (butter or cheese)
**desmenuzar:** to turn into small pieces
**diente de ajo:** garlic clove
**docena:** one dozen
**dorar:** to fry until golden
**dulce:** sweet

## E
**ejote:** string (green) bean
**elotes tiernitos:** a tender ear of green corn
**elotes maduros:** an overripened ear of corn
**empanizado:** breaded
**enchilada:** corn or flour tortilla wrapped around a filling, covered with cheese and salsa
**enfriar:** to cool or chill
**enjuagar:** to rinse
**ensalada:** salad
**escabeche:** food (chilies, fish) marinated in lime juice
**escurridor:** colander
**espaldilla de res:** brisket or flank steak
**especies:** spices
**epazote:** a strong-scented herb used in boiled beans
**espinazo de cerdo:** pork spine
**estofado:** stewed

**estufa:** stove
**exprimidor de limón:** lime (lemon) squeezer

## F
**falda (for fajitas):** flank or hanger steak
**filete:** filleted fish
**filoso:** sharp
**flauta:** an elongated tortilla, rolled and wrapped around a filling
**flor de calabaza:** squash flower
**flor de jamaica:** hibiscus flower
**freir:** to fry
**fresco:** fresh
**frijoles:** beans
**fritangas:** deep-fried food
**frito:** fried
**frito en agua:** poached

## G
**gallina:** hen
**gallina pinta:** a dish made with whole, white hominy and boiled beans
**galón:** gallon
**gorda:** fat; a thickly filled corn tortilla
**gorgojo del frijol:** bean bore
**guacamole:** a relish, filling, and topping made with avocado
**guajillo:** a large, reddish-brown chili; dried and used in red chili sauces
**guisar:** to cook, stew, or stir-fry

## H
**harina de maíz:** corn flour
**harina de trigo:** wheat flour
**harina de trigo integral:** whole wheat flour
**hervir:** to boil
**hoja de orégano:** oregano leaf

**hondo:** deep (as in a deep skillet)
**horchata de arroz:** a refreshing beverage made from steeped rice and sweetened with vanilla
**hoyo:** barbeque pit or hole
**huesos de tuétano:** marrow or soup bones
**huevo:** egg

## J
**jalapeños en escabeche:** pickled jalapeno peppers mixed with sliced carrots and onions
**jícama:** Mexican potato; also called yam bean
**jitomate:** tomato

## L
**laurel:** bay leaf
**leche bronca :** raw milk
**leche evaporada:** evaporated milk
**lechuga:** lettuce
**lentejas:** lentils
**levanta muertos:** any dish (or beverage) that provides resurrecting relief after a hangover
**limón:** Mexican lime
**licuadora:** blender

## M
**machacador (marrito para carne):** meat pounder
**maduro:** ripe or seasoned
**mantarraya:** stingray
**manteca vegetal:** vegetable shortening
**manteca de puerco:** lard
**mantequilla:** butter
**marca:** brand
**margarina:** margarine
**marinar:** to marinate

**mayonesa:** mayonnaise
**masa:** dough
**menudo:** beef tripe soup
**metate:** a flat, stone mortar used to grind grains and seeds
**mezcla:** mixture
**mezclar:** to mix
**michelada :** beer cocktail made with salt, lime juice, Tabasco, and Worcestershire sauces
**molcajete :** a stone mortar
**mole poblano:** a dark sauce made from dried chilies, seeds, nuts, spices, and chocolate
**moledor de frijol:** bean masher
**molino de maíz :** corn grinder
**mostaza:** mustard

## N
**naranja:** orange
**nixtamal or maize para pozole :** whole white hominy boiled in lime and ready for cooking
**nopal :** prickly pear

## O
**olla para frijol:** bean pot
**olla vaporera:** steamer
**orégano:** oregano

## P
**palillo:** toothpick
**pancita de res:** beef tripe
**panela :** fresh, unripened, white cheese made from unpasteurized milk
**panocha:** a dark-colored block or cone of unrefined cane sugar; also called *piloncillo*
**papa:** potato
**papel aluminio:** aluminum foil
**parrilla :** grill or charcoal grill

**pechuga:** breast (usually of domestic fowl)
**pelar:** to peel
**pepino:** cucumber
**pescado:** fish
**picante:** spicy
**picar:** to dice or mince
**pichón:** pigeon
**pico de gallo:** a sour, salty, spicy fruit cocktail
**piloncillo:** a dark-colored block or cone of unrefined cane sugar; also called *panocha*
**pimienta entera:** peppercorns
**pimienta molida:** ground pepper
**pinole de flor:** roasted corn flour
**pinzas:** tongs
**pizca:** a pinch (small amount)
**platanera:** banana grove
**plátano:** banana
**poblano :** a mild, green chili pepper that, when dried, is called *chili ancho*
**pollo :** chicken
**polvo de camarón:** shrimp powder
**polvo para hornear:** baking powder
**popozahui:** a term to describe a green mango beginning to ripen
**portión:** serving
**postre:** dessert
**pozole:** a stew made with pork and hominy in a red chili sauce
**prensa de tortilla:** tortilla press
**puerco:** pork
**pulque :** an alcoholic beverage made from the fermented juice of maguey
**puré de tomate:** tomato puree

## Q

**quelite:** wild spinach
**quesadilla:** a tortilla filled or folded around with melted cheese
**queso asadera :** unmolded, fresh cheese made from packed, whole curds, air-seasoned
**queso de rancho :** mild, white cheese made from raw milk, soft ripened, and lightly salty
**queso fresco oreado :** air-seasoned, fresh cheese
**queso para rallar :** grating cheese

## R

**raja:** a slice
**rallar:** to grate
**ramita:** sprig (of coriander)
**rana:** frog
**ranchero:** country style
**raspado :** grated or shaved
**raspador de queso:** cheese grater
**rebanar:** to slice thinly
**rebanada:** a thin slice
**rábano:** radish
**recado rojo:** achiote paste (ground spice blend made from pounded annatto seeds)
**recalentar:** to reheat or warm
**relleno:** stuffing
**repollo:** cabbage
**reposada:** aged
**requesón :** fresh, mild, soft cheese made from the curds of cooked whey
**res:** beef
**retazos con hueso:** soup bones
**relvover:** to mix
**revuelto:** mixed
**rociar:** to sprinkle
**rodillo:** rolling pin

## S

***sal:*** salt
***salsa:*** sauce
***salsa embotellada:*** bottled sauce
***sancochar:*** to parboil
***sandia:*** watermelon
***sartén:*** skillet
***sazonar:*** to season
***secar:*** to dry
***serrano:*** a small, green chili, medium hot on the Scoville scale
***servilleta de tela:*** dish cloth
***sopa azteca:*** Aztec soup; meat broth mixed with chipotle peppers, tortillas, and cheese
***sopa de arroz:*** literally "dry soup"; rice cooked with chili, onions, and tomato puree
***sope:*** a thick, fried circle of corn dough topped with meat, cheese, and vegetable
***sopitas:*** deep-fried pieces of corn tortilla

## T

***tabla para cortar :*** cutting board
***taco:*** a rolled tortilla folded around a filling
***taco de abañil:*** mason's taco consisting of a tortilla filled with cheese and hot sauce
***tamal:*** steam-cooked corn dough with a filling
***tamarindo:*** tamarind
***tatemado:*** charred (chilies)
***taza:*** cup
***tazón:*** bowl
***tazón hondo:*** deep bowl; serving bowl
***tazón para mezclar:*** mixing bowl

***tejolote:*** a stone pestle used to grind seeds and grains in a *molcajete*
***tendedero de ropa:*** clothesline
***tenedor:*** fork
***tierna:*** tender or unripened
***tepache :*** a beverage made from fermented pineapple rinds
***tocino en barra:*** bacon with rind
***tomatillo :*** green tomato; relative of the ground cherry
***tortillería:*** a local tortilla bakery
***tortillas para recalentar:*** reheated tortillas
***tortita:*** cake (as in potato cake)
***tostada:*** toasted, dried, or deep-fried tortilla
***trigo :*** wheat
***trozo:*** a cut or piece (of meat)

## V

***vaina de vainilla:*** vanilla pod
***vainilla:*** vanilla
***vapor:*** steam
***varita :*** stalk (of celery)
***verdolagas:*** purslane
***vinagre:*** vinegar
***voltear:*** flip or turn over

## Y

***yema:*** yolk of an egg

## W

***wakabaki:*** a soup made with boiled beans and marrow bones

## Z

***zanahoria:*** carrot

# Index

## A

acelgas (Swiss chard), 136, 142
achiote paste *(recado rojo)*, 146
*Agua de Cebada (Barley Water)*, 242–243
*Agua de Ciruela (Plum Water)*, 244–245
*Aguachile (Chili Water)*, 95–96
*Albóndigas de Camarón (Shrimp Ball Soup)*, 25, 160–161
*alubia*, 34
amaranth *(bledo)*, 136
Anaheim pepper *(chile largo-verde)*, 87, 88
ancho, 88
*antojitos* (snacks), 23
*Arroz Blanco (Fried White Rice)*, 124, 142, 167, 168
*Arroz Campestre (Country Rice)*, 121, 143
*Arroz con Leche (Rice in Milk)*, 94, 224–225
*Arroz Verde (Green Rice)*, 122
*Asado de Caballo en Salsa de Tomate (Pan-broiled Horse in Tomato Sauce)*, 27, 183–184
*asientos*, 209, 210
avocado *(aguacate)*, 78
Aztec Soup *(Sopa Azteca/Sopa de Tortilla)*, 27, 204–205
*azufrado*, 34

## B

bananas, 146
barbecued meat *(cochinita pibil)*, 175
barbeque pit, 19
*Barley Water (Agua de Cebada)*, 242–243
basket cheese *(panela)*, 23
*Bean Bone Soup (Wakabaki)*, 196
bean bores, 38
bean broths, 23
bean masher, 17
bean pot, 17, 35
bean spoon, 17
*Bean Tacos (Tacos de Frijol)*, 55
beans
   buying, 34
   cleaning, 34–35
   cooking in pot, 36
   dishes, 33, 36–44
   green beans, 25
   in tostadas, 60
   keeping on hand, 31
   refried, 23, 39–40
   storing, 38
   string beans, 25, 104, 129
   tortillas rolled with, 65
beef bones, 196
beef tripe *(pancita de res)*, 197
beef, shredded, 212
*Beefsteak Charlie (Bistec Carlos)*, 181–182
bell pepper, 86
beverages *(bebidas refrescantes)*, 235–245

*birria*, 172, 175
*Bistec Carlos (Beefsteak Charlie)*, 181–182
*bistec ranchero*, 175
Blanquillo, Benito, 98
*bledo* (green amaranth), 136
blender, 17
*bocadillo plantains*, 146
*Boiled Tomato Sauce (Salsa de Tomate Cocido)*, 75
*botanas* (appetizers/snacks), 23
brands, preferred, 28–29
broiled meats, sauces for, 82
broth *(caldo)*
  bean, 23
  for gorditas, 214, 215
  for tostadas, 58–59, 60
brown sugar, substitutes for, 51
*Burritos de Carne Deshebrada en Chile Colorado (Cortez-On-Foot Burritos)*, 27, 185–186
*burritos de machaca* (meat burritos), 175
*Buttered Rice with Cheese and Corn (Sopa de Arroz a la Mantequilla)*, 123

## C

cabbage cakes, sauce for, 75
*Cabbage Cakes (Tortitas de Repollo)*, 131
cabbage, chicken with, 98, 148
*Caguamanta (Stingray Stew)*, 162–163
*Caldillo (Poor Gringo Soup)*, 201
*Caldo con Albóndigas de Requesón (Cheese Ball Soup)*, 195–196
*Caldo de Caballo (Horse Broth Soup)*, 199
*Caldo de Papas con Panela (Chewy Cheese Soup)*, 202
*Caldo de Pescado (Fish Head Soup)*, 169–170
*canario*, 34
*Capon Overboard in Vinegar (Estofado de Pollo)*, 150
capsaicin, 30, 86
*Carne de Puerco con Nopales en Chile Colorado (Red Chile Pork with Nopales)*, 187–188
carne machaca. *See machaca*
*carnitas*, 209
carp eggs, 158–159
cat meat, 172, 176
cauliflower, 75, 130
*Cebiche (Naked Fish)*, 154–155
*Cebollas al Carbón (Charcoaled Onions)*, 133
cereal, dishes comparable to, 224–225
*ceviche*, 154–155
*Chacha's Pozole for Six (Pozole para Seis)*, 175–178
charcoal grill, 18
*Charcoaled Onions (Cebollas al Carbón)*, 133
chayote (merliton) in soups, 200–201
*Cheap Cheese Green Enchiladas (Enchiladas Verdes de Queso)*, 67
*Cheap Cheese Red Enchiladas (Enchiladas Rojas de Queso)*, 66–67
cheese
  as gordita topping, 214–215
  as tostada topping, 59–60
  in crêpes, 226
  squash in melted, 128
  string beans with, 132

tortillas rolled with, 64
types of, 23
*Cheese Ball Soup (Caldo con Albóndigas de Requesón)*, 195–196
*Cheese Flutes (Flautas de Requesón)*, 211
cheese grater, 17
*Chewy Cheese Soup (Caldo de Papas con Panela)*, 202
*chicharrones*, 209
chicken
   dishes, 142–143, 146–150
   killing and dressing, 247–249
   obtaining, 140
   shredded, 212
*chilaquiles*, 23, 62
*Chilaquiles Rojos (Tattered Tortilla Casserole)*, 62
*Chilaquiles Rojos con Pollo (Tattered Tortillas with Chicken in Red Chile Sauce)*, 149
Chile (musician), 86–87
*chile largo-verde* (Anaheim pepper), 87, 88
*Chiles en Escabeche (Soused Chilies)*, 91–92
*Chiles Rellenos (Stuffed Green Chilies)*, 89–90
chili marinade *(marinada de chile)*, 190
chili sauces, 81–83, 87, 101, 149
*Chili Water (Aguachile)*, 95–96
chilies (chili peppers)
   canned, 29
   charring and peeling, 30
   deveining, 30
   dishes, 85, 89–96
   overview and types of, 86–88

   potatoes with, 112
   stuffed, 23, 75
   toasting, 20–21
*Chilies in Cheese (Rajas de Chile con Queso)*, 96
chiltepín, 87, 88, 95–96
chipotle, 87, 88
*chiquelites* (garden huckleberry), 136
*Chivo Tatemado (Fired Tequila Goat)*, 19, 189–190
chorizo, 41, 42
*cochinita pibil* (barbecued meat), 175
*Coco Helado (Cold Coconut)*, 227–229
coconut, 227–229
*Colache (Squash in Melted Cheese)*, 128
colander, 17
*Cold Coconut (Coco Helado)*, 227–229
*Coliflor Empanizada (Fried Cauliflower)*, 130
Connie Joe (rabbit), 179–180
*Cooked Sauce (Salsa Cocida)*, 73
cooking equipment, 17–21
cooking oils, 28
cookware, 17–18
corn
   greens with, 138
   husking, 233
   obtaining, 126–127, 232
   on the cob, 134–135
corn grinder, 18, 233
corn tortillas, 96, 178
*Corn Tortillas (Tortillas de Maíz)*, 47–48, 94
corn tostadas, 165, 166
*Cortez-On-Foot Burritos (Burritos*

*de Carne Deshebrada en Chile Colorado)*, 27, 185–186
*Country Rice (Arroz Campestre)*, 121, 143
*Cream of Chayote/Merliton (Crema de Chayote)*, 200–201
*Creamed String Beans (Ejotes con Crema)*, 129
*Crema de Chayote (Cream of Chayote/Merliton)*, 200–201
*Crepas de Cerveza (Thin Beer Crêpes)*, 94, 226
crêpes, 94, 226
criollo avocados *(paguas)*, 78
cucumber, 221
cutting board, 18

**D**

*Dangerously Crisp Tortillas with Toppings (Tostadas)*, 56, 165, 166, 178, 214
Delgado, Maria, 154
desserts *(postres)*, 23, 223–234, 226
Diplomat mangos, 230
dishpan, 18
dog meat, 172, 176
Doña María Mole, 28, 144
donkey meat, 183
*Dough Boats with Pork Renderings (Sopes con Asientos)*, 209–210
dove, 140, 144–145
*Dried Carp Egg Cakes (Tortitas de Hueva de Carpa)*, 158–159
*Dry Soup (Pickerel's Rice)*, 119–120, 150, 162, 163

**E**

eggs
  dishes, 97, 99–108
  obtaining, 98
  sauces for, 75, 82
  scrambled, 75, 101–107
*Ejotes con Crema (Creamed String Beans)*, 129
*Ejotes con Queso (String Beans with Cheese)*, 132
*Elotes Asados (Roasted Corn on the Cob)*, 134–135
*Empanadas de Atún (Tuna Turnovers)*, 156–157
*Enchiladas Rojas de Queso (Cheap Cheese Red Enchiladas)*, 66–67
*Enchiladas Verdes de Queso (Cheap Cheese Green Enchiladas)*, 67
enchiladas, cheeses for, 23, 66–67
*Enfrijoladas (Tortillas Rolled with Beans)*, 65
*Entomatadas (Tomatoed Tortillas)*, 63–64
*epazote*, 36
*Estofado de Iguana (Stewed Iguana)*, 18, 191–192
*Estofado de Conejo (Rabbit Stew)*, 179–180

**F**

*Fat Tortillas with Chili and Clotted Cream (Gordas con Natas y Chile Chiltepín)*, 93–94
fatty foods, 208
fire, 18–19
*Fired Chili Sauce (Salsa Tatemada)*, 82–83
*Fired Tequila Goat (Chivo Tatemado)*, 19, 189–190
fish
  dishes, 151, 154–170

obtaining, 152–153, 156
sauces for, 73
*Fish Head Soup (Caldo de Pescado)*, 169–170
flautas, 23
*Flautas de Requesón (Cheese Flutes)*, 211
*Flor de Mayo*, 34
flour tortillas, 36
*Flour Tortillas (Tortillas de Harina)*, 49–50
flute tortillas, 211
food poisoning, 176
fowl. *See* poultry
fowl ticks *(Argas persicus)*, 98
*Fresh Sauce with Lime (Salsa Fresca, Salsa Cruda, Salsa Bandera)*, 72
fresh stingray, 162, 163
*Fried and Refried Beans (Frijoles Fritos y Refritos)*, 39–40
*Fried Cauliflower (Coliflor Empanizada)*, 130
fried foods *(fritangas)*
  beans, 23, 39–40
  dishes, 207, 209–215
  garlic, 31
  sauces for, 73
*Fried White Rice (Arroz Blanco)*, 124, 142, 167, 168
*Frijoles Charros (Horsemen Beans)*, 37
*Frijoles Fritos y Refritos (Fried and Refried Beans)*, 39–40
*Frijoles Guisados (Stir-Mashed Beans)*, 38, 56, 65
*frijoles puercos*, 23
*Frijoles Puercos (Pork-Style Beans)*, 41–42
frog legs, 172, 173–174

fungicides, 233

## G

*Gallina Pinta (Speckled Hen)*, 43, 44
*Gallina Pinta Guisada (Stir-Mashed Speckled Hen)*, 44
garden huckleberry *(chiquelites)*, 136
garlic, 31
gas, 18
gas stove, 18
goat, 19, 172, 189–190
*Gordas con Natas y Chile Chiltepín (Fat Tortillas with Chili and Clotted Cream)*, 93–94
*Gorditas (Little Fat Ones)*, 56, 212–215
green amaranth *(bledo)*, 136
green beans, 25, 104, 129, 132
*Green Chicken (Pollo en Salsa Verde)*, 143
green chilies, stuffed, 75, 89–90
*Green Corn Tamales (Tamales de Elote)*, 134, 232–234
*Green Eggs/No Ham (Huevos en Salsa Verde)*, 100
*Green Rice (Arroz Verde)*, 122
*Green Tomato Sauce (Salsa Verde, Salsa de Tomatillo)*, 76–77
*Green Tomatoes and Cucumber (Tomate Verde y Pepino)*, 221
greens, 136–138
*Greens with Corn (Quelites con Elote)*, 138
*Greens with Tomatoes and Onions (Verdolagas con Tomate y Cebolla)*, 137
griddles, 17–18

guacamole, 78–80
guajillo, 88

## H

Haas avocado, 78
hangover remedies, 87, 169–170, 197, 198, 237–238
Hayden mangos, 230
herbicides, 233
herbs and spices, 24
*Hibiscus Cooler (Agua de Jamaica)*, 239
hominy, 24, 43–44
*Horchata de Arroz (Steeped Rice Water)*, 237–238
*Horse Broth Soup (Caldo de Caballo)*, 199
horse steaks, 172, 185–186
horsemeat, 26–27, 183–184, 212
*Horsemen Beans (Frijoles Charros)*, 37
*Hot Tomato (Tomate a las Brasas)*, 135
*huevos de segunda*, 98
*Huevos en Salsa Verde (Green Eggs/No Ham)*, 100
*Huevos Rancheros (Ranch-Style Eggs)*, 82, 99
*Huevos Resbalados (Slipped Eggs)*, 105

## I

iguana, 18, 172, 191–192
ingredients, 21–28, 31

## J

jalapeño, 87–88
*Jícama (Mexican Potato)*, 219–220

## K

Keith mangos, 230

Kent mangos, 230

## L

Ladrón (dog), 21, 78, 172, 176
lamb, 189
lemon mangos, 230
*Lentejas con Arroz y Queso (Ranch Lentil Soup)*, 203
lentils, 23, 203
lime, 24, 154, 155, 217–222
lime squeezer, 19
*Little Fat Ones (Gorditas)*, 56, 212–215

## M

*machaca*
  burritos, 175
  from horsemeat, 183
  in soups, 201
  potatoes with, 116
  preparing, 21–23, 56
  scrambled eggs with, 105
*Machaca de Ancas de Rana Estilo Benito (Pounded Frog Legs Benito Style)*, 173–174
Machado, Chacha, 175–177
machete, 227, 228, 229
mango, 230–231
mango *zapote*, 230
Manila mangos, 230
Manola (dog), 56, 105
*marinada de chile* (chili marinade), 190
marlin, 87, 164–165
*Marlin en Escabeche (Soused Marlin)*, 164–165
*Marlin Stew (Marlin Estofado)*, 166
*Mason's Tacos (Tacos de Abañil)*, 23, 54

*mayacoba*, 34
meat
  dishes, 171
  for tostadas, 57–58, 60
  in gorditas, 212, 213
  obtaining, 172
  pounding, 31
  salting, 22
  sauces for, 82
  shredding, 31
meat burritos *(burritos de machaca)*, 175
meat pounder, 19–20
merliton, 200–201
*metate*, 18, 20
*Mexican Potato (Jícama)*, 219–220
*michelada*, 237
milk, 93, 94, 224–225
Miriam (author's wife), 86–87, 118, 131, 172, 175, 179, 194, 244
Mole Doña María, 28, 144
mole sauce, 28, 144
*molino*, 18, 20
mortar and pestle, 20
mother-in-law (author's), 87–88, 131
mule meat, 183

## N
*Naked Fish (Cebiche)*, 154–155

## O
*Omelet de Camarón (Shrimp Head Omelet)*, 25, 108
omelets, shrimp head, 25, 108
onions
  charcoaled, 133
  frying, 31
  greens with tomatoes and, 137
  roasting, 20–21

## P
*paguas* (criollo avocados), 78
*Pan-broiled Horse in Tomato Sauce (Asado de Caballo en Salsa de Tomate)*, 27, 183–184
*pancita de res* (beef tripe), 197
*panela* (basket cheese), 23
*panocha*, 51
*Papas con Machaca de Manola (Potatoes with Manola Machaca)*, 116
*Papas Fritas con Verdura (Tomatoed Potatoes with Veggies)*, 113
*Papas Fritas en Chile Colorado (Red Chili Potatoes)*, 112
papaya mangos, 230
*Papered Fish (Pescado Empapelado)*, 167–168
parrot mangos, 230
peppers, stuffed, 23, 75, 89–90
*Pescado Ranchero (Ranch Fish)*, 168
pesticides, 233
*Pickerel's Rice (Sopa de Arroz, Dry Soup)*, 119–120, 150, 162, 163
*Pickerel's Unholy Mole (Pichón en Mole Poblano)*, 144–145
*Pico de Gallo (Rooster's Beak Fruit Cocktail)*, 222
pigeon *(pichón)*, 140, 144–145
*piloncillo*, 51
pineapple mangos, 230
piquín chili, 87
plantains, 146
*Plum Water (Agua de Ciruela)*, 244–245
poblano chili, 87, 88
*Pollo con Acelgas (Run-over Rooster in Greens)*, 98, 142

Pollo con Repollo (Wandering Neighborhood Chicken Runs into Cabbage), 98, 148
Pollo en Achiote (Suicide Hen in Banana Leaf), 146–147
Pollo en Salsa Verde (Green Chicken), 143
Poor Gringo Guide to Mexican Mechanics, The (Pickerel), 19
Poor Gringo Soup (Caldillo), 201
popozahui mangos, 230
pork, 187–188, 209–210
pork spine (espinazo de cerdo), 177
Pork-Style Beans (Frijoles Puercos), 41–42
pork-style beans (frijoles puercos), 23
potato shrimp cakes, 75
Potato Shrimp Cakes (Tortitas de Papa con Camarón), 25, 114–115
potato soup, 23
potatoes
  dishes, 109, 112–116
  in soups, 202
  mashed, dishes with, 147
  obtaining, 110–111
  scrambled eggs with, 106
Potatoes with Manola Machaca (Papas con Machaca de Manola), 116
poultry
  butchering and dressing, 141, 247–249
  dishes, 139, 142–150
  obtaining, 140–141
poultry lice (Menacanthus stramineus), 98
Pounded Frog Legs Benito Style (Machaca de Ancas de Rana Estilo Benito), 173–174
pozole, 175–178
Pozole para Seis (Chacha's Pozole for Six), 175–178
prickly pear, 102–103, 187–188

**Q**

quelites (wild spinach), 136
Quelites con Elote (Greens with Corn), 138
Quesadillas de Flor de Calabaza (Squash Blossom Quesadillas), 68–69, 94
quesadillas
  cheeses for, 23
  squash blossom, 68–69, 94
queso asadera (unmolded fresh cheese), 23
queso asadero (aged, melting cheese), 23
queso blanco duro (hard white cheese), 23
queso de Chihuahua (Chihuahua cheese), 23
queso de Oaxaca (Oaxaca cheese), 23
queso de rancho (ranch cheese), 23
queso fresco (fresh cheese), 23
queso fresco oreado (air-seasoned, fresh cheese), 23
queso Menonita (Mennonite cheese), 23
queso para rallar (grating cheese), 23

**R**

rabbit, 172
Rabbit Stew (Estofado de Conejo), 179–180

*Rajas de Chile con Queso (Chilies in Cheese)*, 96
*Ranch Fish (Pescado Ranchero)*, 168
*Ranch Lentil Soup (Lentejas con Arroz y Queso)*, 203
*Ranch-Style Eggs (Huevos Rancheros)*, 99
ranch-style eggs *(huevos rancheros)*, 82
*raspado*, 244
raw milk *(leche bronca)*, 93
*recado rojo* (achiote paste), 146
Recodo, Ramon, 22
Red Chile Pork with Nopales *(Carne de Puerco con Nopales en Chile Colorado)*, 187–188
Red Chili Potatoes *(Papas Fritas en Chile Colorado)*, 112
Red Chili Sauce *(Salsa de Chile Colorado)*, 81
red chili sauce *(salsa de chile colorado)*, 101, 149
refined sugar, substitutes for, 51
refried beans, 23, 39–40
*requesón*, 23
*Revolcadas (Tortillas Rolled with Cheese)*, 64
rice *(arroz)*, 117–124
   chicken served with, 142, 150
   seafood served with, 162, 163, 167, 168
*Rice in Milk (Arroz con Leche)*, 94, 224–225
rice water, 237–238
*Roasted Corn on the Cob (Elotes Asados)*, 134–135
*Roasted Tomato Sauce (Salsa de Tomate Asado)*, 74
rolling bottle, 20
rolling pin, 20
*Rooster's Beak Fruit Cocktail (Pico de Gallo)*, 222
*Run-over Rooster in Greens (Pollo con Acelgas)*, 98, 142

## S

*Salsa Bandera (Fresh Sauce with Lime)*, 72
*Salsa Cocida (Cooked Sauce)*, 73
*Salsa Cruda (Fresh Sauce with Lime)*, 72
*Salsa de Chile Colorado (Red Chili Sauce)*, 81
*Salsa de Tomate Asado (Roasted Tomato Sauce)*, 74
*Salsa de Tomate Cocido (Boiled Tomato Sauce)*, 75
*Salsa de Tomatillo (Green Tomato Sauce)*, 76–77
*Salsa Fresca (Fresh Sauce with Lime)*, 72
Salsa La Guacamaya, 29, 67
Salsa Ranchera, 29, 67
*Salsa Tatemada (Fired Chili Sauce)*, 82–83
*Salsa Verde (Green Tomato Sauce)*, 76–77
salted stingray, 162, 163
San Miguel avocado, 78
saucepans, 17
saucepots, 17
sauces (salsas)
   bottled, 29
   chili, 81–83
   cooked, 73
   for tostadas, 29
   fresh, 72
   guacamole, 77–79

keeping on hand, 31
tomato, 74–77
scrambled eggs, 75
*Scrambled Eggs and Tortillas in Red Chili Sauce (Sopitas de Tortilla con Huevo y Chile Colorado)*, 101
*Scrambled Eggs with Manola Machaca (Huevos Revueltos con Machaca de Manola)*, 105
*Scrambled Eggs with Potatoes (Huevos Revueltos con Papas)*, 106
*Scrambled Eggs with Prickly Pear (Huevos Revueltos con Nopalitos)*, 102–103
*Scrambled Eggs with String Beans (Huevos Revueltos con Ejotes)*, 104
*Scrambled Eggs with Veggies (Huevos Revueltos con Verduras)*, 107
*sebiche*, 154–155
serrano, 88
shredded meat, 60, 212, 213
*Shrimp Ball Soup (Albóndigas de Camarón)*, 25, 160–161
*Shrimp Head Omelet (Omelet de Camarón)*, 25, 108
shrimp powder, 24–25, 108, 160
side dish, guacamole as, 79–80
skillets, 17
*Slipped Eggs (Huevos Resbalados)*, 105
snacks *(antojitos)*, 23
snapper, 169
snowcones, 244
*Sopa Azteca (Aztec Soup)*, 27, 204–205

*Sopa de Arroz (Pickerel's Rice)*, 119–120, 150, 162, 163
*Sopa de Arroz a la Mantequilla (Buttered Rice with Cheese and Corn)*, 123
*Sopa de Tortilla (Aztec Soup)*, 27, 204–205
sopes, 208, 210
*Sopes con Asientos (Dough Boats with Pork Renderings)*, 209–210
*Sopitas con Verdura (Tattered Tortillas with Veggies)*, 61
soups *(sopas)*
   Aztec soup, 27, 87, 204–205
   bean, 196
   chayote, 200–201
   cheese, 195–196, 202
   dishes, 193
   fish head soup, 169–170
   horse broth soup, 199
   lentil, 203
   *menudo*, 197–198
   overview of, 194
   poor gringo soup, 201
   potato soup, 23
   rice soup, 119–120
   shrimp ball soup, 25
*Soused Chilies (Chiles en Escabeche)*, 91–92
*Soused Marlin (Marlin en Escabeche)*, 164–165
*Speckled Hen (Gallina Pinta)*, 43, 44
spices and herbs, 24
spinach, 136
*Squash Blossom Quesadillas (Quesadillas de Flor de Calabaza)*, 68–69, 94

*Squash in Melted Cheese (Colache)*, 128
steamer, 20
*Steeped Rice Water (Horchata de Arroz)*, 237–238
*Stewed Iguana (Estofado de Iguana)*, 18, 191–192
*Stingray Stew (Caguamanta)*, 162–163
*Stir-Mashed Beans (Frijoles Guisados)*, 38, 56, 65
*Stir-Mashed Speckled Hen (Gallina Pinta Guisada)*, 44
stockpot, 17
strainer, 20
string beans, 25, 104, 129
*String Beans with Cheese (Ejotes con Queso)*, 132
stuffed chilies, 23, 75
*Stuffed Green Chilies (Chiles Rellenos)*, 89–90
sugar, substitutes for, 51
sugarcane, 21
*Suicide Hen in Banana Leaf (Pollo en Achiote)*, 146–147
*Sweet Whole Wheat Tortillas (Tortillas de Trigo)*, 51–52

# T

*Tacos de Abañil (Mason's Tacos)*, 54
*tacos de abañil* (mason's tacos), 23
*Tacos de Frijol (Bean Tacos)*, 55
tamales, 232–234
*Tamales de Elote (Green Corn Tamales)*, 134, 232–234
*Tamarindade (Agua de Tamarindo)*, 240–241
*Tattered Tortilla Casserole (Chilaquiles Rojos)*, 62
*Tattered Tortillas with Chicken in Red Chile Sauce (Chilaquiles Rojos con Pollo)*, 149
*Tattered Tortillas with Veggies (Sopitas con Verdura)*, 61
*Thin Beer Crêpes (Crepas de Cerveza)*, 94, 226
*Tomate a las Brasas (Hot Tomato)*, 135
*Tomate Verde y Pepino (Green Tomatoes and Cucumber)*, 221
tomato puree, 27
*Tomatoed Potatoes with Veggies (Papas Fritas con Verdura)*, 113
*Tomatoed Tortillas (Entomatadas)*, 63–64
tomatoes, 25–27, 135, 137, 221
tongs, 20–21
*totopos*, 82
tortilla basket, 21
tortilla press, 21
tortillas. *See also tortilla type, e.g.:* flour tortillas
   dishes made with, 53–69, 93–94, 149
   griddles for cooking, 17–18
   keeping on hand, 31
   on side, 36
   pozole with, 178
   preparing, 45–52
   scrambled eggs with, 101
*Tortillas de Trigo (Sweet Whole Wheat Tortillas)*, 51–52
*Tortillas Rolled with Beans (Enfrijoladas)*, 65
*Tortillas Rolled with Cheese (Revolcadas)*, 64

*Tortitas de Hueva de Carpa (Dried Carp Egg Cakes)*, 158–159
*Tortitas de Repollo (Cabbage Cakes)*, 131
tostadas
    *Dangerously Crisp Tortillas with Toppings*, 56, 165, 166, 178, 214
    leftovers used as ingredients for, 214
    sauces for, 82
    seafood served on, 165, 166
*Tostadas for Seven*, 56–60
trans fat, 208
*Tripe Soup (Menudo)*, 197–198
*Tuna Turnovers (Empanadas de Atún)*, 156–157
turkeys, raising, 140–141

**V**
vanilla and vanilla beans, 27–28, 224, 225, 237, 243

vegetables. *See also vegetable type, e.g.:* string beans
    as gordita topping, 214–215
    as tostada topping, 59–60
    dishes, 125, 128–135, 137–138
    greens, 136–138
    obtaining, 126–127, 136, 232
    scrambled eggs with, 107
    tomatoed potatoes with, 113
*verdolagas* (purslane), 136
*Verdolagas con Tomate y Cebolla (Greens with Tomatoes and Onions)*, 137
vinegar, chicken with, 150

**W**
*Wakabaki (Bean Bone Soup)*, 196
*Wandering Neighborhood Chicken Runs into Cabbage (Pollo con Repollo)*, 98, 148
wheat tortillas *(tortillas de trigo)*, 51–52

## A Note about the Author

**Miles Standish Pickerel** lived with his mother until he was thirty-six. After brief engagements as an adulterous husband, a neglectful father, and a larcenous employee, he unsuccessfully impersonated a cardiologist, a cattle rustler, and a visiting dignitary from Guyana. Currently, he is at work on the century's first compendium of Mexican mechanics. He lives anonymously in an unnamed city south of the twenty-fifth parallel. He may or may not answer emails sent to poorgringo@sentrybooks.com.

# Discover More Great Titles

at
www.sentrybooks.com

Sentry Books

**A Great West Publishing Company**

**Printed in the United States on recycled paper**
(Despite strenuous objection from the
dendrophobic and eco-unfriendly Pickerel)

www.ingramcontent.com/pod-product-compliance
Lightning Source LLC
Chambersburg PA
CBHW020645300426
44112CB00007B/238